Evaluating the impact of your library

Second edition

Sharon Markless
and
David Streatfield

facet publishing

© Sharon Markless and David Streatfield 2013

Published by Facet Publishing,
7 Ridgmount Street London WC1E 7AE
www.facetpublishing.co.uk

Facet Publishing is wholly owned by CILIP: the Chartered Institute of Library and
Information Professionals.

British Library Cataloguing in Publication Data
A catalogue record for this book is available from the British Library.

ISBN 978-1-85604-812-5

First published 2006
This second edition published 2013

Text printed on FSC accredited material.

Typeset from authors' files in 10/13pt Revival 565 and Zurich by Flagholme
Publishing Services.
Printed and made in Great Britain by CPI Group (UK) Ltd, Croydon, CR0 4YY.

To the memory of

Harry Freedman, who would have taken great pride in
showing everyone his daughter's name on the front of this book,
regardless of the content

Doris and Bertram Blissett, parents of David Streatfield

Contents

Introduction

This book explores a major issue for library and information service managers of all kinds – evaluating the impact of services. When we introduced the first edition of this book we noted that all types of libraries and information services traditionally collect a range of performance information that can tell you as managers something about the efficiency of your services but that a sustained focus on impact was rare, despite the fact that impact evaluation (or as it is sometimes called, outcomes-based evaluation) had recently taken on new importance. What is interesting now is how many library managers are ready to move on to focus on *effectiveness* of services, or the impact of services on users, including remote users.

Why do we need a second edition of the book? The world of library impact evaluation has changed substantially in the past six years. There are more international and national efforts to engage with the impact of library services on users and, as a result, we now know more about the areas in which libraries of all kinds can make a difference to the lives of their users, as we show in a fully revised and updated Chapter 3.

One thing that hasn't changed much is that library and information service managers still find it hard to get a grip on the slippery concept of service impact and many still struggle when trying to address impact questions in their planning. We are continuing to help here and are increasingly getting involved with evaluation efforts in a variety of countries, with active support from professional bodies in the field. This work has given us the chance to develop, further test and refine our approach to evaluating impact as presented in the first edition of this book. Our analysis of the issues and our approach to evaluating service impact that has helped managers in public, education, health and 'special' libraries and information services are still at the core of this book. The approach is designed to help you to understand, construct and deploy impact indicators that relate closely to what you are trying to achieve. The core chapters take you through our rigorously tested process model for impact evaluation, with tools and examples to equip you with all that you need in order to address your own service impact questions. For this new edition, we have drawn on our growing experience of international library evaluation for some of our examples and fully updated others to reflect professional developments. (Where necessary, we have anonymized these examples because they involve current projects, some of which have not yet reported.) A final chapter draws on our experience of working in a range of countries to suggest how national or international impact evaluation can be addressed.

You will find additional tools and materials linked to this book at www.facetpublishing.co.uk/evaluatingimpact. These take account of recent developments in research approaches used to evaluate impact.

We intend this to be a practical book designed to help busy managers to get to grips with impact issues. Therefore, although it is customary when writing books for professional library audiences to adopt an 'academic' tone, we have chosen instead to use the active voice and present tense where possible. We know that some evaluation specialists working on library evaluation at national level found the first edition of this book useful. In offering this revised edition, our aim is to add to the general interest and broaden the appeal without reducing the usefulness of this book for our intended target audience of library professionals.

David Streatfield and Sharon Markless

About the authors

When reviewing the first edition of this book in *Library Review*, Derek Law (2006) offered '. . . a single grumble. The authors have extensive experience, but there are no author biographies and therefore no context . . . The fact that both authors are experts and have wide reputations is expertly concealed, buried in chapter three. The modesty is unbecoming for those unfamiliar with the experts in the area.'

Who are we to argue?

David Streatfield is Principal of Information Management Associates, a research, training and consultancy team established in 1991 and now specializing in impact evaluation of libraries. David has a social science and educational research background and in a former life was a Chartered Librarian (he is still a member of the Chartered Institute of Library and Information Professionals).

Sharon Markless is a Senior Lecturer in Higher Education at the King's Learning Institute, King's College London and at the Centre for Educational and Academic Development, University of Surrey. She is a National Teaching Fellow and an Honorary Fellow of the Chartered Institute of Library and Information Professionals.

Both David and Sharon are Independent Consultants to the Bill and Melinda Gates Foundation's Global Libraries Initiative (GL)[1] and have acted in a similar capacity for the International Federation of Library Associations (IFLA) and for the Global Impact Study funded by the International Development Research Centre and the Gates Foundation. (David is currently helping to plan and manage a cross-European survey of user perceptions of public access computing in public libraries, commissioned by GL.)

They first worked together in 1984 at the National Foundation for Educational Research, where David was already Head of Information Research and Development when Sharon became a Senior Research Officer. Since then they have collaborated on a range of UK national evaluation projects focused on education and public libraries, commencing with the Effective School Library project in 1991 and culminating in this book. This evaluation research is described in more detail in Chapter 3. In addition they have worked together on a range of national education and libraries research projects. Internationally they have helped to develop the Impact Planning and Assessment Roadmap for GL participants, and helped IFLA to develop aspects of its impact evaluation strategy. They have also worked together or separately in providing impact evaluation guidance to library managers (directly or via their GL contract) in various European countries as well as Indonesia, Japan and Vietnam.

Note

1   The Global Libraries Initiative is a major international public library development programme funded by the Bill and Melinda Gates Foundation. It ' . . . helps public libraries provide free access to computers connected to the internet and training on how to make full use of these tools. GL is built on the success of a similar program that connected 99 percent of US public libraries to the internet (American Library Association and Information Institute, 2009; Bertot et al., 2008, 2009). GL works with library systems in selected countries that are committed to providing access to information technology for all citizens and are able to allocate the resources to make this happen. Partner countries demonstrate need for the foundation's support, and have strong library systems, solid infrastructure (such as electricity and broadband internet capabilities), and the leadership, ability, and resources to maintain nationwide services in their public libraries.' (Fried, Kochanowicz and Chiranov, 2010, 57)

Impact and all that: use of some key terms in this book

During our international impact work we have become very conscious of the meaning of words. Three examples are relevant here:

1 There is no established term for 'impact', in the sense in which we use it here, in many of the countries in which we have worked.
2 The Global Libraries Initiative (GL) uses 'assessment' to describe what we present in this book as 'evaluation'. This was problematic for us because we both come from an education evaluation background, in which 'assessment' usually refers to assessment of the academic performance of students.
3 In various Scandinavian countries the term for research 'evidence', which we use in relation to qualitative work, carries the strong sense of forensic proof. (This may contribute to differences in social science research perspective between various countries.)

The language of performance measurement is overstuffed with complex terms that are often used inconsistently even within the same book. Readers have probably come across all the expressions listed below when working on performance measurement. We try to show here how these terms interrelate, how they are used in this book and where impact fits into the overall picture.

Achievement

The term 'achievement' often crops up in the education world in relation to the impact of curriculum interventions or student learning support, to denote attaining a level of performance by effort. This term can overlap with 'impact', but it is unlikely that any library-based intervention or service will entirely account for an individual's 'achievement'. 'Achievement' is also used more technically in education circles to describe performance in a standardized test.

Aims and objectives

It doesn't take long to find inconsistencies in the use of the terms 'aims' and 'objectives'. They are sometimes used interchangeably, even in the evaluation literature. When they are differentiated, people may talk about overarching aims and more specific objectives, but they may also talk about overarching objectives and precise aims. In the interests of sanity (ours and yours!) we define these terms for this book as:

aims – the main and overarching stated purposes of the library service or of the organization of which it is part
objectives – refinement of the aims into more specifically achievable terms, usually expressed as what can be achieved within one, three or (at most) five years.

Assessment

We use 'assessment' to describe judging people's knowledge or skills (and especially their educational performance); 'evaluation' is used in this book to refer to judging systems and services. See also **Impact Planning and Assessment**.

Attribution *see* Causation studies

Causation studies

Attribution studies are aimed at showing that changes would not have happened without the intervention that is being evaluated. Causation studies seek to answer such questions as 'How much better off are recipients *as a result of* the intervention?' or 'Does the intervention have a different impact on different groups?'; 'Did the intervention *cause* the impact?' and 'What would have happened if the intervention had *not* taken place?' There have been very few causation studies of library services, probably because these are expensive, time-consuming and intensely difficult when dealing with interventions (such as providing internet access) that may have a variety of consequences, some of which can't be easily predicted at the outset. These consequences are influenced by a range of variables that are difficult to identify and to control. Causation studies arise from a particular definition of impact used by some agencies (see also **Impact**).

Contingent valuation *see* Value

Effectiveness *versus* efficiency

It is slightly over-simple to say that traditional performance indicators as used by libraries (such as counting loans or occupancy rates) are focused on efficiency and that impact evaluation is concerned with effectiveness. However, this may be a useful distinction to bear in mind, since most library indicators tell us little or nothing about the effects of the services that are being measured or how these are perceived by users.

Evaluation *see* Assessment

Evidence

Evidence is any information or data that are used to answer a question (Carr, 1961). An important point made by Knight (2003) is that evidence is not a special category of information. It is information or data that people select to help them answer questions. As Knight says: 'One person's evidence is another's information.'

Impact

We define impact as any effect of the service (or of an event or initiative) on an individual, group or community. This effect may:

- be positive or negative
- be intended or accidental
- affect library staff, senior managers, users/customers, pupils, teachers, parents or other people.

The impact can show itself in individual cases or through more generally discernible changes, such as shifts in:

- quality of life: e.g. self-esteem; confidence; feeling included; work or social prospects;
- educational and other outcomes: e.g. skills acquired; educational attainment; levels of knowledge.

There are many definitions of impact and ours is not shared by everyone. The World Bank, for example, defines impact as the difference in the 'indicator of interest' with the intervention and without the intervention (White, 2010, 154). In this definition, impact is limited to any difference discerned in the 'indicator of interest' that can be attributed to the intervention (see also 'Causation studies'). We believe that our definition, which underpins this book, is the most useful one to drive evaluation of impact in libraries because it recognizes the complex ways in which libraries can affect and change their users and the wider community.

Impact evaluation
Evaluating impact using qualitative methods.

Impact measurement
Evaluating impact using quantitative methods (numbers). Some good work has been done using this approach, but it is important to remember that quantitative approaches tend to encourage us to focus on providing more to a larger number of people, and on faster or more efficient provision – in other words, unless we are careful they can lead us to concentrate on outputs not *outcomes* (q.v.).

Impact Planning and Assessment (IPA)
When we talk about national and international evaluation in Chapter 11, we discuss the Global Libraries Initiative (GL) of the Bill and Melinda Gates Foundation. The GL team refers to what we call the 'input, process and output model' and 'impact evaluation' as 'impact planning and assessment', following wide (but not universal) US research usage which distinguishes between *impact planning and assessment* and *impact evaluation*. In this view, IPA is seen as the entire process of gathering both qualitative impact evidence and performance data and applying them through advocacy to secure sustainability of services. The term impact evaluation is reserved to describe systematic causation or attribution studies (using a rigorous approach to collecting evidence that shows whether and how an intervention is directly responsible for particular changes or benefits). Unlike other programmes funded by the Foundation, GL focuses on IPA rather than the Foundation's version of impact evaluation.

Input, process, output model

This is the model that most people think of when they discuss performance indicators and the one that is most commonly used in libraries of all kinds. The three key elements of this model (as defined by Wavell et al., 2002) are:

1 **Inputs** – the resources the service requires in order to function (e.g. buildings, raw materials, staff and information).
2 **Processes** – what is done with the inputs; this may involve all sections of the service (e.g. preparing books for loan; cataloguing the collection; preparing an exhibition, educational programme or website; developing partnerships).
3 **Outputs** – the direct result on the service of combining inputs and processes.

Outputs provide a measure of efficiency and are traditionally measured quantitatively (e.g. number of services provided and number of people provided for; numbers of books issued; proportion of the adult population attending learning sessions; numbers of visitors to an exhibition; number of reference enquiries answered). Output indicators are sometimes called service indicators.

The *input, process, output model* originated as an engineering process model. On the whole, this model has survived very well when transferred to other work contexts such as library service management. However, the analogy with the engineering system begins to break down when we start to look beyond outputs. When engineers are producing things and want to look at the overall effects of the process model, they usually do this by totalling up the outputs into 'direct outcomes'. This works well if the process involves, for example, manufacturing computers. If you bring together enough raw materials (inputs) and assemble them on a production line (processes) into working computers (outputs) the number produced is a good indication of the outcome. However, doing the same thing in the library world will not usually tell you anything about the overall effect – or impact.

Laws of impact evaluation

At various points in the book we have offered general points to guide people through the evaluation quagmire, in the form of 'laws of impact evaluation'. These 'laws' are all based on our practical experience of facilitating evaluation workshops involving over a thousand library service managers so far. Unlike real-world laws, they should only be applied if you find them to be helpful.

Libraries (and information services)

This book is intended to help managers of libraries of all kinds. It should also be useful to providers of personal enquiry-based information services, that is, information services that engage with individual enquirers face-to-face, by telephone or by electronic means. The common factor here is that the services provided are intended to have a positive impact on the people served. Rather than employ the ugly acronym LIS in what follows, we have resorted to using 'libraries' in a generic sense in order to avoid constant repetition of 'libraries of all kinds and information services'. We apologize to any information-service managers who find this shorthand irksome. Where the focus is on particular kinds of libraries or specifically on information services we have tried to make this clear in the text.

Objectives *see* Aims and objectives

Outcomes

In the library context, outcomes can be thought of as the consequences of deploying services on the people who encounter them or on the communities served. These outcomes can be those intended or can be different from what was envisaged (unintended outcomes). A distinction is sometimes made between 'direct outcomes' (which are arrived at by aggregating outputs) and what people in the performance-measurement business describe as 'higher order' or 'longer-term' outcomes. Outcomes of both kinds are not always clearly identifiable and they are often confused with outputs, even in the specialist literature. For this reason we prefer to use a more distinct generic term – *impact*.

Outputs *see* Input, process, output model

Performance indicators

A performance indicator (PI) is a statement against which achievement in an area of activity can be evaluated. It focuses on a *significant* feature of a system or service, enabling managers to monitor and evaluate the 'health' of the whole system or service (for example, many economists regard the level of unemployment as a reliable indicator of a national economic system). A range of performance indicators is needed to evaluate complex services such as libraries.

Performance indicators should provide at least one of the following:

- information about the performance of a system
- information about the central features of a system
- information on potential or existing problem areas
- information that is policy-relevant
- information that can be compared with a previous or future time period.

Performance indicators are relatively stable – they usually change only if there are major changes in the aims and direction of the service or in how services are delivered. However, we should be more willing to consider changing our performance indicators, because they are usually difficult to get right first time and take time to develop. Gray and Wilcox (1995) described PIs as 'socially constructed abstractions arising from attempts to make sense of complex reality'.

Processes *see* Input, process, output model

Special libraries

In this book, a special library is any library that is not an academic, school, health or public library.

Success criteria

In this book we refer to qualitative impact criteria as 'success criteria'. Choosing success criteria is the step required before deciding on your impact indicators. Success criteria should answer the questions: 'How can we tell if we are making a difference?' or 'How can we know that we are getting to where we want to be?' If you start off by identifying a series of criteria by which the service might be judged, you will end up with a list of specific qualitative statements (e.g. 'links into the local community'; 'equality of access to resources'). These then form the basis for creating indicators, which are assessable and may be quantifiable. As we will explain later, it is important to start with the judgement criteria rather than with the indicators themselves.

Targets

Targets are the short- or medium-term objectives for a service or activity expressed in terms of the chosen performance indicators. They may be thought of as performance indicators with numbers attached:

- Process targets usually focus on whether pre-specified changes (in what services are offered and how) are actually achieved within a set time period.
- Output targets are often fairly arbitrary and based on recent history (such as the previous year's output level). Such targets look for a specified change over the next time period. More sophisticated output targets take some account of changes in the environment in which services are offered as well as in the resources available to provide them.
- Impact targets are posed in terms of what level of difference the service should make (to the community, to individuals and groups, or to organizations involved). They are focused on what the service has achieved.

Unlike performance indicators, which are relatively stable, targets change as the service moves on. Process and output targets are usually generated by and fit into the annual planning cycle of your organization. However, impact targets may not naturally fit into the planning year. As one service manager said: 'The trouble with government indicators is that they are all geared to the annual financial cycle. Impact does not occur to fit the annual cycle and has to be viewed over a longer term.'

Value
May refer to:

- users (or other people's) views on the **relative value** of the library service, often based on comparisons with other services
- **implied value** – based on performance data
- user views on the **purchase or exchange value** (what they are willing to pay for the library in money or time (using indicators such as the number of hours spent reading articles obtained from the library))
- user perceptions of the **derived value** of the library – e.g. **contingent valuation** of the service, based on how much they say they are willing to pay for services, or to what extent they are willing to accept compensation for not having the services (expressed in terms of amounts of reduction in taxes)
- or, accountants' (or other people's) estimates of the **return on investment** of library services, to calculate the value returned to the service provider or community served for pound/dollar (etc.) invested in the library (e.g. in academic libraries, relating expenditure on library e-resources to research funds attracted by the university).

Value as a concept is often associated with impact; we regard it as a distinct but strongly associated idea. However, the two concepts often overlap, as in Tenopir and Volentine's (2012) work on academic library evaluation, which we will describe later. She emphasizes that multiple methods should be used, both quantitative and qualitative. Her use of the term explicit value equates it with impact, in the sense in which we use it here.

These definitions are offered for use in this book. However, the literature on managing change emphasizes how important it is to use the accepted local vocabulary when you are working with your colleagues. It may be better to put up with a bit of sloppy language when precision isn't vital than to distance yourself from other people by insisting on using your own preferred terms (or ours).

Part 1
The context

1

The demand for evidence

If you are interested in the impact of your library services, or of library services in general, you may like to start by reflecting on where the impetus towards impact evaluation is coming from and how that impetus can itself distort the picture. These issues are explored below. However, if your concerns are purely practical please go on to Chapter 4.

1.1 Why is evidence of impact an issue for libraries (and information services)?[1]

Picture a group of scholars working in the Library of Alexandria in about 50 BC. Now assume that they have been ferried forward in time and deposited in your library today. Will they identify their surroundings as a library? More specifically, will the scholars recognize the printed publications at the heart of your library as equivalent in some way to their scrolls? If so, it seems likely that they will know their surroundings as a library. But what happens if we ship them forward another 30 years and touch them down again? Will your library still be there? Will it be recognizable as a library? Will information technology and the demand for different kinds of interaction between library staff, users and the service have transformed the library beyond recognition?

Even the most sensitive crystal ball is unlikely to offer a clear picture of libraries 30 years hence because of the accelerating rate of change. However, if we can start to gauge the changes in the impact of various services, this will give us an indication of where things are going and help in managing the changes needed to get there.

We don't have to look 30 years ahead to make a case for looking at impact. One common feature of all types of libraries is that there is too much to do and too little time. 'Traditional' performance indicators are important for enabling you to tell whether aspects of a service are working efficiently. However, when a new initiative or project is undertaken, this is usually achieved by prising precious time away from other operational activities. If this is the case, it is doubly important to know whether the innovation is working and how. More specifically, are you using this precious time well? How can your innovation be made to work better? Are there lessons from your current initiatives or projects that have implications for how you deliver the rest of the service? Do you need to know more about them? Asking these sorts of questions should move you towards gathering impact evidence that will tell you whether you are working along the right lines or whether you should be doing different things in different ways.

What are the big factors to be taken into account when evaluating the impact of innovations and the effects of accelerating organizational change? The most immediately obvious and pervasive influence is the accelerating expansion in information and communications technologies. These advances are raising a plethora of questions about library services provision, all of which demand impact evidence if sensible answers are to be adopted. Some of these changes and the questions they raise are reviewed below.

1.1.1 The impact of ICT

Advances in information technology are already making huge differences to the range of services offered by libraries, the expectations of library users and the roles of library staff. We offer below some examples of change in libraries followed by some questions in italic. If libraries are to make real advances in the 'Age of Information' they need to be able to answer many of these questions.

1 Libraries now have much **more information available** to them electronically than even five years ago, some of which could not have been realistically provided without enormous advances in computer power. Some of this information is only available on subscription and some of it is also available in traditional published form, raising a variety of questions.

   - *How much should the library spend on traditional forms of publication as against e-publications and electronic information?*
   - *Do different users (e.g. students seeking information, scholars, recreational readers, people with visual impairment) prefer traditional forms of publication or electronic access – and how fast are these preferences changing?*
   - *Should libraries subscribe to a wider range of electronic publications and, if so, which ones?*
   - *On what basis should they review and update these decisions?*

- *Should collections and services be managed locally or remotely, licensed for a fee or freely available?*

2 Since the internet (or 'surface web') offers more or less ready access to vast amounts of current or dated information, misinformation and disinformation, most of which cannot readily be filtered by libraries (see paragraph 3), this puts a premium on a range of **information literacy skills** that users may or may not have acquired. Users need to be able to select and reject information for a purpose, to identify and take account of biased information, and to decide whether information from a particular source can be seen as authoritative.

- *What is the role for library staff, if any, in helping people to acquire and develop appropriate information literacy skills?*
- *How should they interact with other people, such as teachers, who have a role in information literacy development?*
- *Do different types of libraries (e.g. health, education or public libraries) have different roles in information literacy development?*

3 Library staff should be better equipped than the average library user to **identify high-quality information on the internet**; they may have more time to do so and if they adopt a guidance role they may be able to steer users towards the most appropriate sources (whether these are electronic or traditional publications).

- *Is the way forward for library staff to be proactive in creating websites and multimedia web pages to promote library services and give easier access to various information sources?*
- *Should they go further and seek to set up gateways through which users can identify and gain access to selected, good-quality information sources (helping to construct the 'deep web')?*

4 Libraries of all kinds are increasingly **investing in computer technology** and are reorganizing available space to accommodate this change. Public libraries offer an alternative means for people, and especially less affluent people, to gain access to the internet.

- *Since libraries are not the only potential providers of access to information (alternatives include computer services or basic skills units in education,*

internet cafés or specialist information centres for the general public) to what extent should libraries become computer providers?
- *What effect will increased public access to the internet from home have on library-based internet provision?*
- *Will public access computing in libraries lead to decline in other library services?*
- *Is there a danger of putting all eggs in the wrong basket – such as investing in computer terminals when people are opting for laptops or mobile technologies?*

5   It is widely predicted that developments in information and communications technologies (ICTs) will have great impact on **key areas of library work**, notably: reader development; access by potential service users; information provision; supporting lifelong learning (including information literacy); social inclusion – attracting users from sectors of society that have not traditionally been heavy library users.

- *How can information technologies be harnessed to actively encourage people to read more widely and deeply?*
- *Can library doors be opened to potential readers who are attracted to those doors by their wish for free ICT access?*
- *How can library access best be enhanced using ICT?*
- *How can libraries establish their place in the pantheon of electronic information providers and how high a priority should this be?*
- *How can ICT be deployed to engage with a wider range of potential library users and which should be the priority groups to target?*
- *What is the most appropriate balance between different ICT tools (e.g. mobile technologies; social media; visual content creation)?*
- *Is internet provision no longer the main focus? Public library internet use research in Poland suggests that 'it is not the internet that is the main attractor to libraries . . . classes and events . . . linked to education or social integration . . . may be the force that will allow the library to retain its social role.' (Kochanowicz, 2012, 35)*
- *If libraries become successful in attracting new groups of users, what will be the effect on the existing core users?*

All of these questions are regularly raised by library managers in our workshops focused on evaluating the impact of library services. They usually have the same effect on participants – rather like hitting a brick wall. What rapidly becomes clear is that the traditional performance data collected by most libraries will not help to generate answers to these questions; nor do they equip staff to make operational or strategic decisions in these areas. Most library statistics still concentrate on monitoring the efficiency of the services currently being offered rather than their impact on users. Library managers usually do not have enough evidence of the impact of their current services to be able to tell how well they are doing, let alone having enough evidence to gauge whether a particular new service or intervention is likely to work. Fortunately, we have found ways of addressing these issues, which we will describe in later chapters.

1.1.2 The pressure to evaluate impact

Moving towards the electronic library may be bringing about a transformation in library-staff roles, user expectations, the range of services provided, service delivery methods and visions of access, but this is only part of the change agenda. As Megan Oakleaf writes in reviewing the academic library scene:

> Academic libraries have long enjoyed their status as the 'heart of the university.' However, in recent decades, higher education environments have changed. Government officials see higher education as a national resource. Employers view higher education institutions as producers of a commodity—student learning. Top academic faculty expect higher education institutions to support and promote cutting-edge research. Parents and students expect higher education to enhance students' collegiate experience, as well as propel their career placement and earning potential. Not only do stakeholders count on higher education institutions to achieve these goals, they also require them to *demonstrate evidence* that they have achieved them. The same is true for academic libraries; they too can provide evidence of their value. Community college, college, and university librarians no longer can rely on their stakeholders' belief in their importance. Rather, they must demonstrate their value.
>
> Oakleaf (2010, 11)

But what other factors are fuelling the drive towards impact evidence-gathering? Three of the obvious pressure points might be labelled 'the accountability obsession', 'the value for money drive' and 'the evidence-based working aspiration'. These are more fully outlined below.

1.1.3 A growing focus on performance management and accountability in public institutions

The idea of evaluating performance is not new, but it is more heavily embedded in some areas of work than in others. To take the most obvious example, assessment of student performance is heavily rooted in national education systems at all levels through internal tests, external examinations and, in many countries, through standardized assessment at various ages in schools. Inspection frameworks, for schools through to universities, now require more rigorous collection of evidence as well as the demonstration of analytical judgements based on this evidence. At the same time, national and federal governments are trying to create more consistent institutional management by demanding that all education institutions produce development plans addressing prescribed issues. There is also a growing movement towards evaluating the quality of teaching and of looking more broadly at the student experience within the education system.

The demand for more and better evidence of service efficiency and effectiveness has rapidly extended into other public service areas and is increasingly being felt in libraries of all kinds. The strength and focus of library target setting, benchmarking and efforts at standardization of services varies from country to country, but the trend towards greater accountability appears inexorable.

In this era of increased advocacy of public service accountability by national and local politicians, library managers have to be visibly on top of the evidence – this means not only collecting information but also being seen to analyse, interpret and apply the evidence with the (ostensible) aim of improving library services. How much real improvement results from all this activity will depend upon larger political factors such as the strength of the organizational will to bring about change, but a key contributory element is likely to be how much the evidence collected and analysed tells library managers about the impact of their current services and innovations.

Government libraries in the UK are under intense scrutiny at this time of national austerity measures. Cuts, reorganization and restructuring are commonplace in the drive for efficiency. Libraries need to demonstrate how they contribute to policy, to ensuring that government runs smoothly and effectively, and to decision making. To provide evidence of the precise nature and extent of the library contribution is a real challenge because of the complex processes involved and the volume of information drawn upon at each stage.

The UK National Health Service is preoccupied with accountability and is heavily target-driven. In particular, the mantra invoked when looking at any aspect of the health service is that it should have 'a positive impact on the quality of patient care'. It is sometimes hard to find evidence to demonstrate how this aim can be met by developing library services!

1.1.4 The value for money ethos

The policy concern with public accountability is closely linked to a focus on perceived service effectiveness – but a view of effectiveness that tends to be narrowly defined in cost-benefit terms – getting more for less money. Public services are widely viewed by politicians as requiring constant rationing and reduction, although they usually prefer to talk about 'cutting out waste' rather than admitting that they want to reduce or remove highly regarded services such as libraries.

Within the organization a narrowly finance-driven approach may create a managerial environment in which it is necessary to argue for funding based on 'results'. In this kind of environment the 'results' will again tend to be narrowly defined in terms of increased use or happier users (or, in higher education, increased levels of student retention), rather than what benefits people get from the services or whether different approaches might be more effective.

1.1.5 Rediscovering information

Until relatively recently, the processes involved in managing information in organizations were largely taken for granted. Although Henry Mintzberg (1973) identified three generic information roles among the ten that he attributed to all managers four decades ago, the idea that information should be managed alongside the traditional activities of managing people, finance and material resources was slow to take root.

Again, from the late 1970s onwards, advances in information technology played an important part here. With the advent of affordable mainframe computers and later of networked personal computers, proposals to spend substantial sums of money on efficient organization of various types of information, which had previously been handled less efficiently as an invisible part of various people's jobs, tended to bring these information areas into sharper focus.

In the 1980s, the process of promoting information up organizational agendas was greatly assisted by Michael Porter (1985), who advanced the idea that better information is what brings organizational success. Porter's version of competitive advantage, based on the 'value chain' (fed by strategic information) in turn led to other information-centred formulations such as the 'learning company', knowledge management and 'evidence-based policy and practice'.

How far have these ideas penetrated into the core of library and information management thinking? The idea of competitive advantage gave business information services a powerful advocacy tool and some library service managers have made efforts to reconstitute themselves as higher-status knowledge managers. However, by no means all library services have reached the point where they feel the need to introduce, for example, a strategic information strategy (as distinct from an information technology implementation and training plan).

1.1.6   Towards evidence-based library and information work

The idea of evidence-based policy and practice (EBPP) is potentially more important for the library and information service world, if only because it has taken organizational root in some traditionally strong areas of library service provision, notably health. The core idea emerged in the medical world in Canada and the USA as 'evidence-based health care' and was rapidly transplanted to Australasia and the UK (see Muir Gray, 1997), before being taken up in the education and social care sectors and by some national governments. In essence, EBPP is about systematic collection and interpretation of what is perceived as valid, important and applicable evidence.

It is clear that EBPP is interpreted in somewhat different ways in the various sectors involved. For example, in the UK health sector there is a strong focus on metaclinical evidence as a guide to decision making, but a growing recognition that different evidence rules apply at the public health end of the continuum; in social care and in education the focus is very much on the nature of acceptable evidence, while the UK government emphasis is primarily on securing a range of evidence to help in the formation, implementation and evaluation of policy. However, all these approaches recognize that the policy and practice evidence base draws (more or less confidently) upon a variety of sources, including:

- academic research evidence
- practice-generated impact evidence
- professionally mediated 'best practice' information.

In other words, EBPP concerns are very much the concerns of this book.

When it comes to applying EBPP principles in practice, the key concerns common to all the main public sector applications include:

- availability of sufficient evidence of high enough quality to inform a specific practice question
- synthesis of the available evidence on a key question to provide an overview of the findings
- adequate dissemination of the evidence to enable practitioners to gain access to the evidence in an appropriate form
- identification of gaps in the evidence and strategic initiatives to fill important gaps

- disciplined reporting of the research processes and the evidence in a 'practitioner-friendly' manner, to enable practitioners to gauge the relevance, importance and reliability of the evidence
- fostering of a strategic and operational management climate to encourage EBPP
- introduction of structures and mechanisms to encourage application of EBPP approaches
- professional development support for managers to equip them to find and appraise the evidence
- active debate about the nature and basis of professional knowledge and practice.

All of these components raise issues for evidence-based library work, but some progress has been made. In introducing the first professional textbook on the subject, two of the leading advocates (Booth and Brice, 2004) asked and answered the key question:

> Is it possible to adapt the evidence-based practice model to librarianship and information work? To do so involves applying the results from rigorous research studies to professional practice to improve the quality of services to users.

There is now a well established Evidence Based Library and Information Practice (EBLIP) Conference[2] (heavily dominated by health librarians) as well as a specialist journal *Evidence Based Library and Information Practice*[3] which was launched in 2006. Unsurprisingly, there is also some challenge to the concept and especially the approach to compiling the evidence base (e.g. Banks, 2008) because of a perceived over-adherence to the medical 'gold standard' of randomly controlled trials (RCT). However, Brettle (2012) points out that although the definition of EBLIP offered by Booth (2006) refers to best-quality evidence (generated from research, among other elements) he makes no mention of particular research designs. Booth (2009) himself vigorously rebuts the perception that he favours the RCT approach and offers a flexible framework for evidence-based library work. Once this movement expands beyond the medical world (assuming that this is ever achieved) the whole process might be seen as providing a framework to exploit impact evidence systematically.

1.2   Emerging interest in the management of change

How much change are we really looking at? A decade ago, in her commentary on US academic libraries, Covey observes that:

Development of the digital library precipitates massive change, not only in delivery formats and access methods, but also in work and workflow, staffing, the scope of library instruction, and assessment efforts. . . . Web access and capabilities have brought with them the need for libraries to engage in the design, management, and assessment of multimedia Web pages, portals, and products. . . . Libraries are conducting surveys, focus groups, user protocols, transaction log analysis, and other kinds of research to assess traditional and digital resource use; the usability of online resources; user needs, expectations, and satisfaction; and the quality of library services and facilities. They are grappling with how to assess research and learning outcomes, cost-effectiveness, and cost-benefits.

Covey (2002)

These demands and challenges are now transforming all types of libraries. Specific drivers of change include substantial investment in ICT implementation in libraries of all kinds (including major public access through public libraries programmes such as the US Libraries Initiative[4], the People's Network in the UK and more recently the Global Libraries Initiative in Central and South America (Mexico, Chile and Colombia), Africa (Botswana), Asia (Indonesia and Vietnam) and various East European countries).

If we take the levels of uptake of training workshops in various countries as an indicator of evolving professional development priorities among library staff it is clear that there is burgeoning demand for:

- ICT skills training focused on the changing work of library staff in e-information environments
- education and training focused on the roles of librarians as teachers, trainers and informal mentors, especially in helping people to use ICT effectively
- more help in development planning and change management as services adapt to the demands of increasingly ICT-based services.

The accompanying rhetoric is of transforming libraries and of the penalties if opportunities are missed to establish libraries at the centre of the new information landscape. Interestingly, a decade ago the People's Network chose to move beyond rhetoric in commissioning 'toolkits' linked to training programmes to help library service managers in grappling with the issues of managing change[5]. One central message from this work is that serious attention to change involves gaining greater clarity about what sorts of change are desirable, what change is inevitable and about the effects of change – based on evidence about what works. In this sense, moving towards more effective management of change is leading to greater need for impact evidence.

1.3   What is distorting the picture?

It is obvious to anyone who looks at the issues of evaluating the impact of library services that this is not a problem-free and straightforward process. As we will show in the next chapter, impact is a slippery concept that many service managers find difficult to grasp. But the problems begin even before the individual library service manager starts to get to grips with the concept. We have identified in this chapter some of the factors that are currently pushing libraries towards impact evaluation: the problem is that all of these factors can have a more or less profound distorting effect on how (and indeed, whether) we engage in gathering evidence of impact.

Taking these factors in roughly the order that they were introduced earlier, the gallop towards electronic libraries, the accountability obsession (and the value for money drive) and even the evidence-based working aspiration can all make life more difficult for the manager who wants to get a real hold on impact. There may also be problems with conflicting agendas and with our capacity to get involved seriously in gathering evidence of effectiveness.

1.3.1   Being realistic about evaluating ICT initiatives

We need to decide when collecting evidence is a good idea and what we are doing this for.

Staff of library services are racing to equip themselves as leading providers of access to the internet and to learn the new skills required to help their users to become confident users of electronic information sources. Unfortunately, the base from which many libraries are starting does not help. As David Murray (2003) noted:

> When we roll out a superb development – the People's Network for example – we graft it on to a failing infrastructure and hope the public will see 'new library'. Too often, what they see is a load of new computers and new furniture in a building that's coming apart at the seams.

This problem can be even more acute in developing or emerging countries, where library services have not necessarily developed to anything like the extent of services in Western countries. Putting ICT in place to encourage public access is not enough without ambitious training programmes seeking to transform the roles of library staff from custodian of the place to facilitator of public access and supporter of independent learning, backed by powerful advocacy to transform public opinion of the role of libraries in the community.

Similarly, many libraries are making efforts to engage users with ICT but without sufficient computers or licensed software to take this on realistically. Their staff may be striving to help users but may not themselves have sufficient training or experience in effective internet searching, or in providing one-to-one tuition or small group training.

Impact, in this less than favourable context, is likely to mean 'any change in our users that may have come about despite the unsuitable environment, lack of confidence or competence in some staff and the depredations of years of systematic under-funding'. This may not be important, if the evaluation is being conducted primarily to inform managers about what needs to be addressed first, but there is a real issue about impact evidence collection for other purposes.

Service evaluation is, among other things, a political process, especially if the intention is to use the evidence to secure funds or to account to politicians or senior organizational managers. You may want to evaluate services that are being delivered in heavily unfavourable conditions and present the case for change – if there is a real chance of changing those conditions. To do such an evaluation in less optimistic circumstances may simply provide evidence to be used by others to allocate blame – in your direction.

1.3.2   The obsession with accountability

In the 'value for money' organizational environment, securing a share of diminishing organizational funds may become a ritual dance with its own rules, which may or may not involve presentation of high-quality evidence of effectiveness. In such an environment, presenting impact evidence as part of the case for service development may be vital or it may be more important to go through the motions of doing so. Evidence-based decision making may be a key to success in your organization but it may also be a notion to which strategic managers pay lip service.

Attention to the financial 'bottom line' is of course important for all organizations but, even in the private sector, there is growing concern that if we only think in narrow 'value for money' terms this may result in throwing out the creative and productive baby with the organizational bathwater. The concern does not end here.

Critics of New Managerialism (a term which is usually applied pejoratively) claim that it denigrates professionalism in favour of generic service management, emphasizes public scrutiny of services, opts for complexity in articulating service objectives, and focuses on evaluating apparent effects on 'customers' (who replace 'service users' in the New Managerialist vocabulary) by means of arbitrary service delivery targets. Deem, Hillyard and Reed (2007) characterized the consequent effect on public services as a descent 'from regulated autonomy to institutionalized distrust.' Pursuing this theme, Macfarlane claims that:

> The performative culture is symptomatic of a society in which there has been an erosion of trust in the professions and those working in the public sector. . . The effect has been to create a contemporary research environment that places a strain on many of the virtues essential to the ethical conduct of research . . .
>
> Macfarlane (2009, 159)

(For a more positive view see Boston et al., 1996.)

What can we do to counter the tendency towards top-down control? Good governance requires us to move on from arbitrary performance indicators that may corrupt the services they are intended to evaluate by concentrating effort in inappropriate areas. Instead, we need high-quality evidence gathering about the effectiveness of library services, allied to sound professional judgements in interpreting the evidence and proposing appropriate action (see also Crawford, 2006). The process model described in Part 2 of this book should help to achieve these goals.

One other disturbing tendency that we have noted is for government departments and their national or local agencies to blur the important distinction between evaluating innovative programmes and making the advocacy case to do more of the same. Evaluation of initiatives should help to show what is working more or less well, which elements in the programme need remedial attention or should be more widely adopted, and whether the initiative represents good value for money. If the 'evaluation' assumes the last point and concentrates on showing how everything in the garden is lovely, this ceases to be evaluation and is not a good foundation on which to build a convincing case for development.

The fantasies about total control are not confined to the public sector. Looking at the world of business, Kaplan and Norton (1992) noted:

> . . . because traditional measurement systems have sprung from the finance function, the systems have a control bias. That is, traditional performance measurement systems specify the particular actions they want employees to take and then measure to see whether the employees have in fact taken those actions. In that way, the systems try to control behaviour. Such measurement systems fit with the engineering mentality of the Industrial Age.

How should the business world set about performance measurement in the Postindustrial Age? Their solution is 'the balanced scorecard', which

. . . puts strategy and vision, not control, at the centre. It establishes goals but assumes that people will adopt whatever behaviour and take whatever actions are necessary to arrive at those goals.

We will return to the balanced scorecard in section 3.1 and explore its usefulness in selecting appropriate impact indicators across four important perspectives.

1.3.3   Is evidence-based working the answer?

When Mahatma Gandhi was asked by an interviewer what he thought about Western civilization he answered 'I think it would be a good idea'. Evidence-based policy and practice (EBPP) probably falls into the same category, at least for the immediate future. However, the idea of EBPP is already under challenge.

The contention that basing decisions on evidence (or aspiring to do so) is not enough has been around since evidence-based working was first proposed and is well articulated by Peter Knight (2003). He asserts unequivocally that 'Evidence cannot prescribe action' and that 'It is more fruitful to think about expertise-based practice in complex settings' before observing that 'evidence' is only as good as the questions we ask and calling on higher education researchers to learn to ask better questions. He then navigates into the long-running debate about the relationship (if any) between research evidence and policy decision making, arguing that 'evidence' needs to be *mediated*, because it is complicated, *complemented* because it is incomplete, and *championed* because even strong evidence gets ignored otherwise. Finally, he calls for expertise-based, rather than evidence-based, policy and practice. 'Experts', he says, 'are plainly informed by evidence but they add value to it, by making judgements about cases not directly covered by the evidence at hand and identifying areas in need of study.' They can also, he hopes, 'engage with policy-makers in ways that inert evidence cannot'.

Following on from Knight's arguments we suggest that the appropriate aspiration is towards *expertise-based and evidence-informed decision making.* (It is interesting to note that the main UK centre for EBPP in education[6] prefers to talk about evidence-informed rather than evidence-based practice.)

1.3.4   Beware of 'methodological fundamentalism'

Clearly, New Managerialism is not a universal phenomenon and there has been some reaction against its extreme forms in countries which at first embraced its tenets with the greatest enthusiasm. However, where this approach to public sector management has been even partially adopted, it has fuelled demand for introduction of service impact evaluation to gauge performance levels, often as part of the espousal of EBPP (which, by narrowly prescribing the nature of acceptable evidence may become a convenient rationing device to limit service innovation to proposals which can meet these prescriptions). Some researchers elect to adhere to a narrow conception of evidence-based working (described by House (2005; 2006) as 'methodological fundamentalism'), which excludes all but the most rigid evaluation programmes based on randomized controlled trials and regression discontinuity designs that meet specific (politically defined) criteria.

The problem for US libraries is that, for the research to be taken seriously by the Federal Government, it has to feature in a charming website called the What Works Clearinghouse (WWC)[7], established by the US Department of Education's Institute of Education Sciences. The criteria for inclusion within the Clearinghouse are, to say the least, rigid: the research reports submitted to their review process are classified in one of three categories:

1 **'Meets evidence standards'** – randomized controlled trials and regression discontinuity designs that meet their specific criteria (virtually impossible to achieve in any real educational research project concerned with library or information service provision).
2 **'Meets evidence standards with reservations'** – strong quasi-experimental studies that have comparison groups and meet their other evidence standards.
3 **'Does not meet evidence standards'** – studies that provide insufficient evidence of causality or otherwise fall foul of the WWC criteria.

The nasty trap for unwary researchers is that if you aspire to getting your research included in the second category and fail, you are then consigned to the 'Does not meet evidence standards' group. Not the most promising start to a postgraduate research career![8]

1.3.5   Conflicting priorities

In some cases there may be conflict between the larger policy agenda and organizational priorities. For example, national policy makers may call on organizations to adopt an impact-focused and user needs-centred approach but internal organizational pressures may dictate a more limited and less challenging outputs-focused approach. (We encountered a frustrating example of this phenomenon in one country, where we helped a local team of consultants to construct a public libraries impact evaluation framework, which was accepted by the supervisory committee but watered down as soon as we had left the country.)

Where national policy includes setting targets for a whole sphere of work, such as schools or the health service, these may be so general that they cannot be readily translated into library service contribution terms. We have already noted that health library services usually have only an indirect and diffuse impact on the quality of client care; similarly, although it is possible to show that schools that are equipped with good libraries tend to produce better exam results, it is much harder to show how anything done within a particular school library directly affects student examination performance.

We may also have conflicting priorities about where and how intensively to focus in relation to service impact within our own library service. Should we give attention to areas in which we can readily be shown to be failing, or concentrate on our main successes? Is it astute to focus, for example, on the relationships between academic staff and library staff in education settings or would this be counter-productive?

Since all libraries are short of time, and given that collecting impact evidence takes time and effort, what proportion of the performance evaluation for your library should be focused on impact? Will all the key players agree to spend the time required? There may also be concerns about timescales. Much of the evidence-gathering in organizations runs to an annual reporting cycle but looking at the impact of innovation in any significant area of work may well require a longer timescale. And how well attuned is your organization to the need to gather impact evidence at all? Will going down this road tend to isolate the library from the larger organization?

The key to answering these questions is to decide why you are looking for evidence of impact. If you are doing this primarily to account to the parent organization or to secure additional funding, it is important to choose ways of gathering evidence that will accord to the predominant organizational ethos. If you are gathering evidence to meet external project-funding requirements then it is likely that the parameters will be set as part of the contract award process. On the other hand, if you are focusing on impact primarily to inform yourselves as managers so that you can improve the service, then any evidence that you will find convincing is acceptable.

1.4   Why is it important to tackle impact?

1.4.1   What is driving the change?

We have tried to show that there are a number of different drivers pushing organizations towards evaluating their effectiveness. As we will see later, different approaches to evaluating impact and different types of evidence will be appropriate depending on whether the demand is coming from:

- the federal/national government level (characterized by very strategic and apparently simplistic targets that are prone to change at short notice)
- external inspection regimes focused on service improvement or the achievement of standards
- the institution of which the library service is part (requiring effectiveness priorities to accord with institutional targets)
- the managers of the library service (focusing on greater understanding of what makes services work well)
- the members of, or participants in the service (where the motives for looking at impact may vary substantially).

It is also important to recognize that there are still many work areas where efficiency monitoring is all that is required; when for example:

- there is no pressure to show impact – there are few demands for evidence from inside or outside the organization
- it may not yet be politic to broadcast or share impact evidence (even if individual service managers choose to focus on impact as well as traditional performance measurement 'busy-ness statistics' to inform their own management decision making)
- there is a tacit conspiracy not to look too closely at whether large sums of money are being spent well!

Curiously, one of the areas in which effective performance has not been taken seriously, until very recently, is the implementation of ICT programmes, unless counting 'hits' on a website can be assumed to be evaluating anything. Various surveys of ICT projects have found that there is usually no real attempt to evaluate them and that when any questions are asked they normally stop at the point of establishing whether the installation works, rather than going on to ask whether it could have been done better or was worth doing at all. This situation is now changing fairly rapidly, at least where there is more or less direct competition between traditional and new ways of providing services.

1.4.2 Why move on?

There are several reasons why library services should be giving more attention to impact evaluation:

External factors

1 The political agenda is changing. The drive towards greater accountability may have a distorting effect on service provision – unless we can come up with good-quality evidence about what works and how.

2 There is a danger that externally imposed performance targets will be confined to evidence drawn from output measures and ignore much of what libraries are achieving.

3 Being effective in meeting government priorities (for example regarding social inclusion, lifelong learning and parity of access) may require additional service expenditure. Success in addressing these issues will have to be demonstrated to justify this. Capacity building in communities requires good evidence.

4 There are opportunities for libraries operating in different fields to learn from each other about how to demonstrate success effectively.

Internal factors

1 Choosing targets carefully and gathering appropriate evidence is an important management skill – the process encourages clarity and helps to focus on priorities.

2 Focusing on a limited number of aims and impact indicators should make you question why certain things are not happening. For example, why is the well staffed and stocked library not a first port of call for senior managers in this organization?

3 Where impact targets are integrated into practice this should lead to higher staff motivation, because they can see what they want to achieve, why they are doing things and what success they are having ('this is more satisfying than just jumping through hoops').

1.4.3   What library managers say

We have looked briefly at why there is a growing demand for evidence of the impact of services and at how these pressures can distort the picture. But why do library service managers get involved in yet another time-consuming activity? The evidence from several hundred managers who have participated in our workshops is that they usually get involved for one or more of eight reasons (in descending order of frequency of mention):

1 **Focus for development**. Most managers want to know whether they are being effective and what they need to do to get better.

2 **Survival**. Libraries are no longer automatically seen as 'a good thing' and there is increasing competition from other 'support services', especially organizational computer services and the internet. Libraries are (relatively) expensive to provide – so why bother? Assembling good-quality evidence of the impact of services currently being provided should help to fight off any future threat to libraries – if the threat is current it may be too late to start!

3 **Internal accountability**. Increasingly, parent organizations want to know not just whether their library services are working efficiently but how well they are contributing to the overall organizational goals.

4 **External accountability**. We have already shown that national and federal governments are seeking greater accountability (or control) from public services. They may want to focus on service impact, but even if they resort to more traditional performance measures it may be important to focus on impact in order to show the full extent of the library contribution.

5 **Professional pride/job satisfaction**. The demand for impact evidence from senior management or from government is not universal. Even where there are no external pressures, some managers want to get involved in looking at their service impact because they want to be sure that they are doing a good job – even if there is little scope for development.

6 **Status/profile**. Although this may not be an incentive at the outset, many managers report that one of the benefits of undertaking impact evaluation is greater recognition or more positive feedback from their users. These effects can be quite specific (such as when various school librarians field tested school library self-evaluation materials that mirrored the school self-evaluation framework about to be introduced and were seen by teachers as 'instant experts' on self-evaluation because of this) but asking questions about your service is likely to produce answers – some of which will be encouraging!

7 **Securing additional resources**. Where organizations are demanding impact evidence as part of the resource allocation process, it makes sense to get involved. In any case it will help your argument if you can show that you are being effective in ways that interest the fundholders.

8 **International advocacy**. Impact evaluation provides a basis for advocacy on behalf of public libraries, school libraries, or libraries in general.

2

Getting to grips with impact

If you have decided to do some impact evaluation, or to try out the process, you may want to go straight on to Chapter 4. If you are interested in some of the difficulties inherent in evaluating impact and in gathering and interpreting evidence, read on.

2.1   A metaphor and a model

The language and underpinning concepts of performance measurement are often arcane and sometimes confusing. This is probably because the basic metaphor of performance indicators and targets and the associated vocabulary were developed by engineers when looking at system efficiency and appropriated by accountants to simplify and 'measure' the complex world of managing organizations.

It is hardly surprising that the concepts of performance measurement work reasonably well when the library is considered as a more or less efficient operating system. Unfortunately for the accountants (often operating in their guise of management consultants), libraries do not exist simply to perform efficiently. The performance metaphor begins to break down when we look at what the service is trying to achieve and how well it is doing (or moving beyond easily measured 'outputs'). In suggesting a way forward, we would like to stress that performance measurement based on system efficiency is important for libraries and should run alongside any work on evaluating impact. Efficiency is important – but so is effectiveness.

Figure 2.1 outlines the traditional performance evaluation model. In this model, performance indicators are arrived at by looking successively at inputs, processes and outputs. Pursuing the engineering example, if you are in the business of manufacturing televisions, your inputs can be all the components that go together to make televisions. The processes will then be everything that you do in your production line to assemble the televisions. Your outputs are the completed and working televisions. In this model, if you want to look at the

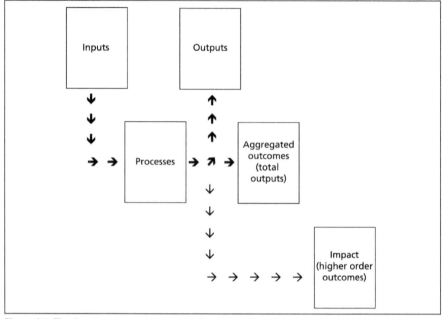

Figure 2.1 *The input, process, output and outcomes model*

outcomes from the production process you can resort to aggregated outputs, by counting the total number of television sets produced (and probably also the proportion of these that work when switched on!).

The engineering process model works reasonably well in complex organizations like libraries – but only up to a point. No amount of aggregation in library settings will usually tell you much about impact. Our next example shows where the problem lies.

If, for example, you are trying to improve the knowledge of a targeted group of children, you might do this by identifying and buying a collection of books on relevant topics and noting how many items you have bought at what cost *(input measures)*. You will then prepare the books for loan and do whatever else is needed to get them into places where they are likely to be accessible to the target children (you might look at the speed and precision with which you do this as *process measures*).

Most of these books will then be used by some or all of the target group and you can choose various ways of measuring how frequently they are borrowed by these children *(output measures)*. But how do you get from there to finding out whether the children know more as a result of your intervention? No amount of monitoring of book loans, however carefully done, will tell you whether the items borrowed were actually read, let alone whether the targeted users were in any way affected by what they read, or whether they learnt anything. In other words, in organizations dedicated to providing services for people, *aggregated outputs* are not usually the same as outcomes.

Some people in the performance indicators business have recognized this problem and tend to resort to other descriptions, such as *higher order outcomes* (or *achievement* in the education world) to describe the world of impact beyond traditional performance measurement. However, recognizing and labelling the problem area doesn't take us very much further. Approaching impact from this direction makes it difficult to focus clearly because most of the evidence gathered is only tangentially relevant, since it concentrates on the efficiency of systems, services and processes. That is why we take a different approach to evaluating impact in this book.

> **LAWS OF IMPACT EVALUATION 1**
> Effective impact evaluation requires clear and consistent use of terms.

2.2 Why is impact such a slippery concept?

It is not surprising if library service managers find it difficult to get to grips with issues about service impact. Full-time academic researchers often run into difficulty with these issues too. Some years ago we were asked to do an evaluation (Streatfield and Markless, 2002a) of a whole national research programme, which was devoted to gauging the value and impact of various types of libraries, and found:

- little attempt to define terms
- no frameworks through which to explore value and impact
- a tendency to move away from value and impact towards reporting and describing activities/processes
- a linked tendency to escape from these problems into national surveys of activities or policies – which tell us almost nothing about value or impact
- problems with the methods chosen to gather evidence about impact.

Why has the library and information research community made slow progress in this area? Part of the problem may be in yawning gaps between the demands of policy makers, the needs of service managers and the interests of academic researchers.

Broadly:

- Policy makers are called upon to find better ways of assessing the benefits of their initiatives and programmes, and the quest to find mechanisms with which to control situations is still being pursued (this was first discussed as a research policy issue in the 1970s – see Caplan, Morrison and Stambaugh, 1975).
- Some parts of the public sector are more outcomes-focused (e.g. education, where there is heavy emphasis on comparative educational attainment); some areas are aspiring to become more outcomes-driven (e.g. health and social care).
- The 'natural' interests of the library and information research community are in exploring and understanding social processes in depth. These may have to give way to the outcomes focus demanded by the 'new managerialism', but this battle has hardly begun.

What is clear is that policy makers, managers, practitioners and researchers are all coming under increased pressure to get to grips with questions of service value and impact. This requires a significant change in how research is conducted. *All* the projects that we looked at in our overview baulked at addressing educational-outcomes impact issues (such as 'before and after' measurements of skills acquisition). Researchers in other practice areas such as education, health and social care manage to conduct such studies. It can be done!

2.3   Overviews of impact

This book is focused on evaluating the impact (or, if you like, 'micro-impact') of your library but there is, of course, a bigger picture, which we will call 'macro-impact'. It is possible to concentrate on the overall economic or social impact of library and information systems, usually for advocacy purposes.

We describe various examples of economic impact studies and social impact programmes later in this book. For school libraries, the Ohio study led by Ross Todd and Carol Kuhlthau (2005), set out to answer the question 'How do school libraries/media resource centers help students with their learning in and away from school?' – by asking them directly. The Rutgers University team in effect orchestrated a mass write-in among high school students in Ohio to an electronic questionnaire, enlisting the help of targeted schools and school librarians. More than 13,000 students responded, many of them giving powerful testimony to the value of school libraries, as reported by Whelan (2004).

When you are assembling evidence of the impact of services it is important to remember that well grounded research evidence can and should be cited to back up your case – it isn't always necessary to reinvent the wheel. You can also use what we know from the research evidence to decide what areas to concentrate on in evaluation work, as we will show in the next chapter.

2.4   Changing how we think of evidence
2.4.1   From hypothesis testing to 'grounded theory'

What we now think of as scientific research is heavily shaped by Karl Popper's proposition that knowledge accumulates by falsification (or refutation) of hypotheses. In the social sciences, the idea of proposing hypotheses has been more or less readily accepted. Unfortunately, the complexities of doing research in the real world, where it is not possible to isolate and examine variables in turn, has led to perversion of Popper's approach in two ways. First, researchers drift into hypothesis-proving rather than hypothesis-challenging; this results in assembling evidence in favour of the hypothesis rather than making rigorous efforts to undermine it. Second, there is a tendency in social science research to rewrite or tinker with the hypotheses during the course of the research, when the work begins to call them into question. Both of these approaches fall foul of Popper's (1969) admonition that 'indefatigable rational criticism of our suppositions . . . is of decisive importance . . . to save us from the allure of the "obvious truth" of received doctrine'.

One answer to the perceived limitations of the hypothesis-based approach to social science research was proposed by Glaser and Strauss as long ago as 1967. Their concept of 'grounded theory' suggests that the theory should come out of qualitative-research data collection rather than being proposed at the outset. Researchers have welcomed 'grounded theory' because it gets them out of the hypothesis straitjacket. Unfortunately, some researchers (including academic researchers in the library and information field) think of it as a licence to by-pass the difficult research questions and to claim that their evidence supports whatever ideas they want to advance. In fact, grounded theory offers a systematic approach based on constant comparisons, theoretical sampling and application of coding procedures.

Since much of the evidence-gathering likely to be undertaken by library service managers is based on deciding in advance what to collect and how the results will be analysed, thinking about grounded theory raises a variety of questions about the nature of evidence and its interpretation. Not surprisingly, we will return to these questions (in Chapter 8).

2.4.2   Emergent evaluation

The approach to impact evaluation that we introduce in this book is sometimes called the simple logic model and is based on identifying impact indicators and collecting evidence against them. However, as libraries increasingly seek to take advantage of ICT developments by introducing new services, design different spaces to engage the community in new activities and venture into teaching and learning in the area of information literacy, they are moving into the area of 'emergent evaluation' in which it is not straightforward to predict where change will appear and therefore, where to focus the evaluation. Rogers (2008) distinguishes between simple logic models and complicated logic models, which she describes as interventions with a multiplicity of components, agencies and causal strands. As though this is not complicated enough, she then articulates a further category of complex interventions and logic models where the paths from action to impact are complex, with disproportionate relationships (where, at critical levels, a small change can make a big difference) and emergent impacts (which cannot readily be specified at the outset). The more advanced library services appear to have all the characteristics of the complex logic model. To what extent should evaluators be encouraged to embrace emergent evaluation when the services being evaluated are innovating?

The good news is that the simple logic model will probably be sufficient for most practical library evaluation purposes, provided that we do not try to establish direct causal relationships between services provided and behavioural changes in users. We may have to accept that we do not always know what will happen or what is likely to happen when we innovate (e.g. by introducing a new computer-based service). In these situations, we may have to start innovating and try to capture as much information as possible about the changes that are happening before we are in a position to decide which changes are important and therefore where we should focus our evaluation.

This problem has been recognized in the evaluation world since the 1970s, when Malcolm Parlett and various collaborators developed the idea of 'illuminative evaluation' to provide flexibility at the early stages of the process (Parlett and Dearden, 1977).

What does this approach entail? There are usually three stages: investigator observation, further inquiry and then seeking to explain. As Parlett and Hamilton (1972) explain:

> During the first, exploratory stage, we . . . become 'knowledgeable' about the scheme. At the second stage this [enables] our questioning to become more focused; communication to be more coherent and relaxed; and, in general, observation and enquiry to be more directed, systematic, and selective.

Elsewhere, they describe this phase as one of 'progressive focusing':

> The third stage [involves] seeking general principles underlying the organization of the programme, spotting patterns of cause and effect within its operation, and placing individual findings within a broader explanatory context.

This approach is put forward in deliberate challenge to the 'traditional evaluator' who:

> examines the . . . formalised plan and extracts the programme's goals, objectives or desired outcomes. From these, in turn, he derives the tests and attitude inventories he will administer. His aim is to evaluate the instructional system by examining whether, for example, it has 'attained its objectives' or met its 'performance criteria'.

The approach to impact evaluation outlined in this book starts from the position of the 'traditional evaluator', because setting objectives for programmes of service provision is an integral part of much service planning. Like Parlett and Hamilton, however, we favour cross-checking in data collection methods ('triangulation' in social science research jargon) because all evidence-collection methods have inherent weaknesses which may distort the results. We strongly favour employing a range of types of evidence, from the statistical to the anecdotal, in addressing impact and recognize that no amount of evaluation will ever provide the full and complete picture or explanation of a programme of service provision and its effects. In terms of reporting the evidence and conclusions, we again like the illuminative evaluators' concept of 'recognition of authority' as more helpful than 'objectivity' and 'generalizability' in weighing up evidence. (We use the word 'resonance' for the recognition by practitioners of what is being described in a setting in which they work.) All these points are explored in later chapters.

We will come back to emergent evaluation in Chapter 6 when we look at impact indicators and in Chapter 11 when we focus on international evaluation.

2.5   What does impact mean?

What form does impact evaluation take in the real world of libraries? Here are some real examples drawn from different sectors of library and information work in the UK. Not all of these cover 'conventional' evidence of library service impact.

Example 2.1 The health service

It can be difficult for UK health libraries to demonstrate their impact on patient care as required by the government. Usually, they can only point to general benefits of their work on the people who are, in turn, influencing delivery or providing services directly to patients. However, sometimes they are lucky. When the health librarian at one hospital tries to find out about the usefulness of the interlibrary loans service to clinical staff he arranges a series of interviews with users. One of these users, a psychologist, reports that he has cut the waiting time before his patients can see him from two years to six months, as a direct consequence of the information provided. This type of evidence fits well into the health culture, since there are specific 'quality of patient care' government targets about cutting waiting lists. The only problem is how best to present this story to senior managers who may be more accustomed to assessing quantitative performance data (Chamberlain, 2003).

Example 2.2 The world of business

One of the major UK employers' organizations operates a proactive library and information service for its staff. At the period in question, one target user group for this service is the staff of the regional offices scattered around the country. These people operate more or less independently but they are brought in to the London headquarters once a year for a week of briefing and de-briefing. Since they are an eccentric bunch of individuals, it is no surprise that this week always culminates in a party of legendary proportions. This event usually takes in half a dozen drinking places, but also sucks in a few key members of HQ staff – strictly by invitation only. The head of the information service is first invited to join this gathering in his second year of running the service. This is a strong endorsement of the perceived value of the service by this maverick group and, accordingly, useful evidence to the manager that he is on the right lines. Unfortunately, this evidence is not likely to feature in any official report, especially since his line manager doesn't get invited!

Example 2.3 Schools

A school librarian wants to find out what the children think of the school's homework club (designed to support them when they are doing assignments or preparing for lessons outside school hours). She wants to know why some children drop out and why others never attend. After piloting a questionnaire, she chooses three groups (regulars, drop-outs, non-attendees) in one year cohort for a survey. The survey shows that the most effective promotion for the club has come from teachers and fellow students (rather than from posters or leaflets); the student monitors (older students) are strongly disliked; access to staff help is valued over access to resources; and a picture emerges of how the homework club contributes to effective curriculum delivery.

As a result of these findings the monitors have been rapidly eased out. Tutors are now equipped with homework club advertisement bookmarks for use on academic review days and parents' evenings, so that the club can be offered as a place of help and so that attendance can be set as a target when action is discussed. Extra teacher support time is given to the club and specific support is planned to help the more vulnerable students when they attend. The result has been a steady core of attendance that no longer changes dramatically from season to season.

This is a classic approach to evaluation – it is time-consuming because it is thorough and it has provided the whole school (not just the librarian) with evidence on which to make decisions. The effect has also been to reinforce the role of the librarian in supporting curriculum development (Streatfield and Markless, 2003).

3

The research base of this work

If your main aim now is to get to grips with impact evaluation in your library, you may like to skip this chapter. On the other hand, if you are interested in what the literature has to say about impact evaluation and, more specifically, if you want to know about the research that underpins this book – please read on.

This chapter looks at some of the main recent advances in evaluating impact in other sectors, how these have influenced our thinking and how they can help library service managers in evaluating impact. We then home in on the library and information research and what it tells us about the overall impact of various types of libraries. Finally, we outline the research base of our own work leading to this book.

3.1   What we know about impact from the management literature

Fortunately, perhaps, we don't have space here to trace all the twists and turns of researchers and management gurus who moved on from traditional performance measurement in a quest to determine the impact of services. Instead, we will look at a few important staging posts along the way.

We have pointed to a shift in focus, away from monitoring processes and outputs using traditional performance indicators (busy-ness statistics) towards 'higher-order outcomes', 'impact' or 'achievement' – or from monitoring efficiency to gauging effectiveness. Earlier we noted the danger of adopting too narrow a focus on value for money or costs as the determining factor. The two main approaches described next arise out of concern to get a broad perspective on effectiveness and to translate this into practical evaluation action. Both versions were generated in the world of business and both are sufficiently widely used to make it worth considering them here.

3.1.1 The balanced scorecard

A useful way of ensuring *balance* in generating indicators comes in the form of the 'balanced scorecard'. This approach was developed in business in the USA as a result of concern that financially based performance measurement systems are likely to produce a 'control bias' (as noted in section 1.3.2 above):

> The balanced scorecard, on the other hand . . . puts strategy and vision, not control, at the center. It establishes goals but assumes that people will adopt whatever behaviors and take whatever actions are necessary to arrive at those goals.
>
> Kaplan and Norton (1992)

Although developed in the business sector, this system provides a useful framework to consult when you are trying to draw up performance measures for the library. The underlying premise is that no single measure (whether financial in business or levels of use in libraries) can focus attention on all critical areas of the service. However, it can be difficult to design a balanced set of measures that gives a comprehensive overview on your own. The balanced scorecard sets out to provide help in this area. It:

> . . . allows managers to look at the business from four important perspectives [and yet] minimizes information overload by limiting the number of measures used. . . . The balanced scorecard forces managers to focus on the handful of measures that are most critical.

The scorecard approach is based on answering four fundamental questions:

* How do customers (users) see us?
* What must we excel at (internal perspective)?
* Can we continue to improve and create value (innovation and learning perspective)?
* How do we look to shareholders (or stakeholders – financial perspective)?

Answering these questions *together* lets you see 'whether improvements in one area may have been achieved at the expense of another'. Even the best objectives can be achieved badly. Using this approach means that you can consider together disparate elements of the competitive agenda such as becoming more customer-orientated, shortening response times, improving stock quality, emphasizing teamwork and developing new services. Viewing performance and management become more rounded. You do not just pursue loans, customer satisfaction or expenditure on fiction in isolation.

The idea behind the scorecard is to formulate targets in each of the four areas below (3–5 targets in each) and to design one or more measures for each 'goal':

1 **Customer perspective (users)**
   Customer concerns tend to fall into four categories: time, quality, performance and service, and cost.
   You need to articulate goals for each of these four areas and then translate the goals into specific measures.
2 **Internal perspective**
   Managers need to focus on these critical internal operations that enable them to meet and satisfy customer needs.
   This part of the scorecard looks at the processes and competencies at which you must excel, for example technological capability; introduction of new ideas; skills; and monitoring/evaluation/consultation mechanisms.
3 **Innovation and learning perspective**
   This looks at the organization's ability to grow, learn, develop and introduce new services. It focuses on measures such as take-up of new services and time taken to develop and introduce new approaches.
4 **Financial perspective**
   With the increase in the pernicious effects of the international financial crisis, libraries of all kinds are wrestling with basic issues of survival. For some library services, such as schools library services in the UK, measures like cash flow, growth in customer base, and income by services provided or by school, are critical.
   [Based on selected quotes from Kaplan and Norton, 1992 and 1993.]

It is difficult to gauge the extent to which the balanced scorecard is being taken up by libraries, although it has been proposed for some rather unexpected areas of practice, such as the assessment of learning outcomes (Bielavitz, 2010).

3.1.2 Business Excellence Model

The Business Excellence Model promoted by the European Foundation for Quality Management offers a structured approach to organizational self-assessment. Although the model started life in the private sector, it has been adapted for public-sector working, and has been adopted in some university and public libraries. There is evidence of government interest in this model within Europe as a means of enacting a 'continuous service improvement' agenda, especially in relation to outcome-based benchmarking.

The main premise of this model, expressed in its nine criteria and 32 sub-criteria, is that:

> Customer satisfaction, people (staff) satisfaction and a positive impact on society, are achieved through leadership driving force and strategy, people management, resources and processes, leading, ultimately, to excellence in results.
>
> Brigham (1999)

This model is one of the starting points for a self-assessment process specifically designed for library service managers and staff developers as part of the research project led by Margaret Kinnell and Bob Usherwood, two of the leading academics in the UK field (Usherwood, Evans and Jones, 1999). The resulting book (Kinnell, Usherwood and Jones, 1999a) is accompanied by a separately published training pack and tool kit (Kinnell, Usherwood and Jones, 1999b) containing 'all the necessary documents for developing a training programme and undertaking a self-assessment within a public information and library service'.

Their version of the model, which also incorporates elements of two other frameworks, offers ten criteria (or managerial domains):

Leadership	Processes
Policy and strategy	Customer satisfaction
Customer focus	Employee satisfaction
Employee management	Impact on society
Resource management	Overall performance

These elements are then sub-divided and a set of issues for exploration is linked to each. Although potentially useful for systematic planning purposes this is an inherently complex model: who is likely to keep all the criteria, let alone sub-criteria, and issues in their heads? Accordingly, we have opted for a more straightforward approach to evaluating the impact of services for managerial and accountability purposes. However, as organizations get more involved in evaluating impact they may well find both the balanced scorecard and the Business Excellence Model useful to ensure that they are working systematically and not avoiding key criteria.

3.1.3   Performance Measurement and Management (PMM) Systems

As the name suggests, PMM systems are generic approaches to integrate performance measurement within management planning rather than specific evaluation systems. We only mention them here because they are frequently cited when business evaluation is discussed. A useful overview of PMM systems, a literature review and a suggested approach to consolidation are offered by Taticchi and colleagues (2010; 2012).

3.1.4   More models

When academics engage with impact evaluation it is quite common for them to try to turn the results into models or research instruments for other people to use. There is only space here to mention two of these ventures, along with one international library development impact evaluation framework.

SERVQUAL

Evaluating service quality in the retail sector has spawned a literature of its own. One of the best-known instruments (despite its horrible acronym) is *SERVQUAL*, which aims to measure perceptions of any service across the five service-quality dimensions identified by Parasuraman and colleagues (1988) as: tangibles, reliability, responsiveness, assurance and empathy. Some of the fundamental difficulties in trying to apply an instrument using this approach have been identified by Robinson and Pidd (1998), who find that:

> The only areas of agreement appear to be that service quality is an attitude and is distinct from customer satisfaction, that perceptions of performance need to be measured, that the number and definition of dimensions depends on the service context, and that negatively worded statements should be avoided.

They conclude that: 'Following a decade of measurement with *SERVQUAL* is it possible that another decade will follow? The answer is probably not.' (This prediction demonstrates that people have greater capacity to persist with messy systems than these authors anticipated.)

Why does *SERVQUAL* continue to rate a mention if it is being found wanting, even in the simplified form that is now favoured? There is a strong tendency by national governments and others to try to produce 'simple' sets of impact indicators that can be universally applied. Two generations of *SERVQUAL* evaluation demonstrate that such a 'one size fits all' approach is hugely problematic.

Inspiring Learning for All

The Inspiring Learning for All[9] framework, sponsored by and developed for the (UK) Museums, Libraries and Archives Council, claims to set out 'what an accessible and inclusive museum, archive or library that stimulates and supports learning looks like'. This framework is primarily intended to cover informal learning and includes an impact evaluation dimension driven by a set of 'generic learning outcomes', apparently derived from the educational evaluation literature, which are described as 'a new research tool to measure learning'. Their generic learning outcomes (or impact areas) focus on 'Knowledge and understanding', 'Skills', 'Attitudes and values', 'Enjoyment, inspiration, creativity' (all of which are areas where we can expect to have an impact, as we will show later) and 'Activity, behaviour and progression'. They have added a set of 'generic social outcomes' focused on 'Stronger and safer communities', 'Strengthening public life' and 'Health and well-being'. The framework is extensive, and offers help in developing research tools (including a research question bank), in coding and analysing data, and in presenting evidence. The future of this framework is in doubt because the Museums, Libraries and Archives Council has been disbanded. However, for the moment the framework is available on the 'Inspiring Learning for All' website and is used in various libraries to focus consideration of what might be achieved in the broadest sense.

The Global Libraries Impact Planning and Assessment Framework

This framework is only accessible to country teams engaged in impact evaluation for the Global Libraries Initiative, but various accounts of the framework have been published (Streatfield and Markless, 2009; Fried, Kochanowicz and Chiranov, 2010; Sawaya et al. 2011). The main elements of this framework are described in section 6 of Chapter 11.

3.1.5 Educational views on impact

One important source of ideas on evaluating services, which we drew upon heavily in our early work on impact, is the literature on monitoring effectiveness and quality in education. This literature predates the current obsession with managing performance and focuses on some key elements that have become central to our model for evaluating impact, notably Fitz-Gibbon's (1996) views on the vital importance of:

- starting with some view of the characteristics and achievements of an effective service (what does a quality library service look like?)
- high-quality information (both qualitative and quantitative) about the services and systems that is specific to your local context – to enable rational decisions to be taken about change and external pressures

- good-quality performance indicators (to enable constant checking of service performance)
- designing these indicators because they are rarely readily available
- revisiting performance indicators as more information is gathered, to check that they are still credible and doing the intended job.

The work in education continues to inform our thinking. Recent ideas in education about evidence-informed practice and, even more importantly, practice-based evidence (Eraut, 2004), as well as about the role of the practitioner researcher in generating valid data, are central to self-evaluation using the model that we present in this book.

In UK higher education, researchers are now asked to demonstrate the impact their research has had and on whom (individuals, communities or organizations) as part of their submission to the Research Excellence Framework which directly affects central government allocation of research funds. Each case is presented as an impact case study tracing the route from original research through research outputs to impact. It will be interesting to see how LIS researchers trace the impact of their work on the library practitioner community.

One area of education in which impact evaluation is actively being pursued is the implementation of e-learning. Research in the field stretches from primary to adult education; from focusing on individual subjects, through institutional evaluation to the contribution of ICT and to national development, taking in both formal and informal education on the way: for example, Voogt and Knezek (2008) look across primary and secondary education, Jean Underwood (2009) reviews the impact of digital technologies on formal education, and Punie and colleagues (2008) review the impact of ICT on learning.

The serious investment of time and money that underpins the development and use of online environments has led to widespread demand for evidence of the benefits (or otherwise) of e-learning (enrichment, engagement/motivation and achievement) and how it compares to traditional methods. Educators are also interested in how e-learning and the digital environment affect learning and teaching processes and learner identity and what factors lead to successful use of e-learning. These issues resonate with library managers and the current educational research should provide insights into both the range of impacts possible and approaches to evaluating them. However, we have a concern about this research: the main focus is often on the processes associated with e-learning and the digital environment, not on its impact on learners or teachers. Such reports concentrate on how to implement change and identify success factors, and how related classroom/institutional/work processes are changing. The difficulties we have already described about evaluating impact are evident, although given the rapidly evolving landscape of e-learning we need more time for impacts to emerge before we can evaluate them.

3.1.6   What we know about impact from the international development literature

Of course, impact evaluation is not being conducted within a library and information services cocoon (nor even within a public services bubble). Fundamental changes in how evaluation, and particularly qualitative evaluation, of international development programmes (and, to a lesser extent, education programmes) is conceived and interpreted have occurred over the past 30 years (Guba and Lincoln, 1987; Shaw, Greene and Mark, 2006). Some of these changes in thinking, especially about the political nature of evaluation (e.g. Taylor and Balloch, 2005; Vestman and Conner, 2006; Abma, 2006;), and about the relationship between qualitative evaluation and government policy (e.g. House, 2005) need to be taken into account in any strategic approach to evaluating library services at national or international levels. Various ideas about the notion of a more inclusive and democratic evaluation embracing a wider range of stakeholders, including marginalized groups, and involving them in designing the evaluations and in interpreting the findings are particularly important (e.g. Mertens, 2003; Greene, 2006). Central here is the idea of preventing qualitative evaluation from becoming just another way of enforcing the existing power relationships between governments and their people. The development studies research also focuses on the convoluted ways in which initiatives play out in complex systems such as education and health, and on the need to adopt a flexible approach to impact evaluation in such situations, monitoring progress and being alert to emerging effects (Patton, 2012). We return to this theme in Chapter 11.

Reflecting on these trends from a library evaluation perspective, it should be noted that although real inclusiveness is a reasonable aspiration at local level, it is scarcely achievable within national evaluations of library services. The best that can be hoped for there is to engage with a range of informants drawn from all the main groups of people likely to be affected by changes in services, including marginalized groups, and to ensure that minority views are accorded weight. This is likely to be more than enough of a challenge for evaluators in many countries!

3.2   Evidence-based practice and the LIS picture

Are library services having any impact overall and, if so, how are people finding out about it? Why does this matter? We need to know what it is possible to achieve and how, so that we can concentrate our efforts where they can be seen to have an effect. It's also important to know how this impact is being evaluated, so that we don't waste time trying to collect information in areas where it is too difficult to make progress or where we can't get at the evidence.

Looking at the evidence should help us to broaden our ideas about what can be made to work and how we can evaluate it. Library managers may be reluctant to engage with service impact if they are unsure what this encompasses and if it looks as though the evidence will be hard to get. Some of these concerns may be reduced by seeing that other people have 'been there and done that'. We hope that the next section will add to your ideas about what you can look at and how.

We referred in Chapter 1 to the beginnings of evidence-based working in the library and information service field. One way in which this manifests itself is through reviews of the research literature. Until fairly recently there was little attempt in the library world to conduct systematic or semi-systematic reviews[10] of the research literature, so that it was difficult to say what the research was telling us overall. Semi-systematic reviews of school libraries (Williams, Wavell and Coles 2001; Williams, Coles and Wavell, 2002; Lonsdale 2003) and of the research on the impact of museums, archives and libraries (Wavell et al., 2002), as well as a systematic review of health libraries (Weightman and Williamson, 2005), have improved this picture. They have been followed by (amongst others) Oakleaf (2010) on the value and impact of academic libraries and other types of libraries; Poll (2011) with a bibliography on the impact and outcome of libraries; as well as Sey and Fellows (2009) with a critical review of research on the impact of public access ICT. (There has also been an attempt in the health libraries field to more clearly articulate various approaches to systematic review by Ankem (2008), Booth (2009) and Grant and Booth (2009). All this activity provides a better understanding of what libraries can achieve and the strength of the evidence that supports any claims.

So what do we know about the impact of various types of libraries and information services? How much does the research literature tell us about the impact of libraries, as distinct from efficiency on the one hand or, on the other, advocacy reports that start from the premise that libraries are a good thing? The short version is:

- a good deal if you are interested in *school libraries*
- quite a lot about *health libraries*

- rather less but in a growing volume for *further and higher education libraries*
- substantially more about *public libraries* than six years ago when the first edition of this book was published – some interesting overview (macro-impact) work, a series of national evaluations and research projects pointing the way towards finding out about the social impact of public libraries and a substantial body of evidence about the usefulness of reading promotion projects
- rather less if you are interested in *workplace libraries* or in *mediated information service* provision (where the information specialist, frequently a specialist in the relevant subject area, works with the enquirer to address the problem).

Although strictly beyond the confines of this book, there is also interesting research being conducted on:

- *User needs* of particular groups of information users. Much of this was conducted in earlier decades, including experimental design and development of specialist information services for social workers, education administrators, sexual health workers and others, using variations on the action research approach.
- Modelling or interpreting the *information-seeking behaviour of users*, brought together in a single publication aimed (unsurprisingly) at researchers by Fisher, Erdelez and McKechnie (2005). More recently the focus is on information-seeking and use on the internet (see below).

The main research findings about the impact of libraries are summarized in a little more detail below.

3.3   The overall research picture

In this brief overview we draw heavily on the literature reviews cited in the previous section. The study by Wavell et al. (2002) consists largely of a review of the literature published during a five-year retrospective period, with a particular emphasis on impact evaluations conducted within the UK. It does, however, include major research in the USA and Australia. The more recent reviews cited are more international in scope, albeit with a bias towards research publications in English.

3.3.1   Overall impact: value of libraries

One major change since the last edition of this book is the amount of attention being given to gauging the economic value of libraries of various kinds. Ten years ago Wavell and her colleagues made a series of significant points about doing economic impact research involving libraries:

- Studies examining *economic* impact sometimes use relatively complex analytical techniques and are conducted by economists or special consultants – now also by researchers.
- Some studies use qualitative and quantitative approaches in which economic impact is not necessarily defined in monetary terms.
- Economic impact of the sector is dependent upon data sources that are often incomplete, inaccurate or unavailable.
- Research concentrates on the public sector and major public spending initiatives.
- Research into the economic impact and value of *business information* is limited.
- Research into the relationship between *public libraries* and town centre regeneration is limited.

They observed that 'much of the evidence is in fact pointing to potential areas of impact rather than actual impact'.

The picture has changed significantly since the British Library published the results of its economic impact study seeking to quantify both the direct and indirect benefits of their services to the nation (Spectrum, 2004). They use the 'contingent valuation' approach to cost-benefit analysis for part of this work. In this approach, respondents are asked either how much they are willing to pay for services, or to what extent they are willing to accept compensation for not having the services. Inevitably, both modes of questioning tend to encourage polarization of opinions, and they have other limitations, which are explored by Holt et al. (1996). As Poll and Payne (2006, 554–5) point out

> . . . most library services have no equivalent on the common market and therefore no 'market prices' can be determined. [Users are asked to] financially rate services or institutions that they never thought of in terms of money.

Nonetheless, contingent valuation and other variations on return on investment are becoming a staple part of the valuation repertoire for libraries (see, for example, Aabø, 2009) as we show below.

Public libraries

There is an interesting practice-based academic debate about whether return on investment approaches are appropriate for determining the value of public libraries (e.g. Aabø and Audunson, 2002; Aabø, 2005; Chung, 2008). Meanwhile, several return on investment (RoI) studies have been conducted on US public libraries, either state-wide (e.g. Griffiths et al., 2004, 2006; Steffen et al., 2009) or focused on particular libraries (e.g. Fels Institute, 2010) showing various rates of return between US$3.8 and $6.5 per dollar spent. The RoI element of these studies is usually one of a range of methods used. Practical help for this type of study is offered by The Library Research Service[11] with both a *Personal ROI Calculator* for individual estimates of RoI, and a *Library ROI Calculator* focused on your library.

Not content with local or regional economic evaluation, Latvia has built on earlier economic valuation work (Paberza, 2010) and conducted a national study covering all of the 800-plus public libraries, using a combination of national statistics on libraries and a contingent valuation-based survey (Strode et al., 2012; Paberza, 2012).

Special libraries

Following the example of the British Library, another major state library, the German National Library of Science and Technology, employed contingent evaluation as a key part of its value and benefits study (TNS Infratest, 2010).

Academic libraries

There has been a surge of activity in relation to academic libraries, accompanied by several bibliographies (e.g. Jantii and Tang, 2011). Some notable examples are Kaufmann's (2008) attempt to measure the return on a university's investment in its library, by focusing on grant income generated by the faculty staff who use library materials. She also tries to confirm the benefits of using electronic resources by looking at the impact on productivity. Luther (2008) has also tried to show the return on investment at one university.

Carol Tenopir and her colleagues have engaged in a cluster of studies in the USA, UK and other countries, focused on the value and return on investment of academic libraries (e.g. Mays, Tenopir and Kaufmann, 2010; Tenopir et al., 2010). Their most recent work extends well beyond economic value and is included in the section on academic libraries below.

3.3.2   Overall impact: libraries and learning

This is another area where there has been recent progress. A decade ago, Wavell and colleagues identified several empirical studies examining the relationship between libraries and learning, focused on reader development in public libraries or school libraries, or on support for learning through reading development in young children and after-school activities.

They aver that evidence from research into learning and library use indicates a positive impact on:

- enjoyment and choice of leisure reading material
- reading development in young children
- academic achievement, particularly in terms of language skills
- acquisition of skills, particularly ICT and information literacy
- broader aspects of learning, such as increased motivation for learning, self confidence and independence.

Their review 'identified greater potential for impact than was actually substantiated by the evidence, particularly in terms of knowledge and understanding'.

Since then, at the generic level, members of the CIBER team formerly based at University College London have conducted data mining studies focused on the search behaviour of information users in e-environments (e.g. Nicholas and Rowlands, 2008).

At HE level, two of the leading international LIS researchers (Bruce, 1997; Limberg, 2005) have independently pursued research into the **information-related behaviour of students** from a phenomenographic perspective in Australia and Sweden respectively, and now collaborate on aspects of information literacy research.[12] Limberg's work is continuing through the EXACT Project (2008–), led by Olof Sundin, which is focused on how people come to grips with the transfer of formal expertise and control of information from libraries to the end-users in Web 2.0 resources, and how end-users justify and uphold trust in the authority of resources used (Limberg et al., 2012). Still within the phenomenographic tradition, Heinström's (2003) work on information seekers using the internet offers helpful characterizations of users – as Fast Surfers, Broad Scanners and Deep Divers – based on how they search the internet.

We have referred to other student-focused impact work under appropriate headings below.

3.3.3   Public libraries

What does the research tell us about public libraries?

Recent impact evaluation work focuses heavily on the effects on users of introducing **public access computing**. Pride of place here, because of the scale of its ambition, goes to The Global Impact Study of Public Access to Information and Communication Technologies[13], a five-year project (2007–2012) to generate evidence about the scale, character and impacts of public access to information and communication technologies. Research teams are looking at the impact of public libraries in this area, but also at telecentres, cybercafés and mobile technologies across several countries. The study investigates impact in a number of domains, including communication and leisure, culture and language, education, employment and income, governance, and health (Survey Working Group, 2012). The programme is led by the University of Washington's Technology and Social Change Group (TASCHA) and the Global Impact Study is part of a broader research project supported by Canada's International Development Research Centre and the Bill and Melinda Gates Foundation.

There is still much to do though in identifying impact in this area. The literature review by the Center for Information and Society at the University of Washington, finds that

> . . . there is limited conclusive evidence on downstream impacts of public access to
> ICTs. The evidence that does exist suggests that the public access ICT model is not
> living up to the expectations placed on it. This is not necessarily because public
> access has had no impacts, but because its impact is particularly difficult to identify
> and measure. As a model, public access to ICTs has experienced success and failure,
> leading to both reinforcement of the belief that the model should be expanded and
> strengthened; as well as claims that public access ICTs are ultimately ineffective or
> even counter-productive from the development perspective.
>
> (Sey and Fellows, 2009)

Meanwhile, large-scale public library-focused surveys on perceptions of or use of public access computing are regularly conducted in the USA (Becker et al., 2010; Davis, Clark and Bertot, 2010; Bertot et al., 2010, 2011; Hoffman, Bertot and Davis, 2012) and increasingly, in other countries such as Finland (Vakkari and Serola, 2012). The country-level impact evaluators employed as part of the Global Libraries Initiative (GL) are gradually becoming more ambitious in their evaluation methods, using pop-up surveys (Romania – Chiranov, 2011), computer-assisted telephone interviews (Poland) and contingent valuation (Latvia). They are steadily reporting the results of their user-focused evaluation work (Fried, Kochanowicz and Chiranov, 2010; Paberza and Rutkauskiene, 2010; Streatfield, Quynh Truc Phan et al., 2012) and the issues that they encounter (Streatfield, Paberza et al., 2012). Their findings are now being translated into advocacy statements covering a range of topics such as helping older citizens to learn digital skills, helping people to find employment and breaking down barriers to e-inclusion. GL has identified six areas where impact efforts can usefully focus (Streatfield, 2012), noting that this list 'addresses the primary areas where public access to technology through libraries can influence peoples' lives'. These areas are:

- education
- health
- culture and leisure
- economic development and work; including agriculture
- communication
- e-government.

(We have more to say about GL in Chapter 11.)

Staying with public access computing, Coward and Fisher (2010) point out that all libraries (and especially public libraries) significantly underestimate their 'reach' when focusing on users since many users are acting on behalf of other people when seeking information. Interestingly, there is now some evidence of a positive relationship between internet use and public library use, again from Finland (Vakkari, 2012).

Other evaluators are looking more broadly at the **social impact** of public libraries. Some interesting early work on social impact auditing, notably by Linley and Usherwood (1998), to help garner qualitative information in a context where 'The [Government] is only concerned with what is measurable and, as a result, tends to ignore a great deal of what is important' has not apparently been replicated since, although it offers a 'tool for enabling sensible measurement of complex outcomes' and a 'technique that makes the enacting process (of libraries) visible'. Instead, there have been sporadic attempts to apply the concept of social capital to libraries, as reviewed by Johnson (2010). As we write, Frank Huysmans and Marjolein Oomes (2012) are starting a large-scale survey-driven approach (but with qualitative research elements) to try to measure their societal value. More specifically, a Swedish research team is studying how public libraries function as social meeting spaces (Audunson et al., 2007; Aabø, Audunson and Vårheim, 2010).

Looking back ten years, evidence from seven UK projects cited by Wavell and colleagues (2002) suggested that the most compelling impact evidence is in the area of personal development – including formal education, lifelong learning and training; after-school activities; literacy, leisure, social and cultural objectives through book borrowing; and skills development and availability of public information. These themes are still prominent in local evaluation efforts but the research evidence about the public library impact on users in these specific areas is still relatively weak, apart from the country impact evidence collection by GL.

3.3.4 Health libraries

As we have already seen, the health libraries field is unusual in taking the idea of evidence-based working seriously and this attention extends to conducting systematic reviews of such areas as teaching information literacy skills to undergraduate students (Koufogiannakis and Wiebe, 2006) or the value and impact of information provided through library services for patient care (Weightman and Williamson, 2005). Indeed, before introducing a review of methods of conducting systematic reviews, Ankem (2008) asserts that 'all systematic reviews in [librarianship] have been published on medical library or medical information topics'. (The danger of making this kind of generalization can be illustrated by citing the work of Zhang, Watson and Banfield (2007), comparing computer-aided instruction with face-to-face instruction in academic libraries, although they reported that differences in study methodology and lack of quality made meta-analysis impossible.) Even with this small caveat the message is clear: if you are interested in an aspect of health libraries impact, check the health libraries literature to see what has already been done.

In the UK, health libraries impact enthusiasts have gone considerably further, in moving on from their systematic review to address the value and impact of information provided through library services for patient care (Weightman et al., 2009) and translating this into best practice guidance and a toolkit (the HEALER Research Toolkit[14]), which is

> . . . a set of standard questions used across health libraries in the UK to provide a valuable means of benchmarking and comparing services, for effective market research[15] in planning and improving the current service and in building up a reliable body of evidence for user perceptions of the impact of libraries across the region. It should also complement other shared surveys such as LibQUAL+(TM)[16] that examine service quality rather than library impact, if these are considered or adapted as additional analysis tools (Urquhart and Weightman, 2008).

The earlier systematic review concludes that health care libraries can influence patient outcomes in various ways:

- rapid diagnosis
- appropriate investigation(s) and choice of drug(s)
- reduced length of stay in hospitals
- avoiding hospital-acquired infection

- avoiding additional outpatient visits

[and that] '. . . clinical librarian and other library services can also result in savings of health professionals' time' (Weightman and Williamson, 2005).

Wavell and her colleagues similarly conclude that good-quality information provision has a positive effect on clinical decision making.

3.3.5   School libraries

When we wrote this section about school library research in 2006 we claimed that there is probably more evidence available about school libraries worldwide than about any other type of library. The series of important state-wide quantitative studies in the USA (many of them orchestrated by Keith Curry Lance), which show positive relationships between well equipped and organized school libraries and aspects of student performance, including exam results, is continuing. As a result, the research paper summarizing this work, *School Libraries Work!* (Scholastic, 2008) has now reached its third edition and is already out of date (see, for example, Lance, Rodney and Schwartz, 2010; Francis, Lance and Lietzau, 2010; Lance and Hofschire, 2012). Meanwhile Ross Todd and his team (2011) at the Center for International Scholarship in School Libraries are using the results of qualitative research into New Jersey's school libraries to 'understand the contribution of quality school libraries to education' in order to 'build momentum for a programme of evidence-based continuous improvement of school libraries'.

Their research portrays the school library and the work of school librarians as essential to learning in information- and technology-intense environments. They confirm earlier research in the UK (Williams and Wavell, 2001) and other countries (Streatfield and Markless, 2002b; Loertscher with Todd, 2003) that good school libraries:

- contribute to educational beliefs and the school culture
- help to shape the school learning environment by (inter alia) offer a different but complementary learning space
- connect students to curriculum learning and their personal interests; teachers to a richer interdisciplinary approach to learning; teachers to each other to provide the best learning experiences for students; and both students and teachers to the wider world of information
- provide library staff as co-teachers and as teachers of teachers
- offer students the chance to develop resource-based capabilities, knowledge-based capabilities, reading to learn capabilities, thinking-based

capabilities, and learning management core capabilities, as well as personal and inter-personal capabilities
• as part of this, to offer inquiry-centred instruction . . . carefully planned and staged to take students though a research journey, carefully diagnosing particular learning needs to ensure successful research.

(our summary of Todd et al., 2011).

Compared to earlier research conducted before the intense shift towards information- and technology-rich teaching and learning environments, their report (29) puts special emphasis on

> the school librarian's role as connector [which] firmly establishes the school as connected to the community, the curriculum connected to the real world, and the school community connected to its stakeholders. In the role of teacher the school librarian makes the ultimate connection among the academic disciplines represented in the school curriculum and the instructional program.

It is interesting how strongly these facets of the role of US school librarians (as represented in New Jersey best practice) align with the key roles identified by more than a thousand UK secondary school librarians in the recent survey of what they do and how (Streatfield, Shaper and Rae-Scott, 2011). Best practice in the UK is associated with promoting reading for pleasure, developing and contributing to information literacy programmes within and across the school, engaging in other forms of active support for teaching and learning in the school, building a range of relevant resources, and helping to develop virtual learning environments.

3.3.6   Academic libraries

This is the domain in which we have seen most change in the level of research activity since the last edition of this book. It is particularly interesting to see that the people conducting the economic value research, described earlier, are tending to get more involved in other areas of impact evaluation. Two examples are:

1 Megan Oakleaf (2010), whose research review gives a broad overview of value in relation to academic libraries which encompasses impact evaluation and includes the impact of public, school and special libraries. This work forms part of the Value of Academic Libraries project (Hinchliffe and Oakleaf, 2010). This work identifies a series of areas in which evaluators should be working and reports relatively few substantial projects.

2 Carol Tenopir and her colleagues whose recent work focuses on the value of the library for academic staff. The Scholarly Reading and the Value of Library Resources project (Tenopir and Volentine, 2012) measures the 'value and outcomes' from access to scholarly publications in six universities in the UK. It seeks to answer questions such as 'What is the value and outcome of scholarly reading for academic staff?' Some of their conclusions are particularly important when considering where academic libraries can make a difference (see pp. 6–8 of their report):

- *The academic library is a convenient and valuable source of high-value article readings.*
- *Based on the value academics place on scholarly reading and the percentage obtained from the library, the library adds significant value to the academic work at the universities.*
- *By contrast, the library is not the primary source for books for academic staff. Even though book readings are often considered even more important to the principal purpose than article readings, book readings are less likely to come from the library's collections.*
- *While the library is not the main source of book readings, it is the most likely alternative if the original book source is unavailable.*
- *The library supports the work of younger academics, since they are more likely to obtain books from the library.*

Looking at the other end of the library telescope, the past few years have produced a series of studies of the information-related behaviour of academic researchers, commissioned and re-presented by the UK-based Research Information Network in various collaborations. These include a mixed-methods study of the information skills training of researchers (Research Information Network, 2008; Streatfield, Allen and Wilson, 2010); and case-study based investigations of researchers in the life sciences (Research Information Network and British Library, 2009), humanities scholars (Research Information Network, 2011b), and researchers in the physical sciences (Research Information Network et al., 2011); as well as a mixed methods examination of the value of libraries for researchers (Research Information Network and Research Libraries UK, 2011), which extends beyond consideration of academic articles to include sections on reading from books and other publications and questions on use of social media. The CIBER team, which focuses strongly on e-information, also extends our understanding of aspects of the behaviour of information users in different academic disciplines, such as business and management (Nicholas, Rowlands and Jamali, 2010).

Despite all this work, when Creaser and Spezi (2012) report on their project involving eight case studies in the USA, Scandinavia and the UK, they conclude that 'Libraries are struggling to find appropriate and systematic ways to capture evidence of their value for teaching and research staff.' They point to two UK exceptions in the work of the CIBER team (using logs, questionnaires, interviews, observation and statistical datasets) to show that high levels of expenditure and use of e-journals are strongly positively correlated to research performance (Research Information Network, 2011a); and that of Dave Patten and the Library Impact Data Project, which is using large sets of data to show the link between student library use and attainment.[17]

Unsurprisingly, there is a steady flow of small-scale research studies focused on various aspects of the impact of academic libraries, mainly on student users and sometimes using innovative methods (e.g., Fisher, Landry and Naumer, 2007).

3.3.7 Workplace libraries

Although Wavell and colleagues find evidence that provision of information by special libraries can have a positive impact on professional decision making, there is relatively little impact evaluation research to amplify the effect of special library services on users.

3.4 What we don't know

The problem at this fairly early stage of moving towards evidence-based library and information work is that there are still aspects that have not been properly investigated – where what we are doing is what feels right or what we have always done rather than what we know works or can be made to work. These gaps in the research may occur because nobody is challenging us to show our worth, because the right questions haven't been asked yet or because the results so far are inconclusive.

Looking at library research on impact generally, although there have been major advances recently, we can still see:

- lots of descriptive and anecdotal evidence and descriptions of best practice
- too little detail of data-gathering methods; absence of systematic and rigorous reporting (this is still a real issue for the field, although advances have occurred since the first edition of this book), and as a result
- often no way of identifying the quality of the data collection through the published reports

- lots of attention to *potential outcomes* rather than systematically assessed impact evidence
- some synopses of impact investigations, but not integrated into a growing body of evidence.

There are still some challenging impact questions waiting to be answered. For example:

- How big is the overall economic, social and educational contribution of libraries to the community?
- What mix of library services works best in different situations?
- What is the overall value of libraries to the country or to society?
- Is this value consistent over time?

These questions may appear to be too big to be addressed, but we already have some answers emerging to the first two of these in relation to school libraries and the third is being sporadically addressed, although so far without clear success.

Example 3.1   Playing for Success

This project demonstrates that we can learn useful lessons from other research areas. It is an old example, but one which uses a quasi-experimental design which is still beyond anything attempted in library research.

The Out of Hours Study Support Project was a UK national initiative, focused on providing homework facilities for schoolchildren, including some projects based in school libraries. National evaluation showed positive impact on academic attainment by the students involved, as well as improved attitudes to school and better attendance at school (MacBeth et al., 2001).

The most rigorous evaluation, of Playing for Success work involving football clubs, encompasses observation, interviews with people involved, questionnaires to pupils, parents and schools, attitude measurement of pupils before and after involvement and tests of their reading and mental arithmetic (potentially a model for future library impact research?). The programme was popular with pupils, contributing to improved attitudes, motivation and self-esteem, and improved academic skills and achievement. School libraries offer a potential base for this type of support, and could aspire to achieve some of these results, even if they do not have the magnetic appeal of football clubs! (Sharp et al., 1999; 2000)

And finally, it is probably still true to say that:

National research evidence of impact does not have much effect at a local level. Heads, Governors, etc., want to hear of local successes and local improvement. They want to see how their students are benefiting . . . You will not be heard until your day-to-day practice is evidence-based; a practice that is directed towards demonstrating the real power of your contribution to the school's learning goals.

Todd (2001)

3.5   Where our model comes from

All of this research provides a context for our own work, which concentrates on helping library managers to get to grips with service impact. What follows now is an attempt to trace our learning path through a series of national research and development projects over the past 30 years.

3.5.1   Getting at impact through research and development

If we look back at various points in our past, as with many projects, the early stages in developing this model are largely accidental. In the 1980s we worked together on UK national research and development focused on what is later called information literacy. Since this work is conducted in schools and further education colleges it is no great surprise that we become very interested in how their libraries contribute to the central activities of their institutions. Our interest is soon translated into another national research project, The Effective School Library, in which we concentrate on the roles of the library staff in the key part of their job, supporting teaching and learning. Our choice of focus forces us to address the issues involved in evaluating the impact of these services in schools (Streatfield and Markless, 1994).

In the final stages of this project we devise sets of performance indicators to help librarians decide where to focus in order to make a positive contribution to teaching and learning in their schools. We quickly realize that it is vital to make direct links between activities and impact. Failure to make these links led generations of school librarians to pursue a vision of what we now caricature as the 'All-singing, all-dancing learning resource centre designed to support students as independent learners' – or 'the Holy Grail model'. (This approach is fine if the school as a whole is committed to a student-centred approach to learning, but our research clearly shows that this model of library provision won't work if the school puts a strong emphasis on traditional teaching.) This project teaches us valuable lessons about the need to base development decisions on a clear view of the impact you can achieve or want to achieve.

Next, we turn our attention to the role of the further education college library/resource centre, in another national project imaginatively entitled The

Effective College Library (Streatfield and Markless, 1997). As part of this project we decide to work with seven college libraries in which the staff already plan to innovate in an aspect of support for teaching and learning (ranging from running information skills workshops to assigning library staff to work as part of curriculum teams). Since each innovation is different, there is a real chance of a mess, with all the libraries going off in different directions. What we need is a process to help people to decide together what they mean by impact and how impact can be evaluated for their innovation. We design a workshop for our collaborators and the process model is born! A common approach to generating performance indicators and targets duly emerges. Now we are in a position to start looking at the real impact of these services on students and teaching staff. Our chosen approach also means that we are well placed to go further down the impact evaluation route by testing this methodology, trying out some performance indicators and evaluating the innovations within the same project (Markless and Streatfield, 2000).

By this time we are in full research flow. Our next opportunity to focus strongly on impact comes with the National Year of Reading, a major programme to celebrate libraries and reading, promoted by the UK government and mounted in 1998–99. We are asked to take on the evaluation of public library involvement in this programme, which sees public library services come back to the forefront of the public sector agenda after years of government-prompted neglect (Streatfield et al., 2000).

What is really striking, when we attend various events organized in different parts of the country during the Year of Reading, is the level of energy flowing through the library staff and everyone else involved. It is obvious that the events are having a big impact – but when we ask what effect an event is having on the promotion of reading in the community we hear only vague answers. Yes, the Year of Reading seems to be working, but nobody appears to have much idea about how to evaluate its impact locally. Why is this?

We find the clue that leads to the answer in the files of 147 annual public library service plans sent in to the relevant government department for England. Our team ploughs through all of these, looking for references to library managers' plans for the National Year of Reading and for the programme evaluation measures to be used to judge the results. There are plenty of plans for events during the Year of Reading, but most of these have no evaluation criteria attached and, where there are any, they are nearly always process performance indicators (numbers of activities, or targets for numbers of people to be involved). Almost everyone has backed away from the more difficult questions about evaluating impact.

Similarly, our national survey conducted as part of this evaluation finds 26% of public library services in which managers report that they have adopted some impact or achievement indicators or targets in relation to the Year of Reading. However, when we follow up by asking them to give examples, well over half prove to be process or output indicators.

3.5.2   Generating an impact evaluation model

We are now convinced that library service managers need help to focus on impact, especially because they are coming under increasing pressure to do so. Not surprisingly, the Library and Information Commission takes the same view! As a result, it funds us to do some development work concentrating on public libraries and on the schools' library services that provide strategic help to individual schools in UK local authorities. For the Best Value and Better Performance in Libraries Project, we engage the interest of various public library services and schools library services management teams with the offer to help them shape up their impact ideas. For this purpose we clearly need a process and one that is robust enough to deal with a variety of services and settings. Fortunately, we have a model ready for this purpose.

We base the first of the workshops for library managers on the process that we originally devised for college librarians. Over the next few months, we try out the processes on various management teams and collect feedback as we go along so that we can strengthen the model. At the end of the project we publish the results as a set of guidance materials.[18]

Over the next four years we further refine the process model by running training workshops for a wide range of library service managers in all kinds of settings. We also run or contribute to development projects based on the model for groups of health librarians developing specific innovations, children's librarians focusing on reader development and further education college librarians interested in benchmarking on the basis of service impact.

We now engage in a two-year rolling programme to help university library staff to evaluate the impact of their programmes and initiatives. The Impact Implementation Programme involves a total of 22 university library teams exploring the impact of e-learning and e-implementation (Markless and Streatfield, 2005, 2008) through annual cycles of workshops and practical impact evidence-gathering, looking at integrated enquiry services, e-information services, subject e-support for research, and support for a wider range of students.[19] This is the point at which we are asked to write the first edition of this book.

Soon after the book is published, we are invited to join a small team of impact evaluation consultants advising the Global Libraries Initiative about 'impact planning and assessment.' This involves helping the central team to develop an IPA Roadmap as a step-by-step guide for impact specialists in grantee countries to do impact evaluation at country level. We are also asked to visit various grantee countries to help plan and implement evaluation programmes, and to help the IPA specialists to ensure publication of the results of their work in academic journals. We are also invited to help IFLA to develop its impact evaluation framework by working with two of their development programmes. Finally, we are asked to help the Global Impact Study to address issues about international impact evaluation (focused on various types of public access computing). All this work enables us to test the robustness of our model in a wide range of contexts, and especially in a wider range of cultures and library traditions. We are able to see how local needs and aspirations can be respected within our procedures. We also see the need to emphasize the use of a clear, agreed vocabulary (hence the extended definitions section in this edition of our book) and the enhanced options for collecting impact data (see Chapter 9).

Our general approach to the generation of performance indicators and targets has helped a growing number of librarians and education managers to get to grips with the fairly complex issues and choices involved. It has also enabled librarians to engage in development planning from the right end – that is, starting from specific time-limited objectives and moving on to set realistic and achievable targets.

3.5.3 Creating a self-evaluation process

Can a free-standing and comprehensive self-evaluation process be developed for libraries? It should be possible to do this, if we know enough about the optimum range of services possible, the key constraints and the main dimensions of process and impact evaluation for these services.

Fortunately, when we were asked (in 2003) to do this for school libraries by the UK government's Department for Education and Skills, we felt that the research evidence about what works in schools was strong enough and that, with the help of 53 schools, we could come up with practical self-evaluation frameworks for primary (age 5–11) school libraries (Streatfield and Markless, 2004) and a more comprehensive and challenging version for secondary (11–18) schools (Markless and Streatfield, 2004).[20] The secondary model offers seven broad areas in which the school library can make a difference, breaks this down into segments, then takes the school library manager through a series of steps to arrive at an evaluation of that segment. Data collection tools are provided to help and the process is rounded off with guidance on how to do better in the chosen area. In some ways that ambitious project provided a dress rehearsal for writing the first edition of this book.

To end this overview on a sober note, having published these guides, the Department for Education apparently loses interest in school libraries. Meanwhile, the Portuguese Department of Education asks for permission to translate and adapt these guides as the basis for their own school library self-evaluation programme, which is still going strong!

Part 2
Evaluating impact

4

Putting the impact into planning

This chapter introduces the model for evaluating impact and makes some points about how to use it. You are then invited to start using the model by thinking about the answers to some general questions. Answering these questions is an important step to take in moving into the impact evaluation model.

4.1   Why do we need a new evaluation model?

The balance between service delivery, detailed consideration of processes and impact evaluation is critical when assessing the success of a service. However, our experience suggests that the balance is usually heavily weighted away from impact evaluation. Ever since we first began to work systematically with library and information service managers on impact, two points have been apparent:

1   **The concepts and terminology get in the way.** People easily become confused about such ideas as efficiency and effectiveness when they try to apply them in practice. Not only that but the terms used, such as inputs, processes, outputs and outcomes (and higher order outcomes) are applied inconsistently, both by managers in practice and in some of the published literature on performance evaluation.
2   **When people identify an area for attention or improvement they can usually come up with a list of things to do to put it right.** Generally speaking, however, people find it much harder to think about the aims and objectives underlying what they are trying to do (that is, what they are trying to achieve by providing services). Unfortunately, this focus on aims is necessary: we need to be very clear about what we are trying to achieve if we want to be able to tell whether we have succeeded. Since people are usually more comfortable with organizing and running activities, their focus on impact often gets fuzzy – when this happens we slide off into identifying process performance indicators (or 'tick off when done' indicators). These

tell us whether things on the list have been done, but they don't tell us whether they were worth doing, or indeed whether they have had any effect.

Our response to these two challenges is to offer a process for people to work through to help to get to grips with impact. We have used this general approach with more than a thousand library and information service managers and have adapted it for all kinds of settings – from school libraries to universities and from public libraries to business and industry.

The good news is that we know that this approach to evaluating impact works! People consistently tell us that our process helps them to work systematically through the issues without getting sidetracked or bogged down in the complexities. Now we are offering you a version of the same general process – please let us know how well it works for you by contacting us at www.facetpublishing. co.uk/evaluatingimpact. If you hit any problems that are not fully covered in this book, you may find that they have been dealt with on the website; if not, contact us there and we will try to help.

4.2   The model

We have adopted a step-by-step approach to generating impact indicators. The idea is that by working through the steps managers should emerge with a set of useful impact indicators linked to what they are trying to achieve. By the end of the process, you should also be well on the way to putting together a workable development plan and an implementation timetable to go with it, whether this is for a library service or for a research, development or pilot project. By the time you have worked through the model once, and have generated your own impact indicators, you will be able to integrate collecting evidence of impact into your planning cycle. The steps in the model are shown in Figure 4.1.

This model distinguishes between the performance measurement activities and processes which are undertaken by many libraries of all kinds and the more challenging stages involved in impact evaluation. We present them here together because both types of evaluation are important for libraries – it is important to know whether the library system is running efficiently as well as whether the service is effective in meeting the needs of users. This book concentrates on the impact of the service on people, communities and organizations: there are other books available if you are interested in service performance measurement (e.g. Poll and Boekhorst, 2007) and an interesting overview of UK academic library practice is also available (Stanley and Killick, 2009).

Each of the steps shown in Figure 4.1 is unpacked in detail in the following chapters. Examples of products at each stage in the process are offered for

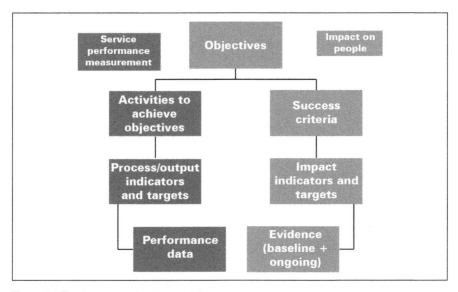

Figure 4.1 *The impact evaluation model*

different types of library service, so the model should be readily adaptable to any project or service management situation.

4.3 Using the model

Managers can use this approach individually, but you will probably gain more if you work through the stages with colleagues. It is possible for a senior management team to work through this model to the data collection stage in a one-day session (assuming that you work in parallel small groups for part of the time), but this is hard going. It may be more productive to tackle the first three stages in a four-hour session and pick up the other steps later.

Six points to watch are:

1 Setting out and agreeing on the aims/objectives and translating some of these into impact indicators will take much longer than you might expect (two to three hours) – if it is done properly.
2 Most, if not all, library and information services tend to start too far down in the model (at the identification of 'Activities (and services) to achieve objectives'). One purpose of this book is to put the impact back into planning. To achieve this it is necessary to spend time on the steps at the top of the model. This is the way to generate impact indicators that will drive your data collection in areas that will provide you with the elusive

evidence of impact that is vital to decision making and real service development. Starting too far down results in:

- *neglect of impact indicators, since these spring from service aims, not services delivered*
- *consulting users and potential users about services (unproblematic and uninformative) rather than about service aims and directions (more contentious and a better basis for developing services).*

3 We recommend you start at the top of Figure 4.1 (with objectives) and work systematically down the sequence, but move sideways to generate appropriate indicators at each of the three steps shown. (We know that many libraries have an overall mission statement but these are usually too general to drive the impact evaluation process.) The chapters that follow adopt this pattern.

4 It is likely that when you reach the evidence collection stage you will find that you don't have ready access to baseline information on where you are now. Our experience with various kinds of libraries is that services seldom have baseline impact information, even about areas that they regard as important for development (because such data are not routinely collected to measure the efficiency of the service). If you want to show that a service or initiative is making a difference you need to collect baseline information to show evidence of progress. Planning is central to ensuring that baseline information is available.

5 If you are using this model for development planning, it will be necessary to collect relevant baseline information in order to be able to set sensible targets. You will need to put systems in place that enable you to collect high-quality management information more easily (e.g. activity-based costing).

6 If you are looking at improving an aspect of your service, you may choose to get over the problem of 'no baseline information' by putting in the evidence-collection mechanisms and starting to innovate. In this way you will have baseline information at the end of the first period of operation (usually, but not necessarily a year) and will then be able to compare later results against this baseline.

We know from experience that this process helps managers to create appropriate impact indicators and targets anchored in what they are trying to achieve. Some library service managers start the process feeling that impact is too big and amorphous to address but soon realize that they can 'get a handle' on it at key points by carefully relating impact indicators to aims.

The process should help to achieve a balance between the necessary service output and process indicators and targets on the one hand and impact and achievement indicators and targets on the other. The next few chapters show how this model can be applied in detail to ensure that you can evaluate the impact of your library or information service. However, here are some questions to help you to orientate yourself before you start.

4.4   And the first question is . . .

Unless you have a strong focus on what you already know about yourselves and the services you offer, you are not likely to learn much more. Even before you start looking at the model you should think about why you are interested in service impact and what you hope to gain from having better evidence about your effectiveness. Putting it bluntly, if you aren't sure why you are doing this why not find something more interesting and worthwhile to do?

What kinds of questions do you need to ask yourself before starting the evaluation? Here are four to start with:

1 **Is this evaluation really necessary and, if so, why?** Who is it most necessary or useful for? Is the main purpose to enhance the effectiveness of the service; to demonstrate (and potentially, to increase) value for money; to justify or account for expenditure; or as feedback to identify other areas for development?
2 **Who should do the evaluating?** Who is likely to be able to obtain the co-operation of key informants and library staff? Is it important to get different perspectives when collecting evidence and interpreting results?
3 **What aspects of the service should be evaluated?** Since you are unlikely to have the resources to look at the impact of everything at once, where are you going to start and why?
4 **When should the evaluation be done – or when should it not be done?** You may want to get a picture of the service at all times of the year and under all conditions, but you will have to balance this against adding to the pressure by calling for evidence gathering when the staff are under maximum stress.

Since this whole process is one of development, we suggest that if you are making a start now, you may find it useful to note your answers to these questions, date your answers and file them so that you can look back later and recapture what you thought at the outset and how far you have moved on.

4.5   How do you currently measure your success as a service?

This brings us to another set of questions. How far has your service moved into the area of performance measurement and impact assessment? Please answer the questions below:

1 Nearly all library services have some sorts of *service delivery performance indicators* (e.g. issues per number of population served; stock size related to registered users, etc.):

   - *What do your service delivery indicators concentrate on?*
   - *Do you use the data collected against each of these indicators and, if so, what for? How do they fit into service management, external reporting or the planning cycle? Do you monitor the data closely and act on them or do they mainly serve to show senior managers that you are 'on the case' (on the assumption that if you produce regular performance monitoring data you must be doing your job of watching how well your service is performing)?*

2 Most library services use some key process indicators linked to delivering services (e.g. 'produce a stock development policy'; 'organize six reading groups'):

   - *Which processes do you try to monitor?*
   - *What process indicators do you have in place? Do they help you to improve your services? How?*

3 Some library services try to measure the impact of specific services (e.g. collecting evidence from participants that training provided for users on the internet makes them better 'searchers'):

   - *Do you collect any evidence of the impact of services? In what areas? How?*
   - *Does this evidence really measure impact?*
   - *Does this evidence help you to improve services? How?*

Again, we suggest that you note your answers to these questions now, date your answers and file them to show progress over time.

Doing information literacy development and evaluation in a university

The university library subject specialists collaborate with lecturers on information literacy (IL) sessions and these are now part of the **peer observation** programme. Combined teams of subject librarians and teachers are developing e-materials to help students deal with IL issues as they arise. Students are recruited to **test and critique materials** before they become part of the i-skills framework, **pop-up surveys** are used to obtain student feedback and the **university student survey** now includes a question on the usefulness of the framework. Library staff began to offer IL workshops as part of the generic skills training offered centrally to postgraduate and postdoctoral researchers initiated with central government funding. These workshops are **observed** and the tendency for library contributions to adopt a behaviourist approach to teaching rather than the constructivist learning approach favoured by the rest of the training is noted. **Surveys of researchers** find some dissatisfaction with the generic approach to skills training. As a result, library staff now work with trainers and with academic development units to develop subject-based IL learning opportunities for researchers (including lecturers in their research roles) as well as for research supervisors, supported by an adapted version of the university i-skills framework developed for students. Regular **focus groups** are held with students, academic staff and researchers to evaluate current offerings and consider further developments. Library staff are currently negotiating with the university ethics committee to secure a **research study** of library-initiated IL support for students and researchers.

5

Getting things clear: objectives

This chapter focuses on the first stage of the model and explains how to work through it when evaluating the impact of your service. Impact evaluation is essentially about three things:

- Focus – being clear about the library's purposes; what you want the service to achieve and for whom (areas of impact turned into impact objectives)
- Indicators – deciding what will tell you that change has happened
- Evidence – being able to show that change has occurred.

The first stage of the evaluation process model is about focus.

5.1 Choosing where to get involved

If you are going to be more effective you need to choose how, where and with whom to get involved. Before you can make these decisions you should start with clarifying the impact you want to make – your objectives. However, you need to do this in the real world, so spelling out the objectives should take into account what is achievable. This means making careful choices and adopting clear priorities.

The basic constraint for librarians is having to spend so much time on managing and operating the library infrastructure. This makes it difficult to step back and look critically at what the library is really trying to do: where should you concentrate your efforts? In which areas might you most fruitfully develop your service? The first step in impact evaluation calls for thought about key foci (success criteria) for your service which you can then turn into objectives.

Lack of time is not the only problem; there are also issues of logistics. For example, in *education librarianship* there will always be many teachers and still more students to every librarian. Moreover, both teachers and students will spend much of their time out of physical reach of librarians, in the lecture room or classroom. Who should you target and how? Again, *public library services* are being called on to meet more and more externally imposed demands within existing resources. What should take priority and what should be left until later? Other types of libraries will encounter variations on these two constraints.

Responding to both these constraints may well boil down to making choices about where to concentrate on being *efficient* (relying on traditional performance indicators to monitor performance) and where it is important to show yourselves or other people that you are being *proactive and effective*, rather than spreading limited time across too many initiatives. A key consideration is to decide where you can be effective. If you are trying to make an impact it is important to find areas that are ripe for action as well as energetic collaborators – or, as educational change guru Michael Fullan (2007) insists, 'Go where the energy is'.

Working through the impact evaluation model brings these choices into the open. So, now for the first step in clarifying your focus.

5.2   The mission

In theory, we should probably look to the overarching purpose or mission statement of the library service to guide our quest for evidence. In practice, although most library services have a mission statement, these are usually bland, often wildly overoptimistic (any statement containing the words 'all users'), and almost invariably too general to be of much help in getting focused. It is not usually worthwhile spending a lot of time refining your mission statement. The main exception here is with a new service or project, where focusing on the mission statement can lead to a useful discussion about what you are really trying to achieve.

The hard work in evaluating impact begins at the next stage: identifying key areas in which you want your service to make an impact and writing appropriate objectives for each area.

5.3   Where *can* libraries make an impact?

The previous chapter on impact research shows some areas where we know that various kinds of libraries can make a difference. This research should help to guide any discussion about what your library can achieve and where to focus your activity. For a practitioner perspective on the same question, we don't have to go any further than the aspirations expressed by all the managers who have taken part in our workshops over the past few years. What do they identify as their key areas of impact? We summarize for four types of library:

5.3.1   Education libraries

Education librarians in schools through to university libraries tend to concentrate on:

- library use of ICT to support teaching and learning (from identification and delivery of e-resources to designing e-learning programmes)
- development of basic skills, key skills, information skills and problem-solving skills work involving the library
- the impact of services designed for postgraduate and postdoctoral researchers (including lecturers doing research)
- collaboration between teachers and library staff; this can be:
  - small or large scale (from team teaching to resource-based learning projects)
  - outside the library
  - requiring new roles/skills (not only for library staff).

Although the issues of the moment do tend to change and are likely to be influenced by the political agenda, these general areas for attention have been to the fore for at least the past decade.

5.3.2   Public libraries

Public librarians tend to concentrate on:

- public access computing
- the impact of proactive cultural and informal learning services (including outreach services)
- key skills (associated with thinking, learning, reading, ICT and literacy)
- lifelong learning
- social inclusion
- reader development
- effective and engaging library space(s).

Useful additional help is offered by Rebecca Linley and Bob Usherwood (1998), whose work on social impact auditing of two public library services in England concentrates on collecting evidence about the value of the library to the community and its impact on people's lives. They focus on four strands:

1 Established functions, including culture, education, reading and literacy, information provision and leisure.

2 Social and caring roles, including personal development, community empowerment and learning, local image and social cohesion.
3 Economic impact, including business and employment information, training opportunities and tourism information.
4 Equity between groups and communities, as well as equity of access.

5.3.3   Health libraries

For health librarians, the agenda is partly determined by government or institutional priorities and partly by what is 'hot' in health librarianship. In the first category come:

* meeting the information needs of staff who are directly involved in delivering care to patients
* clinical outreach (ensuring access to and use of best evidence by clinical teams)
* increasing multi-disciplinary use of services.

In the 'hot issues' area come:

* electronic resources training provided by the library service
* the effects of centralizing various health service information access functions
* working directly with users to encourage independent learners and an evidence-based practice culture.

5.3.4   Special libraries

Special libraries obviously vary enormously in their focus. However, in recent workshops two common themes have emerged:

* being a first port of call for managers/researchers in their organization (and beyond in some cases)
* supporting decision making in the organization (by traditional service provision or engaging with knowledge management).

In addition, legal librarians talk about saving time (and therefore money) for partners.

Step 1   Starting the process

Think about your own library service and decide which key service area or initiative you want to work on now. Use this service area as your focus in working through the impact evaluation model.

5.4   From impact areas to objectives

5.4.1   Specific and time-limited objectives

When we work with library service managers, we always start by identifying key areas in which they want their service to make an impact. These areas then provide the focus for generating *specific and time-limited service objectives.*

'Specific', in this context, means being as precise as possible about what you intend to achieve – what advances you expect to make and with which people. We know from our workshops that if managers stick to broad and general objectives, they get into real difficulties when they are asked how they can tell that they are succeeding. This usually entails going back to rewrite the objectives more sharply so that they know where they are trying to get to.

Your definition of 'time-limited' will depend upon whether you are a strategic or operational manager. (Managerial seniority is sometimes delineated by organizations in terms of the length of time over which managers are called upon to plan and deliver services – more senior executives have longer time-scales.) However, the longest realistic operational planning span in most library settings is between one and three years (even where strategic plans are projected over longer periods).

Before focusing on specific objectives, some library services find it helpful to distinguish between user-focused objectives (such as, to enhance lifelong learning opportunities for young people and adults) and internally focused objectives (e.g. to develop the capacity of staff and the organization to learn and improve).

5.4.2   What else do you need to take into account when setting your service objectives?

Objective setting must take account of the wider working context and overarching organizational priorities. Most library services will be more or less affected by:

1   The national agenda as it affects your service – this is self-evident for libraries in central/federal government agencies, and may be important if you are funded by local/state government (especially if your service is heavily influenced by central government direction). In any case the national agenda will affect specific aspects of your work (e.g. through employment legislation). To give one example, UK public libraries have to

be seen to address centrally imposed accountability measures (such as impact measures and service review processes). Unfortunately these central prescriptions come and go with successive governments – where, a few years ago, there were national impact targets for public libraries, at the moment the UK government is implementing a 'slash and burn' policy for public sector services (such as public libraries) with the result that the emphasis has changed from 'value for money' service provision to saving money by cutting services. (This situation could reverse again if there is an economic upturn.) In other countries, there are European Community opportunities to align public libraries with meeting European policy priorities in the country such as providing support for e-government.

2 The interests of other key stakeholders (and potential partners). It is important to be clear who the stakeholders are and how they will be involved in the process. In business, commercial and other special libraries these stakeholders may be easier to identify and consult than in the public sector. When consulting about objectives, it is important to focus on what you are all trying to achieve and how well (that is, on the quality of the collaboration) – otherwise the focus will shift towards activities. It is even more important to focus on the priorities of the stakeholders and partners and on how libraries can help to meet them.

Despite the need to take all these perspectives into account, it is still vital to keep your professional judgement in play. The wants expressed by community representatives may not fully reflect community needs. You may have to help people to see what is possible, to open up alternatives and present new ideas. (As a schools library services manager observes: 'It is no good talking to school heads about a quality service if they have no idea what quality looks like.')

It is important to be clear on precisely what you are trying to achieve through your programme or service so that you will be able to tell whether you are meeting the objective or making progress towards this. The key to success at this stage in the impact evaluation process is to be realistic in answering these two questions:

1 Does this objective cover what you are trying to do 'locally'? Since all countries and localities are different, there will be differences in your priorities compared to other libraries. Success in changing your service may be different from success in other places, either because of the current state of development of the library service or because of different national or local priorities. Taking the state of development of the library service first: if only a small proportion of potential users make use of the library,

your first objectives are likely to be to increase the membership and engage more people actively in the library's activities. Once you have achieved this you will want to move on to other development challenges. Considering particular 'local' priorities: your central government may want to engage the full range of indigenous communities more fully into national and local affairs, in which case two objectives for the library service may be to attract more people from different communities and to involve librarians from these groups more fully in library work. This may not be an issue at all in other countries or localities.

2 What resources of staff time and money do you have available to meet this objective? A common issue in looking at objectives set by library service managers (we see this most frequently in education libraries) is that managers set themselves objectives that would be admirable – if they had unlimited resources and time! The reality is that library staff who are trying to innovate or develop part of their service also have to run the existing service. They only have limited spare capacity for innovative activity – and for evaluating what they are trying to do.

5.4.3 Some traps to avoid . . .

Watch out for these three things when writing your objectives:

1 Do not set objectives for areas where you have little (or not the main) control over the activities required to meet them.
2 Do not simply adopt the objectives of your parent organization. In most organizations it is politically important to take account of and reflect the overall institutional objectives, but it is equally important to ensure that you specify the part that your services should play within that bigger picture – otherwise you will not be able to demonstrate what your service contributed to the whole.
3 Try to be realistic about *what can be demonstrably achieved*. It is pointless to set ambitious aims for the service, on the lines of 'the local community will read better' or 'children in schools served will achieve better exam results', if there is no way of establishing whether or not any such impact can be achieved, how to go about it, or whether the library service makes any contribution to achieving any change. Simple cause and effect relationships are difficult to establish in the real world but it should be possible to find objectives with which you can show if you are having any impact – usually by asking people!

If you do fall into one of these traps you are setting yourself up to fail, if other services fail. You will also lose out if success is achieved, because you will not be able to show clearly your part in that success.

Do not be drawn into considering precisely how you will collect your evidence at this stage. Writing objectives is about building a realistic vision of what your service might achieve. Looking at the difficulties of demonstrating achievement too early in the process will inhibit your vision.

5.4.4 . . . and the elephant trap!

The biggest and most common mistake that library managers make at this stage in the impact evaluation process is that they prescribe activities instead of objectives – what they will do to get there rather than what they want to achieve.

➜ Task 5.1

It is not always easy to avoid the elephant trap. Which of the following proposals are impact objectives and which ones are activities?

1   To support managers in carrying out their work effectively and efficiently by providing appropriate information
2   To provide access to ICT-based learning through adult learning sessions
3   To enable students to operate effectively in an e-environment
4   To enable health care staff to find the evidence to develop local care pathways
5   To provide materials appropriate to the needs of ethnic minorities
6   To increase the confidence and competence of socially excluded people in using library resources
7   To develop children as readers
8   To secure the library as a main source of information in conducting research in the field
9   To collaborate with managers in the organization in order to integrate the library into their work
10   To develop the skills of library staff in delivering effective user-education.

(Answers at the end of this chapter)

If you think that you have drifted into specifying activities, ask yourself *why* you are aiming to do the activities and what difference they will make to your users and other stakeholders – this should take you back to your objectives.

Step 2   Write your objectives

Write between two and four specific and time-limited objectives for your key service area or initiative. Concentrate on what you want to achieve within one to three years, not on what you will do to achieve your objectives. (Some examples of objectives are given below.)

5.5   Some examples of objectives

These examples are all based on real objectives generated by library service managers in different types of library.

5.5.1   Public library services

- to empower individuals and communities to engage in democratic processes
- to support the study needs of young people
- to build individuals' capacity to engage in lifelong learning
- to embed diversity and equality into all aspects of the library's work
- to engage marginalized groups with the wider community
- to engage the community in reading across generations
- to contribute to the economic regeneration of the locality
- to sustain community cultural heritage and confidence.

5.5.2   Schools library services

- to enrich/extend learning opportunities for all pupils by providing appropriate classroom resources
- to support the development of pupils' independent learning skills
- to enable parity of access to resources across schools
- to help extend the range of teaching strategies used to support literacy
- to develop school librarians and school libraries to support reading and learning within schools more effectively
- to promote wider reading for pleasure
- to enable teachers to use a wide range of resources in the classroom more easily
- to promote effective use of ICT within school libraries
- to survive as a business.

5.6   Why objectives matter

Early on in our workshops, library service managers often ask why they should spend so much time writing impact objectives and why we scrutinize the wording of these objectives in such detail. Are we just being pedantic?

In fact, the objectives drive the whole process of impact evaluation. As Peter Brophy (2002) has stressed, no library should think about trying to evaluate its impact before getting its objectives crystal clear. If you use the wrong words at this point you will find it very hard to move on to the next stage, which (as we will show in Chapter 6) involves asking yourself 'How can I tell if we are succeeding in our objective?' When people hit problems in answering this question, the only way out is to go back and write the objective more precisely.

> **LAWS OF IMPACT EVALUATION 2**
> If we are to focus on impact we need to articulate precisely what we are trying to achieve rather than how we will get there.

> **LAWS OF IMPACT EVALUATION 3**
> If we don't generate specific and time-limited objectives to help focus on impact, we will end up monitoring efficiency instead.

➡ Answers to Task 5.1

1 is an objective but the last four words have slipped into activity; 2 and 5 are activities; 9 is both an activity and an objective – it should be re-written to focus on the library being integrated into managers' work. If a statement includes 'to provide' this usually heralds an activity.

6

Success criteria and impact indicators: how you know you are making a difference

This chapter guides you through stage two of your quest to evaluate impact: choosing success criteria and using them to write specific impact indicators. The key question at this stage is 'How can I tell if I am making a difference?' or, to put it another way, 'What do I want to be judged on in relation to each of my service objectives?' Designing indicators is one of the most critical steps in the whole process of evaluating impact.

Let us start with two more traps for the unwary.

When we talk about the elephant trap in section 5.4.4, this is because we have seen so many library service managers slide from writing objectives into listing what they expect to do to achieve them. We've come to the conclusion that this happens because the driving motivation for most library managers is to provide as wide a range of services as possible for everyone. Where this is feasible there is no problem, but when resource limitations kick in it is necessary to start asking questions about what works best.

The same problem crops up at this stage, but with the subtle difference that people slide from 'How can I tell if the service is making a difference' to 'How well are we doing this?' As Linley and Usherwood (1998) say:

> Even where people have sought to assess the libraries' performance against goals . . . the emphasis [is] on developing indicators of administrative effectiveness, that is of process.

The second trap to beware of is that it is easy to slide into the problems of collecting the evidence needed to inform your indicators, rather than sorting out the indicators and then worrying about the evidence. This leads to library managers shying away from indicators that might be difficult to measure.

Working through this chapter should help you to avoid these traps.

> **LAWS OF IMPACT EVALUATION 4**
> When you are thinking about what impact you would like to see, don't inhibit yourself by worrying about how you will gather the evidence – yet!

6.1   Formulating success criteria: getting the balance right

You should now be ready to translate your service objectives into success criteria. If you have written clear objectives, you should be able to answer the questions:

- What sort of changes am I looking for in the people that I want to reach with this service objective? or
- How can I tell if the parts of the service that are trying to meet this objective are making a difference?

The answers to these questions become your success criteria, which you then turn into impact indicators. Impact is usually about having an *impact on people*, which creates *change*. What sorts of changes in people are you looking for?

These changes may be:

- **affective** (attitudes, perceptions, levels of confidence, satisfaction with the service)
- **behavioural** – people do things differently (e.g. doing something more or less often, asking different types of questions, being more critical or more independent)
- **knowledge-based** (e.g. knowing about key sources of relevant information; knowing what questions different databases can answer)
- **competence-based** – people do things more effectively (e.g. improved search techniques; being able to find appropriate information).

The Global Libraries Initiative (GL) is uncompromising in choosing to focus on changing people's lives. More specifically, they focus on whether and how introducing public access computing into countries and areas where there is only limited internet access can make a real difference to people's lives, and what those differences are. Such a criterion of success is appropriate for an international development programme like GL – but it is also a legitimate aspiration for any library service that engages in developing both physical and intellectual access to information. In the UK, 'libraries transforming lives' is the slogan of the newly formed Community, Diversity and Equality Group of the national professional library body, CILIP. If you can help people to learn how to find, evaluate and use information for whatever purpose so that they are confident information users you have changed their lives!

The people who may (or may not) change are often your users, but depending on your objectives and how you are carrying them out you may be looking for changes in other people, such as your colleagues, senior managers, teaching staff or local politicians. Your services may reach even further: we have mounting evidence that people often use library computers to find information for other people; and in countries where significant numbers of parents work abroad, they, or their children and other relatives, may rely on public access computing through libraries to maintain contact and sustain family cohesion.

Success criteria identify the sorts of changes that you are trying to achieve by addressing your objectives. Impact indicators translate these broad areas into specific pieces of information. The main justification for having the success criteria step in the process before we get stuck into impact indicators is that you are then less likely to lock onto one of the four areas of change above at the expense of the other three.

What we are doing here is similar to what researchers do when they design questionnaires or interview schedules. The first stage in that process is to think of all the question areas you want to cover and to decide whether you actually need to cover them all. Beginners tend to jump straight in and start writing questions, with the result that they don't usually cover all the important areas and may ask unnecessary questions. Similarly, stepping back and asking 'What criteria will tell me we are being successful?' and 'Which of these will do the job best?' should ensure that you get the balance right.

6.2   What sorts of changes will show impact?

Impact may appear at different points on several dimensions, making it more difficult to capture.

Dimension 1: Impact on what?

As we have just noted, changes can appear in behaviour, competence, levels of knowledge or attitudes. These may show themselves through early changes in people's skills or activities, gradually growing confidence and competence over time, through to life-changing experiences (such as learning to love reading, or finding out how to achieve major health improvement) and overall improvements in quality of life due to increased income, saving time or improved social contact.

Dimension 2: Individual or collective impact

The impact can show itself in individual cases or through more generally discernible changes, such as:

- quality of life, e.g. increased self-esteem of library staff or users; greater confidence; feeling included; enhanced work prospects or social prospects
- educational and other impacts, e.g. skills acquired; educational attainment achieved; enhanced levels of knowledge
- impact may also affect specific organizations such as small local businesses or community groups (e.g. survival and growth).

Dimension 3: Speed of change

Impacts can start to show almost as soon as you start to collect evidence, within months, or not for several years:

- Romanian public libraries involved in the Global Libraries Initiative begin to report success stories from users of public access computers installed in libraries as part of that initiative, almost as soon as the new services open.
- However, we know that major organizational change (Fullan, 2007), such as reshaping a library association, will take from three to five years.
- Educational evaluation is usually focused on student performance over a school year or on external examinations which may be taken after learning has been accumulated for several years.

Dimension 4: Depth of change

Impacts are likely to range from smaller changes that may be achieved in the short term to more deep-seated changes that will take time to emerge. Here are some examples of both:

- **Small-scale changes** Library managers engage in more advocacy for libraries; collaborate with new organizations; develop a wider membership base.
- **Deeper changes** Library staff have an increased capacity to undertake a wide range of activities; or engage with partner organizations in complex long-term collaborations.

Examples of success criteria

Objective: take reading out to targeted community groups:

- SC 1 More reading by people in community groups (behavioural)
- SC 2 Increased knowledge of books (knowledge)
- SC 3 Greater staff confidence in promoting reading within community groups (affective).

Objective: to enhance the user experience of using health literature:

- SC 1 Knowing 'what is out there' (knowledge)
- SC 2 Increased user expectation that they can find and understand relevant health literature (affective)
- SC 3 Improved ability to do their job (competence)

Step 3 Write success criteria

Choose two of the service objectives that you wrote earlier (section 5.4.4). Write two or three success criteria for each one. Make sure that you focus on changes in people.

6.3 What is an impact indicator?

In the world of performance management that we occupy, the word 'indicator' is freely bandied about. What is an indicator and how can it help us to evaluate impact? An indicator is a piece of information that indicates something useful to you. Indicators are not produced or used in a vacuum. They are tied to your service objectives. They must be seen in the context of what you are trying to do.

Indicators can only give you clues about the difference you are making. It is extremely difficult to evaluate the actual impact of any service. Human beings are complex and are affected in many subtle ways by each experience. Impact indicators are usually surrogates for impact: pieces of information that provide good clues, telling part of the story. Your challenge is to design the strongest surrogates possible. For example, assume that your service is trying to encourage enthusiasm for books and reading. You may decide to monitor loan levels, but this is a weak surrogate for the impact that you are trying to record. Loans might increase for a number of reasons. A much stronger surrogate, and therefore a better indicator, is users' attitudes towards books – are they more positive as a result of your work?

6.4 What do good indicators look like?

Much has been written during the past 20 years about designing good indicators (for example, Kaplan and Norton, 1992; Fitz-Gibbon, 1996; Woodcock, 1998). Lists of their characteristics abound. Education, in particular, has engaged in many debates about what makes a good indicator.

Example 6.1   Avoid too many indicators and still focus on what really matters: looking at schools

Here is an example from an education workshop for school heads and advisers that we both attended some years ago.

A leading university professor begins by saying that he only needs three pieces of information about a school to know how good it is – examination results, teacher absence rates and levels of truancy (unauthorized absence by students). Not surprisingly this pronouncement is greeted with shock and horror. However, he maintains his position, arguing that these three indicators illuminate the impact of the school on pupils and teachers.

An education inspector at the same workshop replies that he wants four indicators to judge the quality of education and a school's effectiveness: academic progress, pupil satisfaction, positive pupil–teacher relationships and instances of excellence within the learning process. (Neither speaker suggests looking at the number of classes taught, levels of expenditure, staffing levels, resources per pupil or anything else – the educational equivalent of what many library services do.)

They tie their indicators firmly into what the schools should be trying to achieve: progress in pupil learning, a supportive environment for pupils and teachers, and engaging with all pupils in the school.

This exchange illustrates some of the most important factors to bear in mind when you are creating good indicators. Indicators should be:

1 **Directly linked to what you are trying to achieve** – the key areas in which you are trying to make a difference (relevant to accepted and valued organizational goals). This is why we give so much attention to articulating objectives before getting any further into evaluating impact.
2 **Clear and understandable.** Check them with colleagues at all levels.
3 **Generally accepted as reasonable and fair.** You need to agree that the indicators really do tell you about the impact of your service. Are they measuring something over which you have little control (hardly fair), something that does not tell the whole story of what you are achieving, or things of secondary importance in the eyes of your staff or managers? Are they up-to-date? You may be doing invaluable online support work for managers in your organization but this may result in declining use of your physical space or reference material. Do your indicators reflect such changes? (There is always likely to be some discussion about how fair your chosen indicators are.)

4 **Valid** (evaluate what they say they are evaluating). This is more difficult than it seems – for example, a public library registers a surge in use after it runs an awareness-raising programme. It is delighted at this impact until someone notices that most of the new users are in the 18–21 age group, and the local college has just closed the site library nearest to that public library.
5 **Informative, providing significant information.** They should illuminate your successes, highlight changes/trends and throw up warning signs.
6 **As few in number as possible.** They should cover the most significant parts of the service (what really matters). The question to ask is 'What are the most important changes that you are trying to achieve?' However, you also need to make sure that the indicators are balanced. You don't want to choose a very small number of indicators and then find that they pull your attention and even your whole service in the wrong direction (more about this below).

An important issue here is how many impact indicators you really need and how to choose the key areas. If you have consulted over your objectives and prioritized them, it is reasonable to confine your impact indicators to the priority areas in which you are trying to make a noticeable difference and to rely on traditional process and output performance indicators (see sections 7.4 and 7.5) to monitor other areas.

If you could only use one indicator to show the impact of your service what would it be? Faced with this question, the organizers of public library reading groups to encourage reading for pleasure choose 'the % of group members who recommended at least one book to a friend, family member or other group member' as their key indicator. Fortunately, you can usually choose two or three indicators to give you a better picture. However, it is important to avoid choosing too many indicators, because you will need to collect evidence of impact for each indicator and that will take time.

6.5 What do you do if you don't know what impact to expect?

If you are designing highly innovative services, such as experimental e-services offering novel service delivery options, you may not know what changes to expect and what impact indicators to choose. This is because the simple logic model (which is how the impact evaluation sequence can be described) is not designed for situations where you do not know what the impacts are likely to be – until you start innovating. A more complex approach is needed here, which we described in Chapter 2 as emergent evaluation (Rogers, 2008) and which is also known as developmental evaluation (Patton, 2011).

Here, the evaluation follows on from the innovation. As the evaluator, you collect as much information as possible about what is happening until you have built up an understanding of where changes are occurring, so that you know where to focus your evaluation work and to apply the other steps in our sequence. This evolutionary approach to evaluation does not fit comfortably with organizational plans, although it does sit well within the action-research cycle, which is one reason why we advocate this approach in section 9.6.

6.6   What makes a poor indicator?

There are several ways in which indicators can fail to do their job. They can be:

1 **Corruptible** – easily used to create a false impression. For example, library managers assure us that they could massage or selectively use their loan statistics to show a range of desired impacts, from demonstrating the excellent job they are doing to indicating problems in the hope of getting more resources!

2 **Corrupting** – provide an incentive to do disruptive or counter-productive actions; such as when a police force introduces 'time taken to answer phone calls' as an indicator of effectiveness, resulting in a discussion with a distressed robbery victim being broken off to answer the next call! It is also a common occurrence on London trains for all travellers to be turned off at an intermediate station so that the train can run through to the end of the line without further stops – the indicator is 'Proportion of trains that arrive on time'! Your indicators should always encourage positive service. In libraries, corrupting indicators might focus on one or two aspects of the service to the detriment of others. To avoid this, remember that your indicators should reflect the competing priorities that all services have to struggle with.

3 **Inflexible** and unable to reflect diversity and change in your services – how many libraries that are now offering interesting ICT-based services are evaluating them actively to show how their services are changing?

6.7   Some issues to consider before you start writing indicators

1 You should focus impact indicators on changes that you are deliberately setting out to achieve and at which you have targeted resources. These

changes should be clear from your service objectives. Targeting resources should be specific in this context: our work with Global Libraries shows that providing public access computers and ICT training is not enough if you are trying to achieve specific objectives. For example, if you aim to empower women in a community by giving them access to appropriate health information you may have to train library staff to work with women's groups and form partnerships with organizations that are committed to working on women's health issues. This idea of 'intentionality' is important: are you hoping that people will use greater information access in various ways or are you doing things that should encourage this to happen? If you don't take specific actions, what sort of a claim can you make about the contribution of the public library to meeting women's health concerns?

2 It should be possible to find two or three indicators of impact in relation to each objective. Sometimes the same impact indicator can be used for more than one objective.

3 Indicators are provisional. It is very rare to get indicators completely right at the first attempt. We don't usually know enough at the outset about the complex relationships between different factors and different elements of any service. The first time you work through the measuring impact process you may find that some indicators do not tell you what you really need to know while others distract you from the real issues. Change them.

4 Don't be distracted by *how* you will gather the necessary evidence. It is important to resist the normal managerial tendency to consider the 'what' and 'how' questions together. If you lose the distinction, you will probably slide into output indicators (e.g. quantity of loans to socially disadvantaged groups) because these are easier to collect. Once you decide that it is important to evaluate an area of impact you will probably be able to find some way of gathering evidence. (We look at data collection in Chapter 9.)

5 You may have to revisit your objectives when you start to look for appropriate indicators. For example, one service abandons its aim of 'promoting literacy' when service managers consider how much direct effect they can have. Instead, they opt for 'supporting literacy through partner organizations' and the impact indicators flow more naturally.

6 It may be easier to assess impact at some levels than at others. For example, if a schools' library service provides training and advice for teachers from several schools it should be possible to collect some evidence of any change in their awareness and behaviour; it will be much harder to demonstrate any impact on pupils.

7 Some services group their indicators by the strategic, operational or service level at which they are applied (e.g. specific service points; organization-wide). You may like to use this as a checking mechanism to ensure that all the indicators are not clustered at one level – after you have identified your indicators.

8 It is difficult to *measure* some tangible benefits that libraries can bring (e.g. personal development, community empowerment, quality of pupil work). However, indicators of impact do not have to be quantitative and therefore easily measured. Qualitative indicators (e.g. Do members of socially excluded groups feel more able to contribute their ideas to library managers?) can be equally valid.

Please don't forget that, whatever indicators you choose, professional judgement still matters!

6.8 Writing indicators

Writing indicators requires effort: they should be unambiguous – make it clear what evidence you need to collect to see how you are doing – and you should be able to apply them in a sustainable manner so that by collecting evidence year-on-year you can see any trends.

We now discuss some of the choices you have about the form of the indicators that you write.

6.8.1 Different forms of indicators

People write indicators in different ways. This may be based on the accepted approach in an organization, 'how they are always written'; or they may follow guidelines; or someone may attend a course where a certain approach is used. Unless you are constrained by organizational rules, think carefully about the type of indicators that you will find it easiest to work with. Which of the formats below do you prefer? Which will you find easiest to write? Which format seems the clearest?

6.8.2 Indicators as questions

You can find this approach in our school library self-evaluation materials produced for the English Department for Education and Skills (Streatfield and Markless, 2004). For instance, in looking at the objective of improving the standard of pupils' reading, the indicators chosen are:

- Do pupils read a wide range of challenging material?
- Do pupils respond imaginatively to what they have read?
- Do pupils enjoy reading?
- Do pupils show progression in their reading, extending the range and level of material chosen over time?

Questions like these are clear: they focus on important areas of impact for any reading programme; they point you towards collecting particular information; and they can be used over time to signal trends.

6.8.3   Indicators as statements

Indicators written as short statements are common in library plans. An example was on the Their Reading Futures website, (but now only available as a CD-ROM, from tricia.kings@readingagency.org.uk) which offers the following indicators of success for promoting reading among young people, in the form of brief statements:

1 Young people read more widely.
2 Young people become more confident about themselves as readers.
3 Young people have more positive attitudes towards reading.
4 Young people and families have an increased sense of belonging to the community through reading and reading activities.
5 Through reading and reading activities young people are inspired to engage in creative activities.

6.8.4   Indicators as quantities

Many managers are obsessed with numbers. This is partly due to pressure from government departments and other influential bodies that hold the purse strings, and partly because many managers think that the only valid evidence is quantitative. Library service managers should be trying to re-educate senior staff who exhibit this type of tunnel vision. However, there is of course a place for some numbers in the evaluation of impact and it is possible to write indicators in quantitative terms. You could rewrite any of the indicators given in sections 6.8.2 or 6.8.3 above as numbers or proportions (e.g. 'the proportion of pupils who enjoy reading', or 'the percentage of young people who read more widely').

Numbers can only tell you a limited amount, unless you are in a position to collect large-scale data which shows trends over time, and even then it is hard to attribute changes in (for example) patterns of library service use to developments in your service provision. It may be more important to find out about the nature and magnitude of the changes that have occurred rather than just how many people were involved. Quantitative indicators can also pull you into thinking about the numbers too early in the process of evaluating impact. When you come to think about setting targets (Chapter 10) you will inevitably be drawn into enumerating your targets. At this earlier stage, when you are thinking about indicators for evaluating impact, it is often more productive to consider in broad terms the types of information that tell you what difference you are making; this information may or may not be numerical and can be combined to show a fuller picture. Appropriateness and relevance are the principles to guide your choices (Patton, 2012); what types of things do you need to know, how will you use your data and who else will see and use the information you collect?

As we show when looking at the presentation of evaluation findings, the ideal approach is often to combine numbers and stories to give a sense of scale of change and impact.

> **LAWS OF IMPACT EVALUATION 5**
> Beware of formulating too many quantitative indicators. This can lead you to concentrate too heavily on the statistical side of your impact – numbers never tell the whole story.

Step 4   What kind of indicators?

You now need to decide what your impact indicators will look like. For example, which of the following do you prefer?

- The proportion of managers who use the library as a first port of call when needing information about their work.
- Managers use the library as a first port of call when needing information about their work.
- Do managers use the library as a first port of call when needing information about their work?

You can, of course, switch between or vary your formats, as long as you retain clarity.

6.9   Writing your own impact indicators

You have already formulated some success criteria linked to two of your service objectives. You can now use these to write your impact indicators. At this stage you are looking at the sort of changes that you want to achieve (success criteria) and deciding what specific pieces of information will enable you to judge whether you are making that difference. It is usual to write between two and four indicators for each of your objectives.

Later on, when you have written a full set of impact indicators that cover all of your service objectives, you should review them as a package. This gives you the chance to get rid of any overlap and duplication, so that you end up with the smallest set of indicators that still demonstrate your success.

Step 5   Write impact indicators
Revisit the two service objectives and associated success criteria that you have already produced. Use the success criteria to help you to write impact indicators for each of the two service objectives.

Sections 6.10 and 6.11 should help you with this activity. You may prefer to do the task first and then use the information to check or amend your indicators. If you prefer to have all the information at your disposal before you begin, read to the end of section 6.11 before doing the task.

6.10 Getting the words right

Clarity is one of the most important characteristics of a good indicator. Your indicators tell you what evidence you need to collect to see if you are achieving your service objectives. They also establish what you will be judged on. So, your indicators need to be precisely worded to make sure that you do not set yourself up to fail. Our concern with getting the words right is not born out of a desire to be pedantic. It arises from our experience of running workshops for practitioners and from our development work with library senior management teams engaging in evaluating their own service impact. We often spend time with library staff going through their indicators and 'fine tuning' them. How well this time is spent will become evident at the next stage when you begin to plan data collection.

Here are some examples of this fine-tuning (drawn from our workshops), along with our reasons for making the suggested changes.

Example 6.2   Impact indicators for a special library
The library staff drew up the following lists of impact indicators for two of their key service objectives.

Objective 1: To support managers carrying out their work with appropriate information
1 Managers make more challenging demands of the information service.
2 More managers use the service as a first port of call when seeking information (directly or indirectly).

3   More managers know about the specialist information services provided by the library.

4   More managers make appropriate use of the specialist information services provided by the library.

Objective 2: To secure the library as a main source of information in conducting research in the field

1   Researchers make regular use of the research resources of the library (directly and indirectly).

2   Researchers make written acknowledgement of the library in their published works.

3   Researchers recommend the library to other potential users.

4   Users make more challenging demands on the services of the library when conducting their research.

What do you think of the indicators in Example 6.2?

Would you make any changes?

If so, what changes and why?

Try to answer these questions before you look at our comments below.

6.10.1 Commentary on Example 6.2
Objective 1

The first indicator is fine. It focuses on a specific change in behaviour by the group identified in the objective. It should give useful information about the nature of the help that the library service is providing.

Indicators 2, 3 and 4 need some attention. All of them focus on whether the service is having an impact on managers. They all appear to identify significant elements of behaviour and they all lead the service manager towards gathering particular types of evidence. The problem is in the use of the word 'more' at the beginning of each of the indicators. An indicator should keep the options open rather than lead you towards a predetermined outcome. You do not know in advance whether more or fewer managers will make appropriate use of the service. It is probably better to say 'Managers make appropriate use . . .' or 'Managers know about . . .' if only to avoid the temptation of putting your foot on the scales by concentrating on indicators in areas where you know you can show an improvement. As you collect data over time you will be able to see whether more people are behaving as you would want. (The neutral position we are suggesting here will be abandoned when you come to set impact targets at the next stage. As we will show in Chapter 10, that is why targets can corrupt the service they are trying to evaluate.)

Objective 2

The first three indicators should work. However, when we discussed the fourth indicator with the library staff, they decided that although it might be a good indicator of effective use of the library, it would not give them clear information about whether they are achieving this particular objective of securing the library as a main source of research information in the field. They changed it to:

4 Researchers use the library as a first port of call when seeking information.

Example 6.3   Impact indicators for a college library

Objective 1: To enable students to operate effectively in the digital environment

1 Proportion of students using the e-resources.
2 More efficient and successful searching by a wider range of students.
3 Students are confident working with a wide range of e-resources.
4 Students are producing better quality work.

Objective 2: To develop students' ability to find and use appropriate information

1 Students' engagement with their library-based assignments (motivation, interest).
2 Range of resources used by students for their work.
3 Student questions in the library are less basic and more focused.
4 Students are producing better quality work.
5 Students are confident in carrying out their assignments.

What do you think of the indicators in Example 6.3?
Would you make any changes?
If so, what changes and why?
     Try to answer these questions before you look at our comments below.

6.10.2 Commentary on Example 6.3
Objective 1

The first three indicators taken together appear appropriate and manageable, although the first one is a weak surrogate for impact. The library staff decided to keep it in because they hoped to show senior management that more students were being attracted to e-resources. The fourth indicator raised a problem. It is difficult to make a direct link between enabling students to operate effectively in an e-environment and the general quality of their work (although you might like to try). After discussion, the library staff replaced this indicator with two others:

4   Students cite e-resources in their assignments.
5   Students are able to use the web independently to access appropriate material.

They then decided to remove indicator 2 about efficient and successful searching (remembering the cardinal rule about using as few indicators as possible), because it was subsumed in the new indicator 5. When the librarians gather data about students' use of the web they will be able to see the range of students who can use it effectively and whether this range is broadening over time. By the end of our discussion there were still four indicators attached to Objective 1, but they were different:

Objective 1: To enable students to operate effectively in an e-environment

Revised indicators:

1   Proportion of students using the e-resources.
2   Students are confident working with a wide range of e-resources.
3   Students cite e-resources in their assignments.
4   Students are able to use the web independently to access appropriate material.

Objective 2

Again, the first three indicators work. However, indicator 4 raises the same problem as in the previous example – over-extending the reach of the library. In this case they changed it to:

4   Students know about a range of appropriate information sources.

The last indicator also appears a step too far. Rather than expect information-skills teaching to produce students who are confident throughout the process of carrying out their assignments, they decide to limit their aspirations to:

5   Students are confident in finding appropriate material for their assignments.

6.11   Using frameworks to help you choose appropriate indicators

Although your indicators should flow from your own service objectives, there is no need to start the writing process from scratch. You can use existing frameworks to point you in the right direction and give you some useful ideas. Don't follow them slavishly: consult them to see if they contain material that can be adapted to reflect what you want to achieve. Be careful that any model or framework that you use is looking at impact and not only at process (activities you should engage in). In practice, indicators in these frameworks are often a mix of impact and process. Try labelling them as P (process) or I (impact) so that you can see which ones you might borrow.

6.11.1 Inspiring Learning for All

How times change! In the first edition of this book we describe the Inspiring Learning for All framework as 'the jewel in the crown of the UK Museums, Libraries and Archives Council'. Jewel it may be, but the crown has been melted down for scrap. More precisely, the Council was an early victim of the current UK government's austerity measures, which puts the future of this framework in doubt. It aims to describe 'what an accessible and inclusive museum, archive or library which stimulates and supports learning looks like'. The main focus of this framework is on informal learning stimulated by public libraries (as well as museums and archives) and it tries to help service managers to:

- find out what the people that use your services learn
- assess how well you are achieving best practice in supporting learning
- improve what you do.

To help achieve these aims, Inspiring Learning for All identifies a set of fairly traditional generic learning outcomes (in our terms, success criteria) which replicate the four areas of change outlined in section 6.1 above:

- knowledge and understanding (our 'knowledge-based')
- skills (our 'competence-based')
- attitudes and values (our 'affective')
- enjoyment, inspiration, creativity (again, our 'affective')
- activity, behaviour and progression (our 'behavioural').

These success areas are then unpacked into more specific success criteria. For example, 'knowledge and understanding' is broken down into 'knowing about something', and this in turn is categorized as:

- learning facts or information which can be:
  - subject-specific
  - interdisciplinary/thematic
  - about libraries
  - about myself, my family, my community, the wider world
- making sense of something
- deepening understanding
- learning how libraries operate
- giving specific information – naming things, people or places
- making links and relationships between things
- using prior knowledge in new ways.

Inspiring Learning for All also identifies what it calls 'learning outcomes for users'. Most of these can be developed into impact indicators. At the moment, we think that they are not specific enough to enable a clear enough focus on impact and on gathering evidence. Some examples are:

- people enjoy themselves and are enriched and inspired by the experience
- people use the services and facilities to develop their knowledge and understanding
- people develop skills as a result of using libraries
- people become more self-confident, questioning, motivated and open to others' perspectives
- people decide to do something different in their lives.

They also identify some 'outcomes for the . . . library', which are more specific and can be used as impact indicators:

- a broader range of people use the . . . library
- new learning opportunities are created as a result of partnerships
- staff, volunteers and members of governing bodies are effective advocates for learning
- people who work in and for the organization are continuously learning and developing their practice.

A set of generic social indicators has now been added to the site, because:

. . . libraries . . . need to be able to give evidence of the benefit of our services to [the UK government] Treasury and other interested stakeholders. This framework sets out one way of aligning the sector's potential social contribution with key government policy drivers.

The site offers three 'first tier indicators' and sets of 'second tier indictors' as follows:

Stronger and safer communities

- Improving group and inter-group dialogue and understanding
- Supporting cultural diversity and identity
- Encouraging familial ties and relationships
- Tackling the fear of crime and anti-social behaviour
- Contributing to crime prevention and reduction.

Health and well-being

- Encouraging healthy lifestyles and contributing to mental and physical well-being
- Supporting care and recovery
- Supporting older people to live independent lives
- Helping children and young people to enjoy life and make a positive contribution
- Strengthening public life
- Encouraging and supporting awareness and participation in local-decision making and wider civic and political engagement
- Building the capacity of community and voluntary groups.

Providing safe, inclusive and trusted public spaces

- Enabling community empowerment through the awareness of rights, benefits and external services
- Improving the responsiveness of services to the needs of the local community, including other stakeholders.

'Third tier indicators' are offered for each of the second tier set. For example, under 'Health and Well-being: Supporting older people to live independent lives', they offer:

- Older people say that they have learnt new skills which enable them to be more independent.
- Older people say they have participated in and feel ownership of the development of projects and services.
- Older people say that their experiences, work and interests are valued.
- Older people who are living alone / isolated feel that provision enables them to engage with others.

Possible questions to ask and examples of evidence are offered for each item, at third tier level.

The Inspiring Learning for All framework and a range of support materials can be found at www.inspiringlearningforall.gov.uk. We will return to this framework when we look at development planning at the end of Chapter 10.

6.11.2 The Fitz-Gibbon model

Carol Fitz-Gibbon and Susan Kochan (2000) offer a useful way of focusing on impact indicators that works for education libraries, although their focus is on helping schools to improve. In introducing these areas they recognize the danger of confining impact (their 'outcomes') evaluation to what is formally learnt, and ask:

> . . . how do we move beyond the cognitive to a comprehensive list of important and valued outcomes? In attempting to produce a list of education outcomes, we can take the approach of considering the desired sequence of events in the education of a [student], then identify the logical outcomes related to each step in the sequence. The [student] should:
>
> - enrol at the [college/university] and then
> - attend
> - achieve
> - develop desirable attitudes
> - develop desirable skills
> - have a good quality of life while in the [college]; and
> - then progress appropriately onwards.

They then translate this series of events into impact indicators. We have modified these to fit school, college or university library contexts. Examples of impact indicators include:

1 Flow (enrol at and attend):

- *The proportion of students who are formally introduced to the library and then use it compared with those who are not 'inducted'. (If this proportion can be calculated it gives an indication of the effect of induction and its contribution to flow.)*
- *Nature of enquiries/requests for help from inducted versus non-inducted students.*

2 Cognitive outcomes (achieve). One important direct way for the library to affect student learning is through aspects of the student assignment – if library staff make a specific input to assignment preparation:

- *the inclusion and adequacy of any bibliography*
- *the number and range of sources cited*
- *how the sources are presented and used*
- *teacher views of the overall quality of the work compared with that of people who had not been prepared for their assignment by library staff (or possibly of non-library users)*
- *Library support/library resources feature in students' personal development portfolios or plans.*

3 Affective outcomes (desirable attitudes):

- *levels of student confidence in using the library*
- *levels of self-esteem*
- *positive student views of library staff*
- *positive student perceptions of the value and relevance of library services*
- *readiness of students to use a range of resources.*

4 Skills:

- *students demonstrate information literacy skills (sometimes called information literacy scaffolds)*
- *students use information literacy strategies effectively and efficiently*
- *students show independence when doing research.*

5 Quality of life:

- *students form positive relationships with library staff*

- *students show motivation*
- *students engage in the learning process*
- *students' learning is enriched (especially minority groups in terms of ability, culture, language, etc.)*

6 Long-term outcomes (progression):

- *former students use libraries/information services over time*
- *former students recognize continued benefits from their information literacy training when they were students.*

6.11.3 Global Libraries Impact Planning and Assessment Framework

This framework covers the whole impact evaluation process and the main stages are described in Chapter 11. However, the section on impact indicators identifies the main areas where public access computing can have an impact on people's lives (education, health, culture and leisure, economic development, communication and e-government) and gives examples of service outcomes for libraries, short-term impacts (i.e. during the life of the project) and longer-term impacts for each area. These examples are designed to stimulate discussion about what can be achieved through public access ICT in a particular country. Local impact objectives and indicators are formulated in the key areas to reflect local priorities. For example, under **Culture and Leisure**, 'Service outcomes' (equivalent to our 'success criteria') for libraries are identified as:

- Library becomes a social hub for the community
- Library is an attractive place for children, marginalized groups . . .
- Library offers equal access and respect for all
- Developed local content about cultural heritage of local communities.

Short-term impacts on community/users identified are:

- Groups use ICT in the library to plan and promote local activities and advertise local attractions
- Children use and gather in the library in their leisure time
- Marginalized groups use ICT in the library
- Marginalized groups take more part in community activities
- People develop new interests through finding a wide range of online information
- Access and add to information about cultural heritage.

Longer-term impacts on community/society are:

- Community re-vitalization
- Increased socialization of children into the community
- Marginalized groups have more self-sufficiency and self-esteem
- Marginalized groups are more integrated into society
- People feel they have more choices and improved quality of life
- Cultural heritage kept alive.

Another important and useful element of this framework is the pyramid showing levels of potential impact, which is reproduced as Figure 11.2 of Chapter 11.

6.11.4 Looking at the audience

You may find it useful to think about the different target audiences you want to affect. For example:

- for public library services these might include different sorts of individuals (e.g. children, teenagers, parents and children together, single parents and their children, old people, unemployed people), local groups and associations, local ethnic communities, the local authority and local businesses
- for health library services these could include health managers, clinicians, students, patients, staff in allied professions and hospital workers following courses.

Step 6   Test the indicators

Revisit the impact indicators that you have written for two of your service objectives. Show them to two colleagues and ask:

- Are they clear?
- Will they tell me if I am achieving my objectives?
- Are they reasonable things for me to achieve? (Am I reaching too far?)

6.12   Some indicators

Finally, here are some real examples of impact indicators, tied into service objectives. These were all generated by library service managers and may help you now and in the future when you write impact indicators. You may find useful indicators among those produced by people working in other library sectors, which can be readily adapted. For example, you could replace 'clinicians' with solicitors, managers or researchers; and 'socially excluded groups' with any minority group of users.

Example 6.4   Impact indicators for health libraries

Objective 1: More empowered and effective users

1 Users locate relevant material and apply it in practice and when learning.
2 Users ask more sophisticated questions.
3 Users are more confident when seeking, evaluating and using information.

Objective 2: A literature search service that positively contributes to patient care

1 Proportion of clinicians reporting that the search contributes to patient care.
2 Proportion of clinicians reporting that previously unknown evidence has been identified.
3 Proportion of clinicians reporting that the service is useful.

Objective 3: Provision of an effective current literature search process

1 Proportion of clinicians who follow up the search and ask for articles.
2 Proportion of searches focused in the wrong area.
3 Proportion of clinicians reporting that the process of following up on literature cited is straightforward.

Objective 4: To support health care staff in finding the evidence to develop local care pathways

1 Awareness of the evidence base; 'what is out there' and 'where to find it'.
2 Trainees' confidence in identifying the evidence to underpin the construction of a local care pathway.
3 Trainees' effectiveness in identifying the evidence to underpin the construction of a local care pathway.

Objective 5: Targeted staff making more effective use of evidence-based information in clinical practice

1 Staff offer better-expressed clinical questions.
2 Staff offer more challenging clinical questions.
3 Staff are more competent in appraising evidence.
4 The evidence base is being used by targeted staff.

[Would it be better to express 1 to 3 in neutral impact terms?]

Example 6.5   Impact indicators for public libraries

Objective 1: To use public access information for local economic development

1 Use internet to get information about new agricultural techniques and products.
2 Use online information to develop business (find new markets, financial resources, new products, etc.)
3 Reduce business costs (online ordering, new suppliers, etc.)
4 Get jobs or better jobs by searching online.

Objective 2: To ensure access to ICT for people with sensory and mobility impairments

1 Proportion of people with sensory and mobility impairments using libraries.
2 Levels of competence and confidence in using ICT.
3 Levels of interest in e-learning opportunities.

Objective 3: To ensure staff awareness and competence in relation to aspects of social inclusion

1 Staff knowledge about engaging with people who are socially excluded.
2 Staff taking a more proactive approach to meeting customer needs.
3 Staff confidence in engaging with people who are socially excluded.
4 Do people who are socially excluded perceive that they are treated equally and have equal access to resources?

Objective 4: Identified needs of targeted communities are better met by library services

1 Are people from ethnic communities aware of free access to libraries and their entitlement to services?
2 Are people from ethnic communities able to utilize the available services?
3 Do ethnic communities show more confidence in contributing their views to service development within cultural constraints?

Example 6.6   Impact indicators for schools library services (regional services supporting school libraries and librarians)

Objective 1: Enhance teachers' use of resources in the classroom

1 Range of resources used by teachers during literacy/numeracy lessons.
2 Level of teacher awareness of curriculum-related resources.
3 Level of teacher awareness of strategies for using non-fiction resources in the classroom.

Objective 2: Enable wider reading by pupils

1   Reduced dependence on reading schemes or on a limited range of authors.
2   Ability of schools to provide appropriate reading material to pupils with special educational needs or ethnic minority pupils.
3   Ability of pupils to find books in school that meet their interests and needs.

Example 6.7   Impact indicators for school libraries

Objective 1: To develop information literate students

1   More positive attitudes to learning.
2   Capacity to manage difficult learning tasks.
3   Enhanced self-esteem and confidence as learner.
4   Greater motivation.
5   Greater collaboration among peers.

7

Making things happen: activities and process indicators

Here we look at translating objectives into action. It is the most straightforward and least demanding stage of the process for most libraries. We know from our workshops that once people have a clear idea of what they are trying to achieve it is usually fairly easy to think of a variety of ways to get there. Then, when you have decided on what to do, finding ways of telling whether you have done them (process indicators) is not usually very challenging.

7.1 Why activities? Why now?

We have taken up a lot of space in the last few chapters warning you of the dangers of getting sidetracked when you are trying to evaluate your impact by looking at what you do (activities and processes), rather than concentrating on what difference you make. Why are we moving the goalposts now? Activities do matter: you need to think about them and keep them under review. That is why we have written this chapter. However, if you want this stage in the process to support the evaluation of your impact, you need to get the timing and the focus right.

7.1.1 Timing

You should leave any consideration of activities and processes until after you have completed your initial work on objectives and impact indicators. We have seen what happens to impact evaluation when library managers get caught up with questions about service delivery, allocation of resources, allocating staff time and prioritizing among a wide range of activities. Attention slips away from impact with the result that planning once again focuses around provision. For example, the UK public library annual library plans are still replete with specific processes and actions aimed at keeping the services going, enhancing the library infrastructure and activity building. These processes very much reflect the hands-on, operationally focused approach of many library managers. We are not saying that such concerns are not important, just that they need to wait until now, after you clarify what you want to achieve and how you will know you are being successful.

7.1.2   Focus

The danger when considering activities and processes is that you might record everything that you are doing in the general area covered by your objectives. We recommend that you tie activities into the objectives, specifically linking a set of actions to each impact objective. It is not helpful to generate a raft of activities that outline the totality of what you do to achieve your goals. Focus is vital if you want to use any evidence gathered about your impact as the basis for service development. If you want to sustain or increase your effectiveness in a particular area of work or with a particular group of users, you need to know what you did to make a difference in the first place. You are then in a position to decide whether you can do different things, alter the balance between activities or take an entirely different route to your goal. You therefore need to review regularly the activities related to each impact objective in the light of the data you collect about how successfully you are meeting that objective.

7.2   Identify activities

Librarians are good at identifying activities – it is a fairly automatic part of library planning.

If you are working through this evaluation process, you have already formulated and checked your service objectives. It should not take you long to decide on the main activities you need to meet them. Some library services differentiate between various types of processes and activities. For example, they separate out internal business processes, continuous improvement actions and financial actions. If you adopt this approach it may be easier to check that you have included all the main elements of what you need to do to make a difference.

When you identify the activities needed to meet a particular objective, try to strip your thinking of any preconceptions. Try not to assume that any of your services or interventions should continue automatically. Examine them all critically. Look at each objective carefully and ask what you really need to do to achieve it. Do you need to put any additional services in place? Do you need to change your whole approach? You may want to 'brainstorm' other ways of meeting your objectives (or 'get out of the box' in the current management jargon). If you try this, make sure that you get away from the constraining presence of your normal workplace and remember that, in the words of a Swedish group facilitator, 'When you are brainstorming, 50% of your ideas should be silly ideas' or, rather, ideas that may not look realistic at the outset.

Step 7   Turn objectives into actions

Choose two of your objectives and identify the key activities required to meet them successfully.

Example 7.1   Activities that contribute to realizing impact objectives

Specialist information services

Objective: To enhance the quality of policy decision making by education officers in local government.

Activities:

1 Encourage education officers to contribute their policy and management documents to the information exchange, concentrating on new initiatives and 'good practice'.
2 Circulate sets of abstracts of these documents to all the education officers.
3 Provide copies of the full documents to the education officers on request.
4 Encourage recipients to contact the original donors to find out more about the decision-making context.

School libraries

Objective: To enhance the quality of pupils' reading.

Activities:

1 Actively promote reading for enjoyment (author events; reading games; newsletters; themed displays outside the library).
2 Organize continuing professional development for teaching staff (training workshops).
3 Organize a book club that provides positive feedback to pupils on their reading.
4 Collaborate with the school's literacy co-ordinator to plan and deliver lessons.
5 Set up special projects to encourage 13-year-old boys to read.
6 Involve pupils in library stock selection.

7.3   Review the activities

When you have identified the activities that relate to each of your objectives, you should review them as a whole. You will probably find that a number of activities appear more than once, linked to different objectives. At this stage it is useful to note the duplication but to leave it in place. When you reach the action planning stage (see Chapter 10) you can make sure that you are not doing the same thing three times.

7.4   Process indicators

Once you have decided what steps or actions to take you should find it relatively easy to choose the process indicators that will tell you whether you are doing them. Process indicators (sometimes referred to as activity indicators, or, rather confusingly as 'performance indicators') are readily identifiable as the sorts of indicator that can be 'ticked off the list when you've done them'. You use process indicators to monitor your activities, to check whether you are on course or whether you have been sidetracked or slowed down. Not surprisingly, as well as being full of intended activities, library plans are replete with rafts of process indicators that tell you if you are doing them; these are the two 'strong areas' of library service planning.

Process indicators are fairly easy to generate and to collect evidence about. Unfortunately, they do not necessarily tell you if you are meeting the impact objectives that led you to carry out the activity in the first place. For example, if you decide that a round of executive briefings is necessary to ensure that managers make more effective use of the service, your process indicator might be 'the number of briefing sessions that are held'. But this won't tell you whether the messages are getting home and whether they are leading to changes in the behaviour of the managers. (That is why we wrote this book.)

Since each objective is delivered through its own set of activities, every objective will trail a set of process indicators in its wake as well as the impact indicators you have already generated.

Example 7.2   Process indicators

Schools library services

Objective: Broadening the scope of reading material used by pupils.

Process indicators:

- a range of fiction and non-fiction books provided to all member primary schools

- the number of workshops run for secondary school teachers on integrating books into the curriculum
- teachers given advice about choosing and buying books (e.g. what motivates teenage boys)
- the proportion of primary schools in which reading promotion events have been organized
- the proportion of secondary schools provided with multimedia resources to motivate pupils
- the number of contributions made to workshops for teachers run by local government inspectors
- reading lists to support the National Literacy Strategy sent to all schools.

Specialist information services
Objective: To enhance the quality of policy decision making by education officers in local government
Process indicators:

- range of policy and management documents contributed
- number of sets of abstracts of documents sent to education officers
- number of copies of documents requested
- number of copies of documents supplied
- number of enquiries referred to original donors.

When you are thinking about activities and how to tell whether you are doing them (performance), there are usually two areas to focus on: what you are doing (processes) and what level of activity this generates (outputs). (We have already said that outputs provide a measure of efficiency and are traditionally measured quantitatively, e.g. number of services provided and number of people provided for, or numbers of books issued.) These translate into process indicators and output indicators. You may also like to focus on the resources that you are putting into the activities (input indicators), but these usually come into play only when they are combined with other measures as output indicators, as we show below. Don't worry too much about these distinctions. These are all indicators about performance.

7.5   Output indicators

Output (sometimes called service) indicators focus on the amount of business or traffic produced by your chosen activity. In general, in telling you what you need to know about whether things are happening and whether they make a difference, these indicators are likely to be less useful than either impact or process indicators – but they do have a place. Output indicators are usually created by bringing together two or more measures to say something about the level of delivery of the particular service you are looking at. For example, you can combine an input measure (such as number of books purchased) and an output measure (such as number of loans) to produce an indicator of intensity of new stock use. Equally, you can combine process indicators and output measures. For example, you can link the number of book promotion events held at a library (process) to prior and subsequent loans by that library (output). This gives an output indicator of sorts relating to the effects of the events on library loans, but it is a weak one. There are several other factors that may have affected loans. A stronger output indicator is possible if you can link prior and subsequent loans to the actual people who participated in the promotional events. (Even then, of course, you don't know whether people read the books they borrow, let alone whether reading them has any effect on them.)

The distinction between process indicators and output indicators is not always clear cut, so don't spend too much time on discriminating between them. Try to avoid the perennial library management trap of collecting too many output indicators instead of looking at impact.

Example 7.3   Output indicators

Public library services
- net expenditure on the service per head of population
- net expenditure per library visit or telephone enquiry
- number of library visits per square metre of accommodation
- numbers attending training events organized by public libraries
- numbers of PCs accessible per 100,000 of population
- proportion of stock on loan from each service point.

Schools library services
- proportion of stock on loan to each secondary school
- numbers of teachers or librarians attending in-service training events delivered by SLS staff
- number of 'hits' on various parts of the SLS website
- number of schools that have availed themselves of the SLS advisory service.

7.6   Process and output indicators: things to watch

In section 6.4 we gave you a list of the characteristics of good indicators as well as what to avoid when writing them. You might want to revisit our advice at this point, since it applies just as much to process and output indicators as to impact indicators. However, because process and output indicators are easier to write, you will usually encounter fewer problems. It is still worth taking time to ensure that your indicators are:

- informative (giving reassurance that processes are working or warning signs if they are not)
- able to be changed (provisional; since not all performance indicators will turn out to be useful)
- reliable (telling you something useful each time that they are checked)
- accessible and understandable to all those likely to be affected by using them (staff, managers and people to whom the service is accountable)
- acceptable (seen to be fair; checkable)
- cost-effective (the additional costs of collecting data should not outweigh the benefits of using them. Can you use existing systems or data routinely collected by someone else?)

Of course, they should also be as few in number as possible.

7.7   The 'reach' of the service

We suggested in section 7.5 that output indicators are, in general, less informative than process or impact indicators. We also pointed out earlier that the classic 'input – process – output – outcomes' model for performance measurement tends to break down when we aggregate outputs to arrive at the outcomes (unlike the engineering process field where doing this usually works).

There is one significant exception to this rule – if you are looking broadly enough at a library service, or if you are looking at a number of library services, you can aggregate some outputs to provide useful information in relation to the 'reach' of the service. The 'reach' of the service is calculated by looking at your potential clientele and relating this to the actual number of service users. You can also refine this process to look at particular types of potential and actual users, compare the 'reach' of particular parts of your service, or look at the 'reach' in different geographical locations.

National targets for library services tend to be expressed in terms of service 'reach'. For example, in the halcyon days when the UK government professed to be interested in public libraries, the relevant government department offered public library targets that included:

- proportion of households living within specified distance of a static library
- aggregated scheduled opening hours per 1000 population for all libraries

- number of library visits per 1000 population
- annual items added through purchase per 1000 population.

We leave you to judge how useful such targets are.

8

Thinking about evidence

If you are working systematically through this section of the book, you have already done much of the main thinking that you need for evidence gathering. Assuming that you have thought clearly about what you are trying to achieve, how you can tell that changes are happening and what will tell you that the changes have happened, you are more than halfway to cracking the problem of gathering evidence. You now need to decide how much evidence to gather.

8.1   Deciding your approach to gathering evidence

When people are faced with the prospect of gathering evidence the first reaction is often to panic. How can busy practitioners do the work of professional researchers as well? The answer is that you don't have to. Effective impact evaluation involves careful focus on what is important and then gathering the minimum amount of evidence needed to tell you what you need to know. It should be reassuring to recognize that evidence is not a separate category of information; it is information chosen by someone and gathered for a particular purpose.

8.2   The organizational context

The same evidence-collection activities may work in one place and fail somewhere else. When choosing how to gather your evidence, you need to take account of the culture of your organization, current work pressures and how ready your staff are to get involved in this work. Some of the factors to consider are:

1 Other current or imminent evidence gathering elsewhere in the
   organization that may compete or conflict with your efforts. (For example,
   when a university library decides to conduct a survey of part-time and off-
   campus students it knows that services to these users are a big issue for the

university. It suddenly becomes a bigger issue. The governors call for a survey and the central audit team jump straight in with a hurried and poorly designed effort. This produces little of worth, but the library team has to wait for several months for the dust to settle before doing its own survey.)

2 Timing: what are the best and worst times of day, week, month or year to engage with your target respondents?

3 Whether your target respondents favour or dislike particular evidence-gathering methods. Have they been over-exposed to any particular methods (e.g. are they 'allergic' to questionnaires)?

4 Whether the larger organization of which your service is part is averse to any method (e.g. is it disillusioned with focus groups)? This could affect the reception to any report you produce on your work.

5 What methods are easiest for you and your staff to handle (including analysis of the information collected)?

8.3   Finding strong surrogates for impact evidence

When we talk about impact we are usually thinking about the impacts of services on people (service users; providers; others). As we said earlier (in Chapter 6), this entails looking for surrogates for impact because the actual impacts cannot normally be captured directly. We can classify these surrogates for impact by how strongly they convey or reflect the real impact. If we interview someone soon after they have read an online article which leads them to change their diet this will provide a strong surrogate for impact. Sending the same person a questionnaire some time later about the influence of digital resources and asking the right question may result in that experience being recalled and described, but is unlikely to have the same immediacy.

The information collected may provide a good surrogate for impact if it is detailed, specific and accurate. On the other hand, the best evidence you are able to gather may be rather generalized and approximate, that is, a weak surrogate for impact. What do you do if some of your evidence is weak? The answer is to combine it with other stronger evidence so that, overall, you are getting a good impact picture.

8.4   Ethical evidence-gathering

One consequence of working in various countries on international projects that have the potential to change people's lives is that we are now very interested in ethical evaluation. (We have been particularly guided in our approach to ethical issues by Bruce Macfarlane's (2009) challenging book on ethical research.) Most of the ethical issues come to a head at the evidence-gathering stage of the evaluation process or at the next stage of interpreting the findings, so we address these questions here.

International development and education evaluators have been exercised by research ethics, and particularly evidence-gathering ethics, for some years. Ernie House offers various principles of ethical evaluation, starting with mutual respect, non-coercion and non-manipulation, and he argues that evaluators should support democratic values and institutions. He points out that:

> . . . evaluators exercise special powers over people that can injure self-esteem, damage reputations and stunt careers . . .
>
> Evaluators are engaged in contractual situations in which they themselves are vulnerable to people awarding future work. Some people whom evaluators deal with are powerful within the evaluators' career realm. Also, evaluators come from the same social classes and educational backgrounds as those who sponsor evaluations and whose programs are evaluated . . . All these factors increase ethical dangers.
>
> House (1993, 164)

Working in an educational evaluation context, Simons observes that:

> Evaluation has to operate in this multilayered context of different interests, providing information to inform decisions while remaining independent of the policies and programmes themselves. In such a context it is not surprising that ethical dilemmas arise as to which is the best course of action to take.
>
> Simons (2006, 243)

Most of the authorities we have consulted on the ethics of evaluation address these issues from the perspective of evaluating major programmes, usually in the international development or education arenas and from academic bases in higher education institutions. There has been little attention to the political issues raised in micro-evaluation and the choice of ethical responses at local level, whether by academic researchers, consultants or 'embedded' evaluators working in library evaluation settings.

However, some overlap in the roles of service provider, evaluator and advocate is common in library settings. Service managers may advise on policy through their professional associations or direct to government; may manage the evaluators; and are likely to assume advocacy roles. Evaluators may be academic researchers hired for the purpose or employed by the library service or national association; will have to engage with the library profession in their country to gain access to service performance data and help in conducting evaluations; and may have their career prospects affected by positive or negative judgements by library service managers (especially in countries with relatively few academic researchers focused on libraries). Since there are only likely to be a few library evaluators in most countries the relationship between evaluators and managers is likely to be close. Advocates may be library service managers or may be evaluators. The evaluation literature does not for the most part address these circumstances, apart from House (1993), who notes that 'Internal evaluation entails new ethical problems that evaluators have not been able to solve so far and that deserve serious study.' Such close associations between evaluation and practice have implications for library evaluation at all organizational levels and at every stage in the evaluation process.

The ethical library evaluator has a relatively clear-cut, if difficult, role in being resolute in insisting upon careful and rigorous collection of impact evidence. At this stage in the process though, an additional 'political' role is often called for which is to teach the managers involved and the people to whom they report about the nature and importance of qualitative evidence and, in doing so, help overcome political resistance to the qualitative end of impact evidence collection and use. This might be characterized as being resolute in working to overcome barriers to acceptance of the approach. Resolve is also required to ensure that a sufficiently wide range of respondents is drawn upon in collecting impact evidence. Impact evidence gathering should not be just a process of collecting 'success stories': narratives should be representative and fully contextualized. It may not always be clear at what point gathering evidence of success and failure metamorphoses into collecting propaganda for advocacy purposes, but the ethical evaluator should stay alert to this danger.

Writing from a 'deliberative democratic' perspective, House points to another dimension of ethical evaluation which applies when

> . . . the evaluator collects the opinions and values of various participants in the program, such as decision-makers, legislators and participants, and puts these opinions and values together in some unspecified way. How these values and opinions are adjudicated is not clear. This is probably the most common position in evaluation, but one also burdened with ethical problems. Often the result of such an approach is to give the powerful the priority voice in the evaluation, because it is mostly they whose opinions and criteria have been solicited and used. Evaluators must adopt a more democratic stand than this. They must solicit the opinions and criteria of those not powerful and make sure that these are included as well. There is an ethical obligation to include the interests of all.
>
> House (1993, 170)

How democratic is your evaluation?

8.5   Matching the evidence to your needs

Now you will need to think again about why you are gathering evidence and how much to gather.

8.5.1   Why are you gathering evidence?

The usual reasons for collecting evidence of impact are to assure yourself that your work is making a difference or to check on how you are doing compared with other similar services. You are probably doing this to help in your own managerial role, but you may also need to convince other people inside and outside the service that it is making a difference.

8.5.2   But how much evidence should you gather?

The pragmatic answer to this question is 'as little as you need to make good decisions'. Evaluating impact in libraries is about making sensible decisions. Since there is no finite limit to how much evidence it is possible to acquire, there is a real danger that you can spend so much time and energy on evaluating the impact of your service that the service itself will suffer. You have to strike a balance between what you need to know, how well your evidence is telling you this, and how much of your resources you can afford to commit to this work.

Since all library service managers are potentially 'over-tasked', with a long list of things that they must, should, could or would like to do, our own view is that impact evaluation work should concentrate on areas where you are trying to really make a difference. Traditional efficiency monitoring using process and output indicators will suffice for other areas of the service. We put this argument forward because most library service managers have to devote much of their time, energy and effort to maintaining the service infrastructure (e.g. ensuring that service points are open and running smoothly; obtaining and deploying resources efficiently). If this is your situation, any time squeezed out for development activity is precious (and relatively expensive). It follows that much of the impact focus should be on the development work – is it having the sorts of effect that you want? Will it work better if you do some things differently? Can you use this key time better in other areas?

Ideally, as development areas demonstrate their worth they will be absorbed into the infrastructure, and efficiency monitoring is all that will be needed. This leaves you scope to concentrate on the next development area – and its impact.

8.5.3 How much evidence: different purposes

How much evidence you need to gather also depends on why you are collecting it. Standards of evidence will vary for different purposes:

1 If you are gathering information mainly to inform your own management decision making and future planning, we recommend that you apply the resonance test. This involves gathering a sufficient range of evidence to assure yourself that you are on the right lines. More particularly, when you present this evidence to your colleagues they agree that it sounds OK – it resonates with them. (If not, you need more evidence.) We apply this test when doing national research in library settings, by inviting service managers to look at what we are finding and seeing whether the picture that emerges feels right to them – if not, we gather more information in areas of doubt to the level that we feel should convince a reasonable reviewer.

2 If your prime aim is to account to the people who have an overview of your service (e.g. senior organizational managers or local government representatives), stronger evidence will be needed, at the 'enough to convince a reasonable reviewer' level. We have already suggested that you may also need to offer more familiar evidence of efficiency as well.

3 If you are trying to convince other people beyond the library about the effectiveness of your services, you will have to take account of what they regard as convincing evidence even if your own views are different. We believe that qualitative information is likely to be very useful to you in gauging impact but you may have to supplement this evidence with quantitative data if this is what people expect to get. Unfortunately much of the quantitative evidence collected in libraries is about activities and processes (what the library provides and who uses it) rather than about impact. If this is the case, you then have two jobs to do: an education job – to persuade people why your qualitative evidence is more useful; and a development job – to consider whether you want to collect quantitative evidence of impact and how you might do this. (It is usually collected via carefully validated large-scale user-perception questionnaires that are expensive and time-consuming to construct, administer and analyse. This type of evidence is often collected at country level.) We are not saying that qualitative information is always better than quantitative information – only that it sometimes serves different purposes. Sophisticated quantitative performance data and good-quality impact information should complement each other strongly.

4 If you are making a case for securing funds, stronger evidence may again be needed, if you are competing with other agencies or services. Your evidence

gathering will have to be at least as convincing as theirs, even before you report on the effectiveness of your service as shown through that process. Use a combination of qualitative evidence, especially stories of service impact on people, and carefully chosen data from your performance measurement activity to give a fuller picture if you are reporting to a funder or making the case for library support.

5 If you receive external funding for a project, you will have to meet the accountability requirements of the funding organization. In our experience, these requirements can vary hugely, so it is sensible to check carefully to see what is actually required by way of evidence.

6 Finally, if the concern is to convince government, you are likely to have to conform to arbitrarily prescribed targets and data collection methods which may have only tangential connection to service impact. Use the saturation test if you are building a more comprehensive picture – here you collect qualitative evidence until this is only confirming what you have learnt from the earlier evidence. This is much more of a challenge and is only worth trying if there is a realistic prospect of additional resources or support from presenting this evidence. If this is the case you may also want to consider a large-scale questionnaire with carefully constructed impact questions to provide quantitative impact data.

Example 8.1   Types of evidence

A helpful touchstone may be to envisage situations in which you need to convince others:

- The chief executive of your company questions whether you are providing useful information to support senior managers in their work. What evidence can you offer?
- You are talking to a senior education official about the public library role in supporting literacy or promoting reading. Will the sorts of information you assemble convince someone in that position about the difference you are making?
- The University Teaching and Learning Committee wants to strengthen the learning support provided to students. Can you make a convincing case for doing more through the library?

In each case you need to ask what such people usually rely on as evidence.

8.5.4   How reliable is your evidence?

The quantity and types of evidence are not the only issues. You also need to think about the reliability of the evidence that you are collecting. Three criteria for judging evidence (based on Thomas, 2004) are:

1 **Relevance**. Does the evidence constitute information for (or against) a proposition? In impact evaluation terms, does it tell you whether or not the chosen success criteria are being met, or is it actually evidence of something else?
2 **Sufficiency**. Is there corroboration with other instances of the same kind of evidence, or other kinds of evidence? In other words, is the picture consistent or are you making too much of one-off instances?
3 **Veracity**. Is the process of gathering evidence free from distortion and as far as possible uncontaminated by vested interest?

We are not seeking to transform you into an academic researcher with a strong philosophical bias at this point! Instead, we suggest that you use these three criteria as a checklist when you have decided what evidence-gathering methods to use and again when you look over the evidence that you have gathered.

8.5.5   Use other people's evidence

Finally, it is worth remembering that you don't always have to generate your own evidence in order to argue a case or to take management decisions. We have reviewed the main research evidence of the established impact of different types of libraries in Chapter 3. Think about how to use this evidence to support your development work or to argue a funding case.

LAWS OF IMPACT EVALUATION 6
Be political if you are gathering information to convince other people. Give them what they want – until you have persuaded them that your evidence is more useful than what they are used to.

LAWS OF IMPACT EVALUATION 7
The case for impact evaluation is strongest in areas of service development, where time and resources are limited but real change can be demonstrated.

8.6   What counts as impact evidence?

What does evidence of impact look like and how does it manifest itself? When you focus on the impact of services on people, you are looking for changes in their attitudes or behaviour that can be attributed to these services. This takes us directly into the world of social science research. For practical purposes, you will often be combining 'traditional' efficiency measurement data with impact evidence gathered using the social science repertoire.

Borrowing from the social scientists, most of the evidence you can gather is collected in one of four ways:

1 **Observe** – through structured observation, informal observation, self-recording or other means. You will need to observe over time to identify any changes in behaviour.
2 **Ask people questions** – through questionnaires, interviews, focus groups, etc.
3 **Infer** that relevant change is happening. Two commonly used methods are to:

   – *examine documents or other products created by your target groups to see if what your service is doing makes any difference. (The trick here is to look for changes that can be fairly directly linked to what your service offers. For example, if you offer students an introduction to systematic searching for information you could look for general changes in the quality of student assignments. However, more direct evidence of progress can be found by looking at the quality of bibliographies or seeing whether a wider range of sources is cited.)*
   – *monitor the activities of the target groups using output indicators (e.g. participation in events, levels of service use, examination results). The drawback with using this traditional method is that you may find it difficult to show that these changes are influenced by what the service is doing.*

4 **Engage in action research**. Use the above three methods of evidence collection but as part of a systematic cyclical process. This process involves gathering evidence of impact, then collective interpretation of this evidence, leading to service modification, then back round to evidence-gathering and so on, until no significant improvements are found.

8.7   Fitness for the purpose

Before we go into the variations on observation, asking questions and inferring change from the products of people's activities that form the core of the next chapter, it may be useful to think about the relationship between success criteria (and the impact indicators that explore them) and the different options for gathering evidence. It is not as simple as saying, 'If you want to find out about changes in people's attitudes – interview them', or 'Observation is the best way of noting changes in behaviour', but there is a relationship between what you are looking for and how to find it. We can take our four areas of change (affective, behavioural, knowledge-based and competence-based) as a starting point.

8.7.1   Affective changes (attitudes, perceptions, levels of confidence, satisfaction with the service)

You may be able to *observe* changes in people's attitudes, but getting evidence usually involves asking the people who may or may not have changed. In particular, *asking questions* through short and tightly focused questionnaires should work, because they are neutral, but at the same time you are showing interest by asking the questions. If you are looking for evidence about people's confidence (e.g. when using ICT), questionnaires administered before and after your service intervention give people the chance to register changes without any pejorative overtones.

This is the area in which there is most potential choice when focusing on impact because we know that libraries can contribute positively to the quality of life of users in a variety of ways. (See Chapter 3.)

Example 8.2   The education library role in 'life-enhancement'

Objectives: To encourage positive student relationships with library staff and to provide a positive learning environment

Method: A well focused user questionnaire to gather information on:
- the quality of student communication with library staff (e.g. freedom to ask questions; get support in seeking information)
- the quality of ongoing student relationships with specific library staff
- the extent to which the library provides a positive study environment (e.g. appearance and comfort, noise level, etc.)
- the extent to which the library provides more direct support for study/homework (e.g. whether material can be obtained when needed, whether there are adequate photocopy facilities, etc.)

8.7.2   Behavioural changes (people do things differently)

Here, *observation* comes into its own, but you can also *infer changes* by looking at people's work. For example, to see change after an information-seeking input to an education assignment, you can look at completed assignments to see the number and range of sources cited, how the sources are presented and used and how the work compares with previous assignments. If a business library seeks to increase active use by middle managers, any change in physical use can be observed, but it should also be possible to track changes by analysing enquiries and requests for documents.

8.7.3   Knowledge-based changes

To find out if people have learnt anything, you have to *ask them questions*. This questioning can take many forms, including tests, questionnaires and focus groups. Other options are suggested in the next section. Take care not to become over-reliant on post-event questionnaires by participants. These are sometimes called 'reactionnaires', because they only really gauge whether people are positive about the experience. As Burrows and Berardinelli (2003) note:

> While learner interest and motivation are certainly factors in the outcomes of training, there is not a direct relationship between the learner's perception of training and actual learning, especially at the time when the learner has just completed the training experience.

If you really want to find out whether your training interventions have made a difference it is probably best to contact some of the participants a few months later and ask.

8.7.4   Competence-based changes (people do things more effectively)

How can you tell whether people are more competent? You can *ask them questions*, but also ask other people who *observe* them doing things. When asking people to assess their own change you can use the same range of methods as for knowledge-based questioning (including the additional options listed below). To pick up on what other people see, it depends who the people are and whether they are willing to give you feedback. Potential respondents may be work colleagues of the people you are interested in, other students or teachers. Interviews are usually the most viable method for evidence-gathering of this sort, because informants may feel uncomfortable about making judgements on other people in writing.

An alternative way to throw light on the level and variety of user skills (or of skills weaknesses) is to analyse a sample of enquiries recorded by your service. Service records are typically used to review the demands on the service, but they can also be used to tell you about what your users are struggling with. An analysis schedule could be constructed for this purpose.

The comments made about training under the previous heading also apply to learning new skills.

8.8   Other methods of gathering impact evidence

In an impact-evaluation programme, ten teams of UK university library staff used the following methods to gather impact evidence in relation to e-information services and e-learning innovations (Markless and Streatfield, 2006):

1 Where the focus is on the impact of services on students:

- *tests (including online diagnostic tests)*
- *questionnaires and embedded questions*
- *focus groups*
- *interviews conducted while students were conducting searches*
- *student diaries*
- *progress files*
- *student bibliography analysis (adopted in five universities).*

2 Where the focus is on academic staff the choice of methods depends on the purpose:

- *to gather staff perceptions about service impact: structured face-to-face or telephone interview (four universities)*
- *for more specific baseline evidence: focus groups*
- *to evaluate co-operation or collaboration between academic and library staff: records of contacts between these groups*
- *for evidence of change in academic staff: analyse their lists of recommended reading and e-links for students.*

  (One team also undertook an information literacy teaching audit covering the whole university.)

3 Where *specific information literacy inputs* are made by library staff:

- *monitoring of information literacy outcomes or of assignments that require students to deploy a research strategy*
- *observation of student engagement by other library staff.*

A useful observation for busy library service managers was that interviews produce 'fairly instant results' – that is, the evidence can be used almost immediately to improve service delivery.

Finally, we want to re-emphasize how important it is to be clear about the nature of the changes you are trying to achieve (success criteria and impact indicators). This gives you powerful clues about how to collect your evidence.

9

Gathering and interpreting evidence

This chapter suggests which evidence-gathering methods will tell you what you need to know, how to gather that evidence, and what that evidence is telling you. We then offer a warning about confusing evidence with advocacy.

Since it is probably better to adapt a research tool (such as a questionnaire, checklist or observation schedule) for your own purposes rather than start from scratch, we have prepared or selected a range of research tools for use in different types of libraries. These tools can be found at www.facetpublishing. co.uk/evaluatingimpact.

Let us start with a precept: all evidence-gathering methods have inherent weaknesses, so it is important to employ a range of methods if you want to build up a good picture – this is known in the research jargon as triangulation. Even if you are adapting an existing research tool there are a number of things that you should bear in mind when using them to gather evidence. These are considered below.

9.1 Observation

At first sight, it is surprising that library and information research borrows heavily on two of the social science research approaches (asking questions and making inferences) but largely neglects systematic observation as a research method. It is easy to understand this under-use in large-scale research, since systematic observation is time-consuming and can generate huge amounts of data. However, even when people take on small-scale evaluation they usually gravitate towards the questionnaire and the focus group, almost regardless of whether these will provide the sorts of information required.

This is a pity, because in the immortal words of the American baseball player and coach Lawrence 'Yogi' Berra, 'You can observe a lot by watching.' We know from our own experience that observation is a great way to develop ideas about how people use information, how library systems and services can be improved or how people can improve their teaching, training or interaction with service users. It is also one of the best ways of finding out whether your services are really making an impact.

There are several types of observation that may prove useful in evaluating the impact of your services.

9.1.1   Small-scale systematic observation

If you are interested in specific aspects of service use, such as how users find things in your library, or what they actually use your computers or wireless links for, a time-series study may be the answer. This involves gathering small amounts of information at predetermined times, spread over different times of day, week, term or year (depending on how much variation you think is likely). The advantage of this approach is that it only involves a member of your staff remembering (and if necessary being prompted) to collect and record a small amount of information at any one time. This recording can be done by making notes of what is happening from any convenient viewing point, or doing a tour of the relevant part of the library to see, for example, what is showing on computer screens. These records will soon build up into a fairly detailed picture of use, which may differ interestingly from what you predict. There are of course ethical issues involved here, and your organization may have a code of ethics or a research ethics committee that will have to be taken into account. In any case, individuals should not be identified in your observation records without their permission.

A variation on this theme is to record interesting events as they happen. For example, if a particular group of potential users makes little use of your service, and becomes the target for service development, any instance of use by members of that group is relevant evidence.

Although large-scale observation will be too expensive to be feasible, focused and systematic observation of student activity in the library is certainly possible. You could consider watching students doing a library-based assignment; more general observation at prescribed intervals would be useful too. To get real evidence in this way you will need to use an observation schedule designed, for example, to assess the information skills of students. (See sections 9.10 and 9.11 for access to a range of tools to help.)

9.1.2 Informal observation

Front-line library staff and their managers spend a large part of their time in observing what is going on, but there is usually little incentive to note what is happening, even if there is time to do so. All this changes when you focus on particular areas of service impact. Suddenly all observations about that part of the service are 'grist to the mill'. All that is needed is to alert colleagues to the fact that these aspects of service are now being looked at and to invite them to record anything that they see that they feel may be of interest as evidence (ideally for an agreed and limited time period). For this to work, you need to share with them what you are interested in finding out more about and why, so that they are in the picture and can include you in the part of the picture that they see.

9.1.3 Accompanied visits

This activity is regularly used by museums education staff who want to find out how people are really responding to their exhibitions. If you conduct an exit interview and ask people whether they felt lost at all when going round the exhibition, nobody ever admits to it. But if you accompany people round an exhibition, observe what they do and ask a few discreet questions, you will find that most people are confused about where they are and where the exhibition is leading them most of the time! Transferred to a library context the accompanied visit can provide a valuable picture of the interaction between the user (especially the new user) and the institution. Accompanying new users of the service on their first visit may throw some light on the phenomenon identified by former UK Education Inspector Trevor Dickenson who described the library experience as 'intimidation by furniture'.

9.1.4 Taking pictures

Although this is not a separate category of observation, there may be times when taking still or moving pictures of an event or activity will add a lot to the evidence of the impact of what you are doing. Rules governing photography, especially of children, vary from country to country. In the United Kingdom, you now need the written permission from parents or guardians in advance if you want to photograph children in a library.

9.2   Asking questions

'Asking questions' encompasses the ubiquitous questionnaire survey, individual or group interviews, focus groups and such hybrid activities as getting interview respondents to look at a website and relay their thoughts and feelings to the interviewer via the telephone or face to face. With the advent of social media there is now scope to use such activities as blogging as a means of collecting impact evidence remotely.

9.2.1   Questionnaire surveys

We have put these first because this is the method that library service managers tend to go for if they start to think about impact – unfortunately!

Library services have traditionally relied heavily on service-performance (usually output) statistics, such as enrolments and loans, backed by the occasional questionnaire survey. We have viewed hundreds of library service questionnaires and this may be the time to offer some comments:

1 Many questions are too general and too bland to do more than show that libraries are well regarded by users.
2 Others overreach themselves by trying to gather complex information that is more appropriate for interviews.
3 Many are poorly designed – with embedded library jargon, sloppy wording and little variety of task.
4 Very few are adequately pilot-tested to iron out problems before they are used.
5 Most show evidence that they were produced in too much of a hurry. Constructing and testing a properly designed questionnaire from scratch takes at least one person-week.

Overall, too many questionnaires unwittingly project the designers' preconceptions out to potential respondents and have them reflected back by nice people who are trying to second-guess what the designers mean. Questionnaires are a good method of gathering small amounts of specific information through structured sequences of questions – when you already have an idea of what range of replies is likely and have a feel for the language which the people you are surveying use to discuss the concepts that interest you.

What about sample sizes and response rates?

There are no hard and fast rules about the proportion of your total target audience that you need to involve in your survey, although a higher proportion will make it less likely that you will pick up a totally unrepresentative group of respondents. If you want to get an informative response to questions about the impact of specific interventions or parts of the service, 10% of the target group should give you a good picture, if these are selected randomly. (You may want to 'stratify' your sample to ensure that you include particular groups within your target audience, for example, a business library may want to ensure that all the main levels of management are included.)

If you are thinking about bigger-scale surveys and you want to gather statistically significant data (e.g. if you are trying to predict likely future demand for services) you need to get professional advice from people who are expert in conducting surveys.

The most important thing to say about the response rate to a questionnaire survey is that if you get less than 50% of completed questionnaires returned you know nothing at all about the views of more than half of the people that you asked. Making decisions on the basis of a low response rate is another form of guesswork.

Electronic questionnaires

There has been a migration towards e-surveys in the past few years and a corresponding tendency to report the total number of responses instead of the response rate, since this is not known. Even if you send an e-mail containing an e-survey link to your chosen recipient you do not know if it has reached that person (e-mail addresses probably change more frequently than office or home addresses and incoming e-mail messages may be pooled) or who has replied (unless they identify themselves when they reply). Again, since closed questions are easier to handle using survey software than open questions this may encourage 'tick box' responses using radio buttons even when this is not appropriate. Finally, people may respond to e-questionnaires – if they are active internet users and if they have plenty of time to reply (this can be problematic if you are trying to get e-replies from people who are using public access ICT in short pre-booked sessions).

Turning to the good news about e-questionnaires, they are cheaper to administer than their paper-based equivalents and they largely cut out the need for transcription of responses (although you will still need to 'clean' the data by correcting spelling or omitting obvious response errors). It is also relatively easy to encourage respondents to provide more in-depth information.

When we recently surveyed secondary-level school libraries (Streatfield, Shaper and Rae-Scott, 2011) we set out to get basic information from as many schools as possible about the size and characteristics of the school library by sending an e-mail to targeted people. When they follow the link and reply to the basic questionnaire, we then ask the respondents if they are willing to tell us more about their roles and activities as school librarian. Of those asked, 68% click on the link, giving us 1044 extensive accounts of school librarianship today – not usable for generalizing about school librarians, since we don't know precisely how many school librarians were approached and invited to complete the survey, but a valuable pool of evidence about school library practice.

Recent attempts are being made to get over the problem of 'capturing' responses from public access ICT users by using a pop-up survey approach. The ideal is to link this pop-up to the point when the user logs off after completing a task or activity. This is a good point to ask whether they were looking for information and, if so, whether they found it. As in the previous example, it is also a good time to ask if they are prepared to answer a few more questions (which can be varied over time to build up a body of data). The Global Libraries team in Romania use pop-up surveys to help evaluate the impact of public-access computing. They have described what they do and how (Chiranov, 2011) and are now looking at the reliability of this approach, by examining patterns of use through triangulation with other evidence-collection approaches so that they can begin to see who is playing games with them or whether some users are replying over-frequently.

9.2.2   Towards better questionnaires
Below are some ground rules for designing effective questionnaires.

Give attention to the structure of the questionnaire
- Start with a straightforward question to get the recipient to begin replying.
- Try to ensure some variety in the types of question asked (see below).
- Draw skidpaths if there are alternative routes (of the type 'if 'Yes' go on to question x', with a line showing the route) to make sure that every eventuality is covered. Then choose whether to leave these lines in to help people move through the questionnaire.
- Group related topics into modules.
- Move from the general to the specific in each section (usually).
- Make the structure clear to the respondent by using headings.

Choose the question types to fit the purpose

The main options are:

1 **Closed questions**. These can be 'yes' and 'no' boxes or a wider range of
   categories that you offer people to choose from. Make sure that each
   category is distinct and that all eventualities are covered. If you are
   completing a questionnaire and find that your preferred response category
   is not provided, what does this say about the competence of the designers?
   A useful catch all category is 'Anything else? Please say what', but only if
   you leave enough space for people to add their own categories.

   • *Closed questions are becoming more common with the increased use of
     electronic questionnaires linked to analysis tools that can aggregate replies
     almost instantly. Unfortunately, the ease of access to such tools can lead to
     closed questions being set when open questions are more appropriate.*
   • *A common type of closed question involves time periods (e.g. at least
     weekly, at least monthly, less than once a month) or age ranges (e.g. 1–20,
     21–30 etc.) It may sound silly, but a common fault with this type of
     question is to offer overlapping categories (e.g. up to 20, 20 to 40).*

2 **Open questions**. At its simplest this may be a 'Why is this?' after a closed
   question. However you phrase the question, it must be unambiguous – your
   aim is for the respondents to understand it and to reply in their own words.

   • *Don't forget that you will have to analyse all the replies to open questions
     and that categorization of the replies and then synthesis take time.*
   • *There are several research data analysis tools available to help process
     qualitative information. Even so, there is no substitute for engaging with
     the 'raw' replies to ensure that you understand what the evidence is telling
     you.*

Example 9.1   The hazards in setting closed questions

This example is from an electronic student self-assessment tool:

Using search engines

If your search gives you too many hits do you:

☐ Look at the first few items?
☐ Narrow your search by adding additional search terms?
☐ Try a different search engine?

☐ Give up searching?

This question almost slipped through, although it did not include one of the best ways to proceed: review the search terms and modify them to increase precision.

Use checklists or response scales where appropriate

These are a form of closed question. Most common are:

- **Simple checklists**, for example:

  What was the **main thing** you were doing in the library today?

Working on a course project or assignment	☐
Reading related to my course	☐
Other reading	☐
Exam revision	☐
Looking for specific information in the library	☐
Using the internet for coursework	☐
Using the internet for personal interest	☐
Photocopying	☐
Just visiting	☐
Other: please say what!	☐

  Please tick one box only

- **Likert scales**: a set of choices to record strength of agreement/ disagreement, for example:

  By 2020 sophisticated subject-focused search engines will be the normal method of gaining access to internet resources.

Highly likely	☐	☐	☐	☐	☐	☐	**Highly unlikely**
Highly desirable	☐	☐	☐	☐	☐	☐	**Highly undesirable**

  Please tick one box only in each row

- **Thurlstone scales**: forced choice to agree/disagree, for example:

  Are you confident when using **health websites**?   ☐ Yes   ☐ No

- **Semantic differential**: seeking quantitative measures in areas that are usually addressed through qualitative means, by offering scales between extremes, for example:

The Company Information Service is:

Good	☐	☐	☐	☐	☐	☐	**Bad**
Unfriendly	☐	☐	☐	☐	☐	☐	**Friendly**
Active	☐	☐	☐	☐	☐	☐	**Passive**
Relevant	☐	☐	☐	☐	☐	☐	**Irrelevant**
Slow	☐	☐	☐	☐	☐	☐	**Rapid**
Reliable	☐	☐	☐	☐	☐	☐	**Unreliable**

Please tick one box only in each row

These scales have to be carefully constructed to be effective. It is probably better to use ready-made versions than to invent your own.

- **Guttman scales**: statements arranged in sequence to gauge the strength of the respondent's view, for example:

Within your subject discipline:

Electronic textbooks will completely replace paper-based textbooks within ten years	☐
Electronic textbooks will gradually replace paper-based textbooks	☐
There will continue to be a place for paper-based textbooks alongside e- textbooks	☐
Paper-based textbooks will be preferred to e-textbooks for the foreseeable future	☐
There will be a reaction against e-textbooks in favour of paper-based textbooks	☐

Please tick the box that most accurately reflects your own view.

Instructions and wording

It is important to heed the following advice:

- Offer clear and consistent instructions for completing the questionnaire (this is easily forgotten if questions are considered individually). For closed questions, do you want people to choose one box (e.g. the most important category for their work) or all relevant boxes?

- Pay attention to question wording (avoid ambiguities; negative statements in the question; jargon, except that of the respondents; and enmeshing two or more questions together).

To summarize, the overall aim of the evaluation questionnaire is to obtain relevant information efficiently. You need active co-operation from your target group when doing this. Anything that will help people to co-operate with you by carefully completing and returning your questionnaire should be actively encouraged. This takes time, planning and attention to detail – even before you reach the data-analysis stage.

> **LAWS OF IMPACT EVALUATION 8**
> Questionnaire surveys are ideal for projecting the compiler's preconceptions and prejudices and having them confirmed by an invisible audience. They are also quite useful for collecting small amounts of information from a sample of respondents or all respondents within a target group.

9.3   Interviewing

According to Michael Brenner (Brenner, Brown and Canter, 1985) 'the research interview is an artificial conversation designed to collect research-relevant data.' The element of artifice is provided by the fact that one person is answering all the questions and the other one is asking these questions and recording all the answers. As to data collection, it follows that anything (within reason) that helps to achieve this end is desirable and that all other behaviour is not. As we show below, respondents sometimes have to be taught their role as respondents, especially if they are inclined to be flippant or to wander from the question.

There are four main types of research interview:

1 In the **structured interview**, all questions are asked in a predetermined order from a prepared schedule and each time a question is asked this should be done in the same way and with the same emphasis. This type of interview is probably the norm in library service evaluation.
2 In the **exploratory interview**, the question areas are predetermined but the respondents are allowed some latitude to answer in their own way. The interviewer may probe for more information in promising areas. The exploratory interview is particularly valuable at the early stages of evidence-gathering to identify issues and find out what concepts and terminology various groups of people use. (For example, 'information literacy' is a good phrase to use with education librarians but not with lecturers – in the UK

they prefer 'study skills', 'library skills' or even 'problem-solving skills' – elsewhere you can find out the preferred terms by doing exploratory interviews.)

3 A **semi-structured interview** is a one-sided conversation in which the respondent is allowed free rein as long as the interviewer considers that what is being said is, or might be, relevant. This works well with experts, who usually have a strong theoretical basis to their thinking that will be explicated by letting them talk. The 'Catch 22' here is that although reliability is likely to be improved by increased structure, too much structure may inhibit responses or produce little of consequence.

4 **Passive interviewing** is important in library service evaluation but isn't usually recognized as interviewing at all. Most library staff who are involved with users, and many who aren't, receive lots of passing comments about aspects of the service. In some libraries, staff are encouraged to note down relevant comments and these may be fed into reports. For the most part, such comments are not recorded because there is no reason to do so. As we have suggested with informal observation above, all this changes when you focus on particular areas of service impact. Once there is a focus, all comments about that part of the service are potentially useful. You will need to alert colleagues to the fact that comments on this aspect of service are now relevant (again for an agreed and limited time period), introduce a mechanism for recording the comments (such as a set of forms at each service point) and, ideally, provide an incentive to your staff to keep these records!

9.3.1   Designing an interview schedule

If you are going to use structured or semi-structured interviews, first you will have to choose or design your interview schedule. Here are some of the ground rules for interview-schedule design. Most of them also apply to planning your question areas for semi-structured interviews:

1 Ease the respondent into the interview. For example, you can start with a question about their work responsibilities to get them talking comfortably, assuming that this information is relevant. Don't ask for personal information early in an interview.

2 Adopt a logical structure by grouping questions into sections and proceeding from the general to the specific.

3 Share this structure with the respondents so that they know where the conversation is going. Offer a brief introductory outline of the areas to be

covered; this can be reinforced as each new section is reached (e.g. 'Now I'm going to ask you some questions about how you use information at work').

4 Vary the bill of fare. You can combine closed questions (such as 'Do you ever go to the company information centre?') and open questions (e.g. 'What kinds of use do you make of that service?'). You can vary the respondents' task further by, for instance, asking them to select replies and tick boxes on response cards or to choose one of a set of descriptive vignettes that matches their own information-related behaviour; or again you may want to show people an information publication and ask them for comments.

5 Make sure that the questions are clear and in spoken English, rather than the more formal written version, which sounds stilted when it is read. (Which form is being used here?) Try to avoid using negatives in questions (they can be confusing); and choose any jargon deliberately to reflect respondents' usage. Library and information jargon should be avoided (asking lecturers about serials has been known to elicit strange responses!)

Test out the schedule in pilot interviews. Try to avoid:

- questions that are difficult to ask (too many questions in one, sentences that are too long, tongue-twisters)
- questions that are difficult to answer (e.g. that contain unfamiliar words or phrases, that ask for generalizations or abstractions, hypothetical questions; don't ask busy operational staff about how they divide up their time – they probably don't)
- questions that invite distortion (leading questions that carry assumptions that the people interviewed may not share; don't ask respondents about the opinions or behaviour of other people).

Most of the principles outlined here also apply to questionnaire design.

9.3.2 Setting up and administering the interview

Let us assume that your 'victim' has agreed to be interviewed. What next?

1 Choose a neutral venue if possible (a meeting room or spare office is ideal). If you have to use your respondent's office, avoid the 'client chair' on the other side of the desk: if necessary move it to one end of the desk so that you are not in the usual 'grilling position'.

2 Check that the interview is still convenient (this is especially important for telephone interviews – anything may be happening at the other end!) If there is a problem, reschedule the interview. You want a respondent who is concentrating on your interview.

3 Ask if any telephone calls can be diverted to save time (if you think this will work).

4 Make sure that the respondent knows who you are and what you are trying to find out in general terms (an introductory letter is usual but a reminder may still be needed).

5 Explain that the respondent can refuse to answer any question if they wish.

6 Explain whether the interview is confidential: a common phrase is 'We will not be reporting anything in a form that could lead to your replies being identifiable.' If a respondent later baulks at a question, it may be enough to remind them that the interview is confidential to get a reply.

7 If you wish to record (on tape or electronically), ask permission and say how you will use the recording. Position the recorder where your respondent can reach it and show them how to turn it off if they want to say anything off the record.

If you have organized and conducted the interview well, it is very rare for people to curtail the process. Only a few respondents will cavil at particular questions and only one or two interviews turn out to be useless.

9.3.3   Doing the interview

Once you have chosen the type of interview, you can do a lot to create good interview conditions, 'train' the respondents to perform their task and reduce incomprehension or resistance. In the end, though, to be a good interviewer you need be effective in the five main areas of research interviewing:

1 **Ask the question**. Read the question at 'slow normal' speed and in a neutral tone, but with emphasis on certain words to help the respondent understand the question.

2 **Listen to the reply**. This is usually the easy bit because the replies should be interesting if your questions are good. Don't get distracted if the respondent sounds boring: the most monotonous replies can turn out to be full and revealing.

The other three areas – non-directive probes and prompts, recording answers and feeding back complex replies – are covered in more detail below.

Non-directive probes and prompts

Ensure that the respondent *answers in full* by using non-directive probes or prompts. The aim here is to get answers to the question without influencing the answers accidentally by putting words into people's mouths or directing them towards one kind of answer.

Non-directive probes

If you want someone to answer a question in more depth, try a non-directive probe, such as:

1 **The silent probe**. You ask a question and get a superficial or cryptic answer. Wait, with pen poised. This is all that is usually needed to get the respondent to elaborate. Even a ten-second pause can feel like eternity if you are on the receiving end.
2 **The encouragement probe** (semi-verbal). You make a noise to show that you are listening and interested – such as 'ahah' or 'erhem' if you are working in the UK. Each country has its own variations on 'acceptable noises'. This is a concession to the one-sided nature of the conversation. It can be disconcerting if you are being interviewed and are talking away but getting no response at all. The sorts of grunts advocated here seem ludicrous when written down but work well in practice. As soon as you move away from non-verbal cues you are in danger of influencing people's answers. For example, if you say 'yes' from time to time, are you agreeing with the respondent?
3 **The elaboration probe**. You can ask a respondent to explain an answer, but take care not to offer your own interpretation in case they just take the easy way out and agree to your version. Often, all you have to do to get someone to be clearer is to repeat the part of the answer that puzzles you. If that doesn't work, add 'What did you mean by that please?'

Non-directive prompts

You ask a question and the respondent doesn't answer. Try one of the following non-directive prompts:

1 **Give time** for the person to answer. Strictly speaking, this is not a prompt, but remember that your respondents are hearing your question for the first time. They may need time to think; keep silent to encourage them to do so.

2 **Dealing with a challenge**. If the respondent asks whether your question means A or B you have a quick decision to make. Your main options are:

- *Repetition. If you think that the respondent hasn't fully grasped the question, you should repeat it.*
- *Interpretation. If the respondent asks which meaning is intended, try saying 'Whatever it means to you'. This usually works (but make a note of the problem – you may have to revise the question later).*
- *Neutral adjudication. If the respondent is still struggling, reword the question (and make a note of your exact words so that you can review the* question and answer afterwards, and if necessary discard both).

3 **Predetermined prompts**. Pilot the interview questions properly in advance to make sure you are aware of potential hazards. You are then in a position to prepare definitions or clarifications in advance and give them when asked.
4 **Challenge prompts**. People aren't always consistent in their replies during an interview. If you think that a reply is inconsistent with something said earlier, refer back to the previous answer and remind the respondent what he or she said. This is usually enough to get an explanation.

Record the answers

The huge beginner's mistake is to forget to do this (we have large amounts of videotape evidence to prove it!). You should take notes even if you are recording the interview as this will help you to make sense of the replies at the time and give you a quick route into the interview. Remember that it takes about five hours to transcribe fully one hour of a recording. If you are not recording by other means, try to capture as much as possible of what people say in their own words. This should be the hard job. If you are finding it easy you are probably not probing enough – so why bother interviewing?

Feed back complex replies

You should do this to make sure that you have understood them and to prompt further comment. This takes confidence but is well worth doing.

All of these areas can cause difficulties, but most people can get to perform better in each one through focused training and reflection on their own performance.

Points to watch while interviewing

1 **Body language**. You can convey alertness as well as interest in what is being said (or the opposite!) through your posture. More specifically, you can show that you are listening by establishing eye contact. To signal that you have 'switched off' (if someone is talking too much or wandering from the point) simultaneously look down and stop writing.
2 **Pace**. You can control your own speed of speech as well as the length of the pause after your respondent has finished a sentence before you ask the next question. Aim for a relaxed, deliberate and thoughtful tone to the encounter.
3 **Neutrality**. Do not show agreement, disagreement, approval or disapproval at anything the respondent says. Over-concern with establishing a friendly relationship can reduce an interview to a sociable chat.

9.3.4 The critical incident interview

This special form of structured interview is most useful to find out about interactions between library service users and the services used. It is used in libraries as a way to evaluate enquiry services or to focus on the reading behaviour of academic staff (Tenopir and Volentine, 2012). Some advantages of this method are that respondents find it easier to answer questions if they are talking about a particular incident and that it is easy to build up a picture of their behaviour in context (e.g. where else do they look for information apart from libraries and which do they rely on?)

The standard approach is to select 20–50 substantial enquiries (not requests for contact addresses, etc.) which form the critical incidents. Then:

1 Arrange telephone interviews with the enquirers.
2 At the beginning of the interview, remind the enquirer about the particular contact with your service (using the enquiry record completed at the time). Two difficulties here are:

- *The enquirer may only have hazy recall of the particular incident (options: proceed and hope that memory returns or negotiate discussion of a more recent and memorable enquiry).*
- *The enquirer may not think of the chosen enquiry as an enquiry at all! They may think that it was a conversational gambit or part of an information exchange with library staff (if this is the case, proceed but record the different interpretation of what was going on).*

3 Glean contextual information. Ask the enquirers why they were seeking that information at that time (what triggered them to make the contact, or what was happening in their organization or in their own life that brought this to the fore). Also ask what other information sources were tried and why.

4 Evaluation: what useful information, if any, did the enquirer get from any of the sources tried and why was it useful? (And if relevant, how did your response compare with other people's?)

5 Quality assurance: how well and how politely did your staff respond? (People do tend to remember outstandingly good treatment as well as the opposite.)

6 Impact: did the enquirer use the information provided by your service and, if so, did anything happen as a result?

7 General comments on the enquirer's experience of your services.

This way of looking at enquiries tends to give a better picture of how the service fits into the evolving world of a range of users, as well as of the main factors that lead people to make enquiries. The approach also provides a way for enquirers to make direct comparisons of services (including such elements as format and presentation). It can produce occasional but powerful information about the real impact of information on people's life and work, because it offers a very specific and direct focus for the user to make a judgement.

More strategically, you can readily translate sets of interviews into case studies as evidence. Perhaps most importantly, service managers report that they find this type of information useful in evaluating and then fine-tuning their services in ways that traditional evaluation approaches don't touch.

9.3.5   Conducting a semi-structured interview

All the tactics outlined in section 9.3.3 apply equally to semi-structured interviews. In addition, you can use **directional probes** to obtain **retrospective elaboration or clarification**. Refer back to earlier remarks made by the respondent but in neutral terms, such as: 'Earlier you said . . . could you tell me more about that?' (elaboration) or 'What did you do as a result?' (clarification).

This tactic should be used sparingly. Try to use the respondent's own words whenever you refer to something said earlier.

9.3.6   Telephone interviews

The individual face-to-face interview offers the most straightforward route to gathering relevant information. You can explore issues in depth and can note and analyse the fine points of people's responses. Unfortunately, the face-to-face interview is expensive of your time, especially if the likely respondents are geographically scattered.

Telephone interviews offer many, but not all, of the advantages of the face-to-face encounter and can be more efficient to organize and carry through. They can also be an effective means of garnering evidence, as long as the ground rules are observed. Most of the preparatory steps are the same as for the face-to-face interview. The following guidelines are important:

1 Explain to the potential respondent what you are trying to achieve and why, preferably in the initial contact letter (or e-mail).
2 Suggest how contact should be established. If you write to introduce yourself and your project, say that you will phone to find out whether the recipient is willing to be interviewed and when is a convenient time.
3 Always follow up by phone within the period that you specify. The aim at this point is to allay any concerns about being interviewed and to arrange a convenient interview time. Try to offer a realistic estimate of the amount of time required for the interview (based on your pilot tests of the interview). Be ready to do the interview on the spot if that is what the respondent strongly prefers.
4 When dealing with people at work, it will take two to three contact calls on average to catch up with your potential 'victim' if that person is at operational or middle-management level. In general, the more strategic the respondent, the higher the average number of contact calls required.
5 Always phone when you said you would phone, reintroduce yourself (you are only one of many voices at the other end of the line) and check to see that the timing is still convenient. If it isn't, reschedule the call.
6 The main irritant here is that the respondent may not be playing by the same rules! Relatively few people book telephone interviews into their diary in the same way as face-to-face interviews. They may have completely forgotten the appointment and be away from the office or even on vacation when you dutifully phone up. The good news is that if they do miss the appointment a plaintive message to say that you phoned as promised is usually enough to get better co-operation next time. Be ready for the conscience-stricken respondent who phones back as soon as they return to the office, all ready to talk.
7 Try to avoid interviewing people on their mobile phone. Apart from the obvious matter of cost, this kind of contact diminishes any influence that

you might have over the environment in which the respondent is trying to concentrate on (or even to hear) your questions.

8 Conversely, phoning someone at their office or home should ensure a reasonable environment for the conversation and is the best possible way of reducing the effects of the 'Great Interrupter' – the telephone! (Even so, the occasional respondent will interrupt the call to field another one.)

Conducting the interview again follows the lines of the face-to-face version but with several constraints. Naturally, unless you have the latest in cellular technology, you can't see your respondent. This means that you miss all of the small clues of body language and facial expression that add texture to the interview. Similarly, the respondent can't see you. Any pause at the other end of the telephone line feels much more lengthy than it actually is, so, if you are taking detailed notes (and if not, why are you bothering at all?), tell the respondent what you are doing.

Although respondents usually appear to concentrate quite carefully during telephone interviews, a lengthy interview will feel longer. The ideal length for a telephone interview is probably about 30 minutes, whereas a 45-minute version face-to-face would probably not feel long.

The other constraints are more psychological in character. Many people do not like speaking on the telephone (and this includes some library service managers); some seem to find it more difficult to develop a train of thought on the phone and a few have evolved such a staccato telephone manner that it may be hard to hear or interpret what is being said or to coax out much useful information.

With advances in information technologies, it is now practicable to conduct video interviews with anyone who uses appropriate technology (e.g. Skype) and to record the conversation electronically. There are also advantages when using a computer for 'ordinary' telephone interviews – principally cost, hands-free operation if you use a headset and interviewer mobility (any quiet space with wireless access will do). It is also possible to 'share' documents and files during interviews.

9.4   Getting impact information from people in groups

One way to get at impact is to bring together a group of users of the service to pool their thoughts on how your services affect them. Don't let this turn into a test of who has the loudest voice or most articulate opinions.

9.4.1   Brainstorming

Two ways to pick people's brains and still retain control over the process are individual and structured brainstorming.

Individual brainstorming

Group participants round a table and invite them to think about their answers to a carefully chosen question, such as 'What are the key improvements that need to be made to the library website to ensure that people take notice of it?' Ask them to write their individual replies on sticky notes, using one sheet for each idea, and to pool the results in the middle of the table. Then invite them to cluster the sheets in whatever way they think works (there will be overlaps; get participants to stick these together), sorting out what the statements mean as they go along and labelling each cluster themselves (this will tell you how they describe the concept.) You can then focus discussion on each of these clusters in turn, using open questions such as 'What are the issues or concerns here?'

General points to remember:

- Focus the discussion on the clusters and listen carefully to each person in turn.
- Ensure that someone is recording the discussion – you are too busy!

Just because people are assembled as a group doesn't mean that you have to work with them as a group, as the next example shows.

Structured brainstorming

To carry out structured brainstorming (such as the Nominal Group Technique outlined here), seat participants (ideally about 7–12 people) in a horseshoe formation around a table, with you and a flipchart standing at the open end. Ask them to record their responses to your evaluation question (as for individual brainstorming above). However, this time you ask them to record their answers in short phrases on their own note pads.

Don't give way to the temptation to rush this stage. Allow a good five minutes for them to come up with ideas. When people stop writing, ask each person in turn to offer one item to the pooled list. Write these in their words on the flipchart, numbering each one. Keep going round until people run out of ideas (usually 30–60 ideas). Be inclusive; if in doubt, write it up on the flipchart.

Display all the sheets as you go along. Put off any discussion of the ideas until the next stage.

Sooner or later someone will buck the rules and try to launch into a long explanation of their idea. Ask that person to summarize the idea in a short phrase and say you will collect it next time around, then move on to the next person. This is a good process control mechanism to ensure that the group stays nominal (a group in name only)!

When all the ideas are in, look at each flipchart sheet in turn and ask the group to see if they are sure what each phrase means (some ideas may be too cryptic). Stress that you don't want them to say if they agree or disagree with the propositions at this stage. Then the group may wish to link a few overlapping ideas. Next, invite people to choose the five most important items from the list (important for them individually, or for your service – you decide beforehand). When they have all chosen the appropriate numbers, either get them to tick their five choices on the displayed sheets, or you record their numbers in priority order (most important first – use a different coloured pen) by writing numbers 1–5 for each person on the displayed sheets. (You may then like to weight these scores from first choice = 5 points downwards, using another different colour, and add up the total points for each idea.) You are now ready to discuss participants' high priority items.

General points to remember:

- Actively discourage discussion until after the prioritization stage.
- Timings: individual recording of ideas 5–10 minutes (this will feel like 5 hours the first time around, but you must give people time to think); round-up of ideas c. 30 minutes; ranking 5 minutes; scoring (ticking, or you writing) 5 minutes; ranking (offer a break while you do this) 5 minutes; discussion c. 30 minutes.

Both the activities just described can work well as part of a focus group.

There are literally thousands of tried and tested group activities, including many that are specifically designed to collect and prioritize information. Consult a friendly trainer about what sorts of impact information you are trying to obtain. Most trainers have a good repertoire of group activities for particular purposes.

9.4.2   Card sort activities

Meanwhile, if you want to get people to try to prioritize and discuss propositions, various types of card-sort activity should give you focused information (and they are fun to do).

To stimulate discussion about general service impact or the effect of specific services on users, generate your own set of key propositions in relation to your theme; then type and stick each proposition on 5 in. x 3 in. cards or sticky notes (about 20–24 propositions are ideal; number them to help in de-briefing later). Divide people into small groups (not more than four people); then ask them to sort one set of the cards per group in response to your research question. Your question should be about the impact of the service on them as users. You can get them to do this in one of several ways, such as through a self-directed or more structured nine-diamond task:

Self-directed

Ask people to organize the cards into a meaningful pattern, shape or flowchart, adding their own ideas on blank sheets if they wish. Then de-brief each group in turn by asking them to explain what they have produced and why, picking up on points of similarity and difference between groups.

Nine-diamond task

Ask people to reject all but nine of the cards (they can substitute their own ideas on blank cards at this point) and arrange the chosen nine in diamond formation (the words below each represent one card) in descending order of importance or priority:

FIRST

SECOND TIER

THE THIRD TIER

FOURTH TIER

FIFTH

The idea of this nine-diamond activity is to encourage people to prioritize without wasting time over the 'in-between' rank order (for example, by trying to exactly rank the three items in the third tier). De-brief across the groups by asking what people placed first and why, what went into the second tier and why; what people threw out easily and why; and what they added in (if anything) and why.

When the process is complete, the diamonds can be 'translated' into weighted scores (and the totals for each item added to represent the overall priorities across the participants) as follows:

Items on Tier 1–5 points
Items on Tier 2–4 points

Items on Tier 3–3 points
Items on Tier 4–2 points
Items on Tier 5–1 point.

You can then compare the results of different groups doing the same exercise, and thus gather information about the impact of services. General points to remember:

- You will need one set of cards per group and a 'master' list for yourself.
- Allow ample time (25–30 minutes) for people to sort their cards (including small group discussion).
- If members of a group can't agree on priorities, ask them to remember and report back what they disagreed about at the de-briefing stage.
- If you are working with several groups, wait until the second one finishes, from there on invite the groups as they finish to look at each others' output – but keep them away from groups that are still working.
- When all the groups have finished, start the de-briefing. Allow ample time for debriefing (a rule of thumb is 15 minutes if there are two groups, then 5 more for each additional group).
- Use a flipchart to catch most of the content and, if possible, get a colleague to take notes of the discussion.

This exercise is a good way of equipping people with the concepts that they might not otherwise have. This will enable them to discuss the chosen question in a general way. Requirements for the nine-diamond activity:

- space for participants to work in small groups
- enough time (about one hour) to conduct the activity
- a facilitator for the activity (following the steps set out above)
- a note taker to record the feedback from groups
- sets of slips/cards
- a flipchart and working pens.

Example 9.2   A set of nine-diamond concepts used in an education library

In this case the aim is to get students to say which of the following elements of the service make any difference to them when they are studying:

1 Borrow books from the library
2 Consult reference books in the library

3   Use CD-ROMs in the library
4   Get internet access from the library
5   Get internet access to library resources
6   Use social media-based services provided by the library
7   Read magazines/journals
8   Have e-journal access arranged by the library
9   Have e-book access arranged by the library
10 Use the library enquiries/help desk (use locally preferred term)
11 Take part in library induction
12 Use photocopy facilities in library
13 Use computer print facilities in library
14 Get guidance on how to use PCs/search the internet from librarian
15 Participate in training sessions by a librarian on how to use the library/search for information
16 Read current newspapers
17 Read back-files of newspapers, including e-newspapers
18 Borrow videos
19 Obtain interlibrary loans via library
20 Consult the library catalogue
21–23   Blank cards for students to add their own thoughts.

Evaluation rationale
The approach is designed to throw light on which library services make any difference to students and why. This should enable students to convey whether and how they are functioning as independent learners and whether the library is recognized as encouraging this approach.

9.4.3   Structured focus groups
The main problem in working with groups is other people's time. You know what questions you want answered, but the people you want to talk to are usually busy and may not see library service development as their main concern – especially if they are generally happy with the service now on offer.

Participants in focus groups often complain that they don't have enough cohesion, or, in other words, the events lack sufficient structure to allow people to focus on the task in hand. The answer is to design and facilitate the activities carefully to help people give you the impact information you want.

You can overcome both these problems through the right choice of activity and a flexible approach. The people targeted for your questions may be busy but they probably come together in groups for meetings, education or training purposes. If so, the prospect of doing something a bit different may be intriguing.

Most evaluation calls for focus groups to be made up of various categories of potential service user; in other cases the expertise of the participants is at a premium.

How easy is it to get **a representative group** together to focus on impact? This depends on whether people see your evaluation question as intrinsically interesting. If not, your best bet may be to link up with another activity that brings some or all of your target group together, or you may have to resort to offering incentives to participate. You may also wish to 'pick off' parts of your target group in different sessions if, for example, you want to involve high and low status people and if this difference is likely to get in the way of everybody contributing. However, choosing the right activities may remove the need for this type of separation.

With **expert groups**, people will get involved if they see your topic as relevant and as a high enough priority (you will have to make the case and the initial approach carefully, explaining why they are the best people to get involved and what the benefits to them will be). A way forward is to identify one or more 'champions' who will be sufficiently interested in your evaluation to pave the way to other people. Setting up strategic focus groups requires a longer timescale to prepare the ground and to get into people's diaries.

9.4.4   Putting the spine into focus groups

The two key elements in running focus groups that work are setting up the conditions that enable people to concentrate on the job in hand and choosing the right activities. We have already said that good trainers will have a repertoire of structured activities to call upon. In talking to trainers about what you want it is important to remember the main difference between an evaluation focus group and a professional development event. Your main concern is to pick the brains of your participants rather than to give them a positive learning experience, although the two are not mutually exclusive.

A general rule for effective focus groups might be 'the less opportunity for unstructured discussion the better'. As to activities, options include brainstorming or card sort activities, as already described. In addition, you could try small group generation of cartoons, diagrams, posters or bullet points encapsulating their responses to carefully worded questions. As with card sorts, these provide opportunities for plenary exploration of issues, but there is also scope to get small groups to explain their ideas to each other (tape the discussions), or for them to write in sufficient detail for the next group to be able to understand and add to what the first group produced (doing your recording job for you).

Unlike general discussions, all these activities will give you concrete impact information which has been fully endorsed by the participants.

Example 9.3   The short, sharp focus group

A series of short structured focus groups is used in a UK health service region as part of the review of its library services.

We target various groups of staff and consult administrators to find out where and when these people meet as part of their normal work. Then we contact the meeting convenors and ask for half an hour at their next meeting. The offer we make is that if they give us time to help review recent library service provision we will guarantee two things – we will finish within half an hour and people will find the activity interesting.

Steps

1   Arrive with a set of 20–25 cards, each identifying a specific library service or aspect of provision, such as:

   • 'Ready access to photocopy facilities when studying/researching' or
   • 'Being able to browse contents pages of journals and request copies of articles of interest'.

2   Clear a table and position it so that people can stand round it. Explain the purpose and invite people to help identify where the library makes a difference and areas where it needs to have more impact. If the group size is appropriate (5–12 people):

   • Deal out the cards to the participants as though they are playing cards.
   • Explain that the table will be used to prioritize, with the top end as high success and the bottom as needing attention.
   • Ask people individually (and all together) to put down 'their' cards anywhere on the table according to their view of its success.
   • When this starts, tell them that they can put items above, below or beside cards that are already there but not move anything that is there.

   This usually takes three or four minutes.

3   Now ask all the participants to look at the card layout and challenge anything that they think is placed too high or low by turning it face down. If anyone is unsure about what a card means (since they all consist of short phrases) they should turn it over too. This usually takes another three to four minutes and

results in about five to eight cards being turned over. Record the remainder of the session (tape recorder or a colleague taking notes).

4 Starting at the top of the table, turn over the highest face-down item, read it out to the group and ask why it was turned over. You know that:

- someone wants an explanation – in which case ask the group what they think it means (important: don't offer your own explanation – you are there as an evaluator not as an expert); or
- there are at least two views about the relative importance of the item – invite a discussion and see if you can get a group consensus about where the item should be placed. If not, put it on one side and record that the group can't agree about it.

5 Continue working down the table until all the items are face up.

Through this process you lead a focused discussion about recent service impact, concentrating entirely on areas of difference or lack of understanding. The participants are equipped with a set of concepts through which to consider library service performance (probably for the first time ever). They agree on a ranking list of relative success, to which you can fairly easily assign scores so that you can compare results from different groups. They almost certainly find the activity interesting – and you have done the whole thing in half an hour or less. If the group finishes early, complete the task by asking them: 'If only one of these items can be addressed over the next three years, which should it be and why?'

9.5   Collecting stories and constructing case studies as impact evidence

9.5.1   Why collect stories?

Why should we be interested in case studies and people's stories when we are looking at the impact of libraries? All of the collection methods described in this chapter contribute to the 'library story of change' – but there are many stories behind this story. As the UK evaluation expert Peter Brophy (2008) observes,

> When we seek to measure the performance of our libraries, the challenge is to capture the rich pictures that retain the essence of our achievements, without losing the richness of their contexts . . . That is the contribution that narrative can provide.

You can collect stories to give a much richer picture of how the services are working and how well or badly they are being received. Constructed **service case studies** can be built up by gathering stories of how various managers plan, set up and deliver their library services (and their view of how users respond to these services) – offering a chance to illuminate the essential elements of this 'hidden world'. At the same time, service users can be encouraged to tell **their own stories** to build up a nuanced and detailed picture of how people see the services on offer, where these services fit into people's own 'information worlds' and what real differences these services make, if any.

These two types of story can be used in various ways:

- Service case studies will show **service staff** that their problems and successes are being recognized, give them a chance to signal other problems and provide a way to report their own good practice
- User stories will help **service staff** to understand better where they can make a difference and how
- Service case studies and user stories should help **managers of libraries** to celebrate their successes, as well as to see what issues need to be addressed, where there are service development opportunities and what needs to be done next
- Service case studies will give **stakeholders** (such as policy makers) concrete examples of how services are being provided, and user stories will show stakeholders what differences they can make to people's lives by supporting these services – making the advocacy case
- If you start collecting **stories of both kinds** early on in your evaluation work they can also help to form questions later in your evaluation.

Information on how to conduct service case studies can be found in the collection of additional evaluation tools and materials for this book at www.facetpublishing. co.uk/evaluatingimpact.

9.5.2 Collecting stories from users

The main decisions to be taken when collecting stories from users are about choice of story-tellers, how to collect the stories and how to edit them.

Choosing the story-tellers

The aim is to identify people who should be able to tell you a good story about the library. Good, in this context, means that the story-teller offers you something interesting about one or more of the following:

- what led them to use the service
- whether/how people help them to use the service (or to interpret what they find)
- what use they made of the library at the outset
- how library services have changed them – for example:
  - has their use changed over time?
  - where do library-based information services fit into their overall 'information world'?
  - has contact with the library or any of its services changed their lives at all?
  - what do they do differently now as a result of having library access?
  - have your library services changed the way they use or view the library or libraries?
- whether they are involved in any social or community information-sharing
- what other people are doing with library-based services
- what changes they would like to see in library services.

How can you choose story-tellers who may be able to provide these types of good story? Two characteristics of such people are that they have probably used library services more than once (library staff may well know them) and that they are likely to want to share their story, if approached in the right way.

The obvious way to find suitable story-tellers is to ask your librarians to nominate people who might have stories to tell, using the criteria set out above. Ask them to suggest people from a range of types (e.g. young to old, different occupations, different ethnic groups) depending on what your evaluation is trying to achieve.

An alternative is to invite people to record their experiences of using libraries when they visit the library website, or ask your librarians to invite people to record their experiences on a website.

Collecting the stories

It is difficult to give more than tentative advice on how to collect stories from library service users. They may be oral or written and may be elicited or heard by chance, in an interview or in a naturally occurring conversation. In her exhaustive review of this field, which she calls 'narrative inquiry', Susan Chase (2005) sees this as encompassing 'multiple methodologies in various stages of development and [offering] plenty of opportunities for exploring new ideas, methods and questions'.

Some of the options and their pros and cons are:

1 Ask people to respond to **questionnaires** – these are easy to administer once you get past the problem of how to get them into the right hands, but questionnaires are usually better for getting small amounts of information from a large number of respondents. When used to collect people's stories you usually end up with many more unanswered questions inspired by the replies you receive.
2 Invite people to post their experiences of using library computers on a **website** – this is an appropriate way of addressing people who are using public access ICT and you may get a lot of useful replies, but you exclude non-technology users, have no control over the relevance of their replies and cannot easily analyse the responses by category of respondent. If you ask people to identify, for example, their age, gender or job this will put some people off.
3 Conduct **interviews** with people – this is a good way of getting high-quality stories but it is expensive to conduct (interviewer time and travel costs) and it is better to use trained interviewers who are less likely to skew responses by asking leading questions or prompting people to talk about what the interviewer wants rather than what the respondent sees as important.
4 Arrange **focus groups** to get people to share their stories – this is another good method because people spur each other on to tell more, but again a skilled facilitator is preferable to make sure that everyone contributes and that the conversation stays on track.
5 Ask people to **write their own stories** (on a website or on paper), again offering headings to stimulate replies – the stories should be valuable but this is an onerous task and you may get a poor response (unless you can provide a small financial incentive!).

Editing the stories

Stories from users can be heavily edited examples of good news, if used for advocacy purposes, but a more balanced picture is needed for impact evaluation. Stories can reflect many of the situations and understandings of the people telling those stories. Ethnographic researchers talk about capturing people's authentic voices, which implies much less editing by the people collecting and presenting the stories. However, David Silverman (2007) points out that

> . . . telling someone about our experiences is not just emptying out the contents of our head but organizing a tale told to a proper recipient by an authorized teller.

In our role as 'proper recipients' we should pay careful attention to what we are doing as well as considering what the storyteller is trying to achieve. You may want to ask a researcher to prepare a report on the stories to ensure that the important messages about the impact of services and implications for future service development come through without losing the directness of the users' stories.

Think of your user case studies as part of your impact evidence, not as an end in themselves. As Robert Stake (2004) stresses,

> Good case study research follows disciplined practices of analysis and triangulation [that is, comparing the stories with your other types of evidence] to tease out what deserves to be called experiential knowledge from what is opinion and preference.

IFLA recently launched a new version of their Success Stories Database[21] which documents library achievements and projects in five categories:

- Libraries as access point
- Libraries as ICT learning centres
- Libraries for continuing education
- Libraries for specific needs
- Libraries for cultural heritage.

For more detailed coverage of stories as research evidence see Brophy (2009).

9.6   Action research

What is action research? McKernan (1991) claims that:

> Action research is carried out by practitioners seeking to improve their understanding of events, situations and problems so as to increase the effectiveness of their practice. Such research does not have the writing of research reports and other publications as a primary goal. Action research aims at feeding the practical judgement of actors in problematic situations. The validity of the concepts, models and results it generates depends not so much on scientific tests of truth as on their utility in helping practitioners to act more effectively, skilfully and intelligently.

This is only one view of what can vary from rudimentary research conducted by practitioners dragooned into undertaking fieldwork on behalf of academic colleagues, through to real professional development based on the idea of the reflective practitioner focusing on service impact.

Action research makes the direct link between process and impact. It is essentially a cycle of reflecting, theorizing and acting. The people involved move through stages. You

- identify a problem or challenge
- gather evidence about the nature and dimensions of the problem (don't spend too much time here!)
- then interpret this evidence together
- look for ideas on what changes to make (practice elsewhere and published research)
- make changes to the services
- then collect further evidence about the impact of these changes

and so on until you feel that you have made enough progress.

Through action research, practitioners get evidence to discern what is happening at the moment and how well it is being received. This gives them scope to develop ideas about how to improve the situation and then turn them into new strategies and activities, which are evaluated in their turn. This cycle leads practitioners into exploring the different effects of various processes.

When it is done well, action research keeps practitioners focused on what they are trying to achieve. This approach should work in any library context; we have been able to see it working in various settings, from a semi-formal work group of health library managers to a formal impact evaluation programme involving 22 university library teams (Markless and Streatfield, 2006, 2008). Another instance is described below.

Action research is especially valuable when you are looking at 'messy' areas where there are no clear ways forward yet. With all the continuing developments in e-information, e-learning and information literacy work there is no shortage of such areas in libraries. The usual impact evaluation approach of comparing progress against a baseline starts to break down when the services provided to try to move on from the baseline are themselves changing and evolving rapidly. Action research enables you to engage in a rolling evaluation programme that accepts that yesterday's baseline is just history. With this approach you can change where you start from (your baseline) as well as where you are trying to get to (target) with each round of activity.

Since your rounds of activity are dictated by what you are finding out and wanting to change, they are not usually locked into the annual planning cycle – so it follows that your baseline and targets do not automatically tie in to any annual planning or reporting cycle. It is important to make this point if you are called upon to make an annual report on any action research programme that does not follow an annual cycle.

There are various helpful books on action research, such as McNiff and Whitehead (2010).

Example 9.4   Education librarians as action researchers

A small group of UK professionals (a school teacher, school librarians, further education lecturers and a college librarian) who recently completed their MA in Education discuss how they can continue to develop their practice. They want to keep up the momentum gathered during their Masters studies. The group feels that attending short staff development courses won't do: these tend to be too superficial. Reading may be interesting but won't necessarily galvanize the group into activity or provide the links between theory and practice that they want. They decide to set up an informal action research group and asked their MA tutor to facilitate termly meetings.

Ten years later the group is still going. Members of the group have:

- enhanced the after-hours support that they provide
- collaborated with colleagues to integrate the teaching of 'learning strategies' into subject courses
- developed new approaches to assessing student information literacy
- enhanced the handling of group work differentiated according to the ability of the students in the college library
- become a focal point for literacy across the school.

The group meetings are held on Saturdays and attendance levels are high. Group members are clear that these improvements in their educational practice are due to adopting action research strategies.

Group members encourage each other to investigate aspects of their practice in a carefully structured and focused way; they read relevant research but are also supported while they question its relevance to their own contexts and develop their own ideas out about what they read. They use a variety of data-gathering techniques both in their initial investigations and when evaluating the impact of their changed practices. Group members openly report their difficulties and hold up their own development and their emerging ideas to critical scrutiny.

Despite working in difficult contexts, faced with increasing demands on their time and, in some cases, with decreasing budgets, engagement in action research has stopped group members from feeling powerless and de-professionalized. They are able to enhance the quality of their work in areas that they care about and in ways that accord with their educational values. Recently the group feels sufficiently empowered to collaborate in writing a book about school librarianship, championing the need to continually move forward, be innovative and think laterally (Markless, 2009).

9.7   Doing it!

The actual evidence gathering is relatively straightforward, once you have decided what you want to collect and how. Don't forget that you are not the only people in the evidence collection business.

9.7.1   Getting help

Can you use partners to help you to collect evidence? Here are some ideas:

1 If you want people to give you feedback about how resources are used by others, tell them what you would like them to look out for in advance, then ask for that information later (this is particularly important if you are asking busy teachers to help).
2 Some strategic managers monitor impact evaluation developments; others write reports that may be useful if you can tap into them.
3 Corporate performance monitoring teams in your wider organization may be collecting evidence themselves – can you 'ride on their coat tails' by getting them to ask questions that you want answered?
4 Some people (librarians in your own and other sectors, booksellers? museums staff?) share some goals with your service and may be ready to collaborate over information gathering. Other libraries are likely to be looking at the same impact issues. Why not collaborate with them to produce better tools?
5 Other people may have directly relevant evaluation expertise. For example, many trainers rely on the Kirkpatrick evaluation model, a four-level framework devised by Donald Kirkpatrick and presented in four journal articles published in 1959–60. This model has been the subject of a great deal of analysis and testing – any professional trainer is likely to have useful views on evaluation.

9.7.2   Practical difficulties in gathering evidence

These are some of the difficulties that crop up when service managers engage in evidence collection:

1   Capturing evidence in **busy libraries** – this is the most common problem and it cannot be solved, but it can be managed. The problem affects both staff and users: if staff are really busy, any additional evidence collection is likely to be abandoned. From the user point of view, if your service is busy, users are less likely to want to be interrupted by your attempts to gather evidence. A careful balance is needed here – sometimes it is important to collect impact evidence of the service under stress; in other cases evidence from busy times is necessary to give the full picture. If you don't have to collect evidence at peak periods it obviously makes sense not to; where you have to, explaining to your staff and to users why it is necessary to do so and acknowledging that this creates problems should help you to get support.

2   Unless you are collecting data on a large scale, impact evidence is different in kind from most traditional library evaluation data. Most impact evaluation involves using qualitative research methods where concerns such as getting a large enough sample of responses are less important than getting **robust evidence** that meets the resonance test (see section 8.5.3 in the previous chapter). This type of evidence is usually the best that is achievable, not, as is sometimes assumed, a poor second best. Getting this message across to people who are used to traditional busy-ness statistics may be hard work, but can be done.

3   One pitfall is in the temptation to try to establish **cause and effect** relationships – this is *much* harder than it seems! We can learn something here from another field in which people struggle with demonstrating causal relationships and usually fail – education inspection. You may find it useful to adopt the approach and language of the UK education inspection teams, who look to see whether an activity is 'bearing upon' or is 'linked to' a service objective. A (positive or negative) link can be inferred if there is usually an improvement or decline in a situation when a specific service or activity is introduced or withdrawn.

4   Whether you are asking people questions or observing them, it is important to behave in an **ethical** manner. Difficulties can arise if people don't know what you intend to do with the information they give you or don't like the questions you ask. (You should be safe if you follow our guidance in section 9.3.2.) They may also object to being observed. You can head off complaints by putting up a poster to say what you are doing and (in general

terms) why. There are also hazards in collecting evidence from or about children. You may have to obtain prior permission from parents and the organization where you encounter the children may have specific rules about contact. If you have ever tried to photograph 22 children working with library materials when one of them has failed to bring the necessary parental authorization but keeps getting into the picture, you will know how frustrating these necessary rules can be.

5 If you work in a health, social care or educational organization, there are likely to be **protocols** governing all research done there. You will need to check to see whether your evidence gathering falls within the organizational definition of research and, if so, how to get your activity cleared.

> **LAWS OF IMPACT EVALUATION 9**
> Effective impact work is not about gathering lots of evidence. It is about focusing on real impact and about rigour in collecting, analysing and reporting data.

9.8 Analysing data

We need to make a distinction here between quantitative data, which is usually fairly easy to organize into tables, and qualitative data, which is inherently more difficult to analyse. There are, of course, plenty of statistical packages and data analysis tools to help with this work. These tools range from the best known statistical aid, the Statistical Package for the Social Sciences (SPSS)[22] to the new generation of data analysis tools. These newer tools can help in various ways, such as by giving easy access to data and extensive automation of clerical tasks at one extreme, or helping with qualitative analysis by combining 'subtle coding with qualitative linking, shaping, searching and modelling' at the other (e.g. NUD*IST and NVivo respectively).[23]

However helpful these tools are, and some of them are very helpful, there is no substitute for the evaluator developing a thorough understanding of the evidence. One effect of the widespread adoption of data analysis tools is that it is now too easy to do a superficial job of organizing the qualitative evidence and turning the results into a slick report. The reason why we advocate using qualitative methods to gather impact evidence is that this can give you subtle and nuanced evidence as well as powerful testimony in key areas. This can only be achieved if you do enough work with the qualitative evidence to really understand what it is telling you. Unless data analysis tools are used carefully they can get in the way of the real picture. If you are doing relatively small-scale qualitative evidence gathering, you may be better off cutting and pasting pieces of text and (physically or electronically) sorting and re-sorting them until useful patterns start to emerge. We still regard highlighter pens and scissors, as well as plastic or cardboard folders, as useful adjuncts to the evaluation data sense-making process.

Analysing the evidence

IFLA wants to see whether its Building Strong Library Associations Programme is effective. They want to know what works and what is having the most impact on the staff and members of the Association, including attracting new members, as well as the effect of the programme on key stakeholders in each country involved in the programme. Clear data that shows whether more members are joining the Association, evidence about whether greater numbers of people are being more actively involved, and a picture of organizational change (if that is what is happening) are likely to be the guiding themes. IFLA will also want to know whether the training and support provided is effective.

Country programme evaluators are encouraged to construct a matrix of evidence to enable them to see how much qualitative and quantitative evidence and of what kinds they are collecting in these areas. An example is given below. (The elements in their matrix will depend upon each country's decisions about objectives and impact indicators.)

Evidence of:	LA members	LA officers	LA staff	Librarians who are not members	Other key stakeholders
Changes in level and types of involvement with LA					
Changes in value of LA					
Changes in what LA does and how					
Views on BSLA and its training					

Countries are encouraged to identify the types of evidence they have available and then consider how to present the evidence in each box to tell IFLA what it would like to know. The matrix can also be used to organize evidence for use in local advocacy.

When we referred to 'grounded theory' as an alternative to the hypothesis testing approach to research in section 2.4.1, we glossed over what many regard as the main contribution of Glaser and Strauss when proposing this approach – being systematic in analysing qualitative evidence. They identify three kinds of coding as being at the heart of their approach:

1 **Open coding** (the initial process of breaking down, analysing, comparing and categorizing data – labelling, grouping and re-grouping incidents or events to form categories and properties).
2 **Axial coding** (teasing out hypothetical relationships between categories and subcategories).
3 **Selective coding** (assembling the categories into the core category that becomes the basis of the grounded theory – which might be described as making sense of the data).

Interestingly, the two authors have since diverged in their approach, with Glaser challenging Strauss and his later collaborators (see Glaser, 1992) for, in his view, forcing data into a preconceived framework. Whether you choose to embrace grounded theory or not, it may be helpful to distinguish between these three types of coding, as well as to be wary about forcing your evidence into predetermined categories.

9.9   Interpreting and presenting your evidence
9.9.1   Ethical interpretation of data
We discussed some of the issues in ethical presentation of data in the previous chapter.

9.9.2   Another difficult area?
According to the respondents to Covey's (2002) survey of US academic libraries:

1 Interpreting research findings is a particularly thorny problem, exacerbated when the data are imprecise or in conflict with other data or known trends, and when the research subjects are few or unrepresentative of the campus population.
2 Even when evidence is carefully analysed and interpreted, managers may struggle with deciding how to organize and present it to an audience for consideration in decision making and strategic planning.

These difficulties are still with us! However, if you work systematically through the process described in this book you should not be faced with imprecise or conflicting impact evidence. By thinking carefully about who you want to get evidence from, and on how best to get that evidence, you should avoid getting your evidence from the wrong people. This leaves the question of how to present your evidence.

9.9.3   What is the main message?

When reporting findings it is tempting to follow the same sequence as in the interview schedule or questionnaire. This may work, if the original lines of questioning are logical and if they provide a coherent route through the evidence. The question to ask at this point is 'What are the most important findings from this evaluation?' You may then have to change the way in which you report this evidence to get your message across.

9.9.4   Organize your findings

The key points to consider are: Who needs to know? Who do you want to influence with your impact evidence and who else has a right to know?

Most people tend to take a 'one size fits all' approach to reports of evaluation findings. The usual pattern is start with as much evidence as you can put together, follow this with detailed conclusions and then add recommendations for action. What we know from much work on research dissemination is that this approach works for almost nobody. You need to ask how the key people you want to influence take their information on board. Even in these days of advanced e-communication, people find out a lot by talking to others. Can you boil down your key messages to a set of brief oral proposals and follow this up with an e-mail? Can you get a champion with influence in your organization to speak up for you instead? Is there a decision-making meeting to influence? If so, what is the ideal length and type of report?

Assuming that you need to produce a written report, the guiding principle is – the shorter the better. Get your messages right. For strategic decision makers: try to put over your key findings on one page, with another page for recommendations for action. For operational managers: again offer key findings, show briefly how you reached them, and tailor your recommendations for action to that level. Make the evidence that informs your findings available for the few people who want it (as an appendix or on a website). Keep the raw evidence to compare it with next time – but don't be tempted to show how much work you have done by circulating this. Some examples of what can be achieved are the leaflets on public libraries and e-government[24] or public libraries and access[25], published by the Policy and Access Center at the University of Maryland and based on the Public Library Funding and Technology Access Survey (Hoffman, Bertot and Davis, 2012).

Here is an example of how to combine different types of evidence to tell an impact story, from Romania.

Example 9.5   Combining qualitative and quantitative information

In January 2011 IREX Romania concludes a collaboration agreement with the state Payment and Intervention Agency in Agriculture (APIA), aimed at using the computers donated to public libraries as part of the Biblionet program [the Global Libraries Initiative in Romania] to fill in online the agricultural subsidy applications managed by APIA.

Throughout 2011, around 17,000 farmers fill in applications for agricultural subsidies at public libraries, the total value of the subsidies reaching €20 million. On average, the farmers save two days each by filling in the applications at the public library, a total saving of 34,000 days.

How is this working? Here are some examples. The APIA expert from Braşov talks about the opening of the APIA centres:

> The space is more appropriate than the office from Braşov, where there are five inspectors and no space at all for something like this. The entire procedure is much faster, the technology is much better and organized. The working conditions are much better thanks to the internet connection and the space.

Librarian Gabriela Ticoiu describes changes in the library:

> The initiative brings more people to the library, new members join. Many have just now found out about the library features: computers, the internet and new services.

Petrean Petre, librarian explains:

> During a meeting with the representatives of IREX Romania organized by Dolj County Library, a possible collaboration with APIA was suggested. This idea was taken up with the mayor and the decision was made to fill in the subsidy applications locally. The initiative is praiseworthy, particularly if we take into account the applicants' old age, the distance and transportation possibilities and the long waiting-time at the APIA centre (22 km away), and we should also not forget about the waiting conditions there . . . all this shortens the time taken to fill in the applications. Initially, the filling in of applications was promoted in public meetings organized by village . . . then, to prevent crowding, appointments were made. At the end of the action, 200 applications to obtain the subsidy have been completed.

What the farmers say about this new face of the library:

> The library's activity has improved; the librarian is more efficient and can support the citizens with up-to-date information. The new equipment is used to inform the population. Before enabling the submission of subsidy applications, the library had a standard, book-loaning image.

The librarian should be trained to help the citizens with other services, such as the online payment of invoices. Moreover, it would be helpful to find a method to submit online applications for documents (income records, tax certificates) by public institutions, considering that two trips to Craiova are required to obtain such documents (60 km).

The welcoming space in the library and the state-of-the-art computers make the library the ideal place for this activity. While they wait in line, the farmers can browse through a book, access the internet or find out about the new services provided by the library – programmes for pupils or different cultural events. (Chiranov, 2012, 63–64, edited)

The combined quantitative and qualitative evidence makes a stronger story than either type of information in isolation.

9.10   Sources on research methods

There are a number of more or less readable general publications on qualitative or quantitative research methods which are of use in evaluating the impact of libraries. Three works that we often recommend are Judith Bell's simple but sound introduction *Doing Your Research Project*, written for the UK Open University (2010); then, for people who have a more specific focus, Robert K. Yin's *Case Study Research* (2008); and finally David Silverman's aptly titled *A Very Short, Fairly Interesting and Reasonably Cheap Book About Qualitative Research* (2007). If you want titles on varied topics such as effective action research, critical discourse analysis or using focus groups in research, then the Continuum Research Methods[26] series of short guides may provide the answer.

9.11   Finding research methods e-resources

One of the big growth areas on the internet is in websites offering a variety of tools to help with social research in general through to valuation. Online journals, such as *Information Research*,[27] are becoming more frequent and, fortunately, this growth has been accompanied by a burgeoning of websites offering guidance to what is available. Here, the range of potentially useful disciplines and methodologies comes into play: a quick round-up of useful sites covers:

• the social sciences generally (Research Resources in the Social Sciences,[28] including its own search engine)
• social research (Bill Trochim's Center for Social Research Methods,[29] or Resources for Methods in Evaluation and Social Research,[30] selected by staff at the University of New York, Albany)

- information systems research (Qualitative Research in Information Systems[31] – a subsidiary site of *MIS Quarterly*, which claims to offer 'useful information on the conduct, evaluation and publication of qualitative research')
- research methodologies (Kay Vandergrift's *Research Methods on the World Wide Web*,[32] offering 'sites selected because they address methodological issues and theories').

What about the library and information research methods fraternity? Continuing the pattern of useful websites being constructed by individuals we have *Researching Librarian*,[33] covering 'resources to assist librarians undertaking research'. For the broader information services and systems field there is *InformationR.net*, covering information management, information science and information systems. This site offers access to a hugely valuable series of free *Electronic Resources for Information Research Methods* [34] maintained by Juliet Drennan.

For public libraries, the *Counting on Results* project was formerly funded by the Institute of Museum and Library Services in the USA to develop new tools for 'outcomes-based evaluation'. The website is still accessible.[35]

Two value calculator tools are offered by the National Network of Libraries of Medicine: the Retail Value Calculator[36] (How much would it cost to replace your library services on the retail market?) and the Library Value Calculator[37] (How much benefit does your institution, your user, receive for every £ spent by the library?). Some other research tools are mentioned in Chapter 3.

Finally, there are additional tools and materials linked to this book. To find them go to www.facetpublishing.co.uk/evaluatingimpact.

9.12   Evidence or advocacy?

There is one danger in how we go about collecting evidence and in looking at what it tells us. Even experienced researchers can get into a mess by confusing advocacy and evidence. When we started doing social science research, one of the best pieces of advice we received was to try to treat each new research situation as 'anthropologically strange'. To do this you start out by telling yourself that, however familiar a situation seems to be, you do not really know what is going on until you have gathered and looked carefully at the evidence. In other words, we should look at library services in the same way that a social anthropologist is expected to look at a group or tribe, by asking 'What appears to be going on here and how can I make any sense of it?'

Most of the time this doesn't create too many problems. If you have worked through the process so far, you should be ready to ask yourself what sorts of evidence will help to show the difference you are making. But evidence-based decision making can quickly degenerate into only picking evidence that will support a desired decision. Government bodies are especially likely to blur the distinction between service evaluation and advocacy – but they are not the only culprits, as our own experience shows.

Going back some years to the Effective School Library research project referred to in section 3.5.1, we hit a problem when we reached the evidence analysis stage. Normally, there is a pattern to doing research, whether it is small-scale evaluation of a service or a large national project. After the initial energy buzz from getting the work started, you begin to get anxious (perhaps even depressed) when you see how much evidence is building up – will you ever make sense of it and will it tell you anything useful? Then, by the time you settle down to analyse the evidence and draw out the findings, the evidence speaks to you and the report writing or evidence presentation stage is usually straightforward.

When we reach this stage with the Effective School Library the evidence doesn't fit together. We start again but still can't make sense of what we are looking at. Then we start to think about why the analysis isn't working – and the answer suddenly becomes clear. Because we have worked for several years with school libraries we have unwittingly shifted from a research position to an advocacy stance. Everyone in the school library advocacy field at this time is busy calling for school libraries to be turned into learning resource centres designed to support students as independent learners. (We now refer to this as the 'Holy Grail model' because it is a more or less distant aspiration that is unlikely to be fully achieved.) As we noted earlier, this approach is fine if the school as a whole is heavily committed to a student-centred approach to learning, but our research evidence clearly shows that this model of library provision won't work at all if the school puts a strong emphasis on traditional teaching. We want the Holy Grail model to work, but the evidence tells us something else.

As soon as we stop being hopeful advocates and turn back into realistic researchers it becomes clear that a different and more nuanced model is necessary to take account of the evidence that we have gathered. The evidence shows that schools differ in their approaches to teaching and learning and that what works well in supporting these vital activities in one school won't work at all somewhere else. The result is a 'horses for courses' approach to school library development that takes full account of where the school is now, what its teaching and learning priorities are and what level and type of library service can support these priorities. We learn important lessons in this project about the need to base development decisions on the research evidence about impact.

All of which brings us to our next 'law':

LAWS OF IMPACT EVALUATION 10

Beware of the Holy Grail! To gauge the impact of a service you need to know what change it is making, not what you hope it might do – evidence not aspirations.

We have deliberately not suggested any specific activities (or steps) for you in this chapter because the whole focus is on you doing it!

10

Taking stock, setting targets and development planning

This chapter starts by looking at how to review the impact indicators generated through the process in order to keep the whole thing manageable! We then focus on setting realistic impact targets and conclude by considering where and how development planning fits into the process of evaluating impact.

10.1 Taking stock: reviewing your impact and process indicators

Before you move on to select your targets, it will be useful to stop and review all your impact indicators. There are four main dimensions:

1 **Range**. Do your indicators reflect the full range of what you are trying to change and give you enough of a picture of whether your services are working efficiently?
2 **Number**. Have you generated too many indicators? Publications on managing performance usually recommend 15–20 'key' indicators (including both process and impact indicators), with any others considered as secondary. If you go much beyond that scale it becomes difficult to gain and retain an overall picture of what is going on. Too many indicators can also lead to diverting over-much energy into collecting evidence rather than running your service.
3 **Relevance**. Do all the indicators really tell you something useful and contribute to the overall picture? Are you still collecting 'traditional' performance data because you have always done so? Are any of your indicators only used as the basis for making management reports?
4 **User focus/service focus**. Do you have a balance between 'outward-looking' user-focused indicators and 'inward-looking' system enhancement indicators?

No matter how much care you take in writing and reviewing your indicators, they may not all work. All indicators ought to be regarded as provisional at the outset. They should be monitored to see if they are leading you to really useful information. If not, change them or ditch them.

10.2   Setting targets for impact

Impact targets aim at improving the effectiveness of the service; they focus on discernible differences in impact on people in significant areas of use of the service. They are different from process targets, which record what people have done. Impact targets can be concerned with the whole community served or parts of it. See also the definitions offered in 'Impact and all that: use of some key terms in this book' on page xv.

10.2.1 Baseline information, what baseline information?

Whenever we work through this model with library service managers, we have to stop at this point. The reason is that when service managers look closely at what they want to achieve and at the sort of evidence that will tell them whether they are getting there, they usually do not have the baseline information about where they are now that will enable them to set sensible targets (e.g. What proportion of your current ICT users are unemployed or elderly? What proportion of health workers are effective information users? How many members of reading groups are avid readers when they join a group?).

When we work as consultants to help a management team to work through the process, there is usually a pause of several months at this stage so that people can go off and assemble baseline information. If you set targets without sufficient baseline information you are guessing in the dark. You are also potentially setting yourself up to fail.

10.2.2 Writing impact targets

You are now in a position to consider setting realistic but challenging targets: you know how the service is currently performing in key areas (baseline data collected on your impact and process indicators) and you know where you would like to be. However, quantifying the improvements you want can be difficult – and target setting should not be about 'plucking figures out of the air'. Your targets should be sufficiently challenging to stretch the service but not so far out of reach as to be demotivating.

When setting targets it may be helpful to consider target zones. A study for the National Foundation for Educational Research in England and Wales (Arnold, 1998) sums up the idea of target zones clearly:

- **The historic zone.** Targets in this zone are those that are behind current performance, which is hidden to the extent that others are not aware of its quality. By this means, standstill can be represented as improvement – it is a means of 'domesticating' any threats that targets may offer.
- **The comfort zone.** Targets in this zone seek to keep improvement very much within reach. They often reflect a belief that there is really no need to improve.
- **The smart zone.** Targets in this zone are sufficiently ahead of the present state of play to make a difference.
- **The unlikely zone.** Targets in this zone seek large improvements through 'determination and high aspiration, or recklessness'. They can be a recipe for high risk and high stress.

It needs no guesswork to arrive at which of these zones is the ideal, although in practice library services show very different aspirations in their target setting. Impact targets lend themselves to more precise quantification than process targets and are nearly always expressed as a quantity or proportion. The wording of the targets should not be too difficult if you are happy with your indicators. Whereas an indicator is couched in terms of:

- the number of staff confident to . . .
- the number of staff with knowledge of . . .
- the proportion of schools satisfied with . . .
- the number of unemployed people/retired people/teenagers using . . .

the targets state what specific improvement is being aimed at:

- 5% more managers are satisfied with the quality of communication with library staff, compared with the previous year
- 90% of participants in user training focused on internet searching report that they are now more confident when conducting searches
- 30% of partner organizations have a better understanding of the contribution of the library service to their joint work.

Occasionally, it may be possible to set targets without including a 'target figure' (if, for example, you aspire to generate a love of books among a particular group of people). However, there is no point in setting targets unless you have some way of finding out when you have reached the level of success at which you are aiming. This can be achieved by other means, such as a thorough and systematic qualitative research study focused in the target area – but this is likely to be more lengthy and resource-dependent than impact evaluation against quantitative targets.

Your targets should specify the time period over which they are to be met (usually one year, or three to five years in a strategic plan). Do not automatically try to fit your impact target cycle into your annual planning cycle – it may not fit! As one service manager said: 'The trouble with national audit indicators is that they are all geared to the annual financial cycle. Impact does not occur to fit the annual cycle and has to be viewed over a longer term.'

10.2.3 Some issues

1 You may find it helpful to consult any available benchmarking information (see section 12.6) when you consider the level at which to set targets. How are similar services performing? There may also be clues about achievable levels in the results of national/federal/state research.
2 It is easy to wander into fantasy land when setting targets if you don't take full account of the existing resources available to deliver and the competing priorities within your service. You may want to have much greater impact in a particular area of work, but over-committing your resources in a particular area may lead to unwelcome distortion of the service or to missed targets.
3 If too many impact targets are adopted at the same time this will lead to failure, because too many targets will cause confusion rather than concentrate effort. Each impact target is likely to drag a raft of process targets along in its wake, because you have to do things to meet targets and will probably want to ensure that these are done.
4 Targets are not always about 'more of . . .'. You may deliberately set targets that maintain current levels of impact or, in some cases, choose a lower level of impact (e.g. if the user group or its expectations have changed).

10.2.4 The target snare

The trouble with targets is that as soon as you focus on them they start to have a distorting effect. This phenomenon is well stated by Marilyn Strathern (1997), who draws on what is known as Goodhart's Law by asserting that 'When a measure becomes a target it ceases to be a good measure.' The original version of this Law is a bit more convoluted; as stated by Charles Goodhart (1983), one time Chief Adviser to the Bank of England: 'Any observed statistical regularity will tend to collapse once pressure is placed on it for control purposes.'

How can this conundrum be solved? The best that we can hope to do is to remember that targets are not sacrosanct; they have been chosen by managers for a specific purpose and are only useful as long as they help – in this case, as long as they help you to improve the service.

```
LAWS OF IMPACT EVALUATION 11
If impact targets are not helping, change them or ditch them.
```

10.2.5 Imposed targets

So far, we have assumed that you are interested in setting targets for the active development of your service. However, we have to acknowledge that there is an increasing tendency for targets to be imposed from above (e.g. in the UK, improvements in literacy and in public access to ICT in libraries are both government-driven). It is important to recognize that imposed targets are usually prescribed as a control mechanism by government. As a result, such targets tend to be very general, arbitrary and subject to abandonment or change as political circumstances warrant. Service managers usually have to subscribe to imposed targets, but we believe that it is also important to persist with more appropriate development-driven targets in our rapidly changing world. As Carol Taylor Fitz-Gibbon (1996) observes:

> The imposition of targets or the development of ossified plans is not the approach which seems to fit best with the ideas of complex systems thriving in a region of complexity on the edge of chaos.

She may be talking about schools rather than libraries but the description seems highly appropriate for libraries in the 21st century!

Targets can also be imposed by the larger organization of which the library service is part (e.g. pharmaceutical companies usually have a strong information agenda; local/state authorities have their own priorities too!). Although such targets are likely to feel less distant, it may be problematic to embrace corporate targets wholesale. Targets that are not 'owned' (or at least influenced) by the people who have to meet them can alienate more than motivate. It is not surprising that imposed targets are sometimes called 'in-house terrorists' – they can spread panic and discontent!

10.3   Process targets

Process targets are concerned with changes in what the service does and how. Planning tends to be dominated by process targets in much the same way that services generate a lot of process indicators and hardly any impact indicators. However, you will always use more process targets than impact ones; and indeed it is a mistake to adopt too many impact targets because each one inevitably drags related process targets along in its wake.

We tend to write process targets in one of two ways:

1 Focus on task completion – e.g. you may decide to develop a new stock selection procedure or to put new monitoring/data collection mechanisms in place.
2 Focus on increased or decreased activity – e.g. attend 20% more curriculum meetings; consult 10% more non-users of the service.

10.4   Development planning

It may be a little disingenuous to claim that once you have worked through this model the development plan writes itself. However, it should now be a much less difficult task to express the initial aims and processes as time-limited and specific objectives linked to realistic targets, and to be confident of knowing when the service has achieved what it set out to do.

Our model offers a framework for strategic and service level planning. If it works, it will help you form a clear view of what you want to achieve, and support your exploration of the processes that should help you get there. Using the model then leads you to collect the data that will tell you how you are currently performing in each key area. With all this information you should be ready to plan effectively. If you work through our model you will come to the development plan in its proper place – at the end of the planning process. This makes the development plan more meaningful, not just a document based on 'historic fiction plus 5%'.

Further points:

1 There is a difference between maintenance and development. Most development plans that we have seen present managers with a mass of activities and targets all labelled 'development'. This makes 'real' development very difficult; you can end up engaged in lots of activity but with little sense of getting anywhere. You will need to make choices about which areas of work should be maintained (which could be linked to a set of maintenance targets or standards) and in which areas the service should

try to move forward. The baseline data that you collect to illuminate your current impact and performance, will help in this work.

This distinction can be empowering in itself, giving a renewed sense of purpose. If you separate maintenance from development, you can identify how much resource will be 'used up' in maintaining essential services and infrastructure, and how much spare capacity will then be available to support development activities.

2 The basic constraint for librarians is having to spend so much time on managing and operating the library infrastructure. This means that you probably do most development work 'at the margins', at least in the early stages of the work (unless additional development funding can be secured). One characteristic of successful initiatives is that they become part of the normal work over time ('the institutionalization stage' in educational change-speak); occasionally an initiative may lead to the library operating differently, but this is unusual and is in any case likely to take around five years to achieve.

3 You will have to prioritize. Inevitably you will not be able to do all that you want to immediately. You will need to decide on criteria for prioritizing (for example, focusing on where the library is supporting corporate priorities, or government initiatives, or deciding to tackle areas of 'worst' performance).

4 Development planning should lead directly to more detailed action planning. Many development plans are not implemented because they are left at too high a level (not nailed down to the practicalities of implementation). Once you have decided what key changes are necessary to ensure the development of the library service and what your targets are, you will need to plan the tasks required to implement these changes. You should try to ensure that:

- *key tasks are defined and understood*
- *necessary actions are listed*
- *accountabilities for each action are defined and accepted*
- *performance targets are set for each action*
- *performance measures for each action are identified and documented*
- *mechanisms are in place to review the achievement of targets and to feed the review into future planning activities*
- *timescales for each activity are set.*

(based on Kinnell, Usherwood and Jones, 1999a)

10.5   Planning your impact evaluation

10.5.1 Some challenges

In looking at US university library attempts to evaluate their services ten years ago, Covey (2002) listed some of the pitfalls in managing evaluation:

> Respondents reported frequent breakdowns in the research process because of inadequate planning, particularly in scheduling and marshalling the resources needed to complete the project. Poor planning created problems that cascaded through the . . . process and, when compounded by inadequate skills, doomed it to failure or only partial success.
>
> They focused on the resources needed to gather, analyse, and perhaps interpret the data. Resources needed to manage the project and complete the process – to document and present the findings, develop plans to use them, and implement the plans – were not addressed at the same level of detail.
>
> Limited resources typically restricted implementation to solving only the problems that were cheap and easy to fix.

The picture they painted is not a picture of a culture of assessment or of an organization in which assessment is a core activity crucial to the library's mission.

10.5.2 Meeting these challenges?

If you are undertaking a significant amount of impact evaluation work, this will have to be carefully planned. As the Covey comments show, it is easy to overlook or under-prepare aspects of this work. You may find it useful to look at the planning checklist provided as part of the Inspiring Learning for All (www.inspiringlearningforall.gov.uk) programme (see section 6.11.1 above). This is what it involves:

- Debate what you mean by learning in the context of your library.
- Set up a team to lead the process.
- Audit your service provision using the Inspiring Learning for All checklists to identify your strengths and areas to improve.
- Identify evidence to demonstrate that you meet the stated goals of Inspiring Learning for All and decide where there are gaps in your evidence.
- Develop an action plan to improve your services and overall support for learners.
- Assess learning outcomes for users; for this you can use the generic learning outcome system which is fully explained in the 'Measure Learning' section of the website; the evidence of learning outcomes that you collect will feed in to your action planning and support your advocacy work.

- Develop a convincing case and an advocacy strategy that will help you to win support for learning both internally and externally.
- Feed this back to develop individuals, teams and your organization.

If you want a more generic plan for your impact evaluation programme we offer one in section 8 of the next chapter, based on the experience of the Global Libraries Initiative.

Part 3
The bigger picture

11

Doing national or international evaluation

This chapter is aimed at people who are interested in evaluating libraries at national or international level. The issues covered, including changes in thinking about international development impact evaluation and about ethical evaluation, and current developments in evaluation of public access computing, may also interest other readers.

11.1 Looking at the national and international picture

In this chapter we try to draw out some of the lessons that we have learnt from our impact evaluation work in various countries, and especially our international work for the Global Libraries Initiative (GL) and the International Federation of Library Associations (IFLA). We have tried to be cautious in generalizing too far because no two international projects are alike but some of the impact evaluation issues are likely to recur in some form in any large-scale projects.

(For more information about the Global Libraries Initiative see the note (1) to the introduction of this book. More information on the two IFLA work areas with which we have been involved, can be found in this note[38].)

11.2 Negotiate the terminology

Our international evaluation work has made one thing clear: the technical terms that we have suggested at the beginning of this book will not work across the board. We know from our involvement with impact specialists in different countries that some of the terms that we use, such as 'impact' and 'advocacy', do not readily translate into several East European languages (for instance Lithuanian or Romanian), at least if we wish to convey the same sense. Other terms, such as 'assessment', are used in particular and conflicting ways by different parts of the evaluation community (in UK education research, where assessment normally relates to student performance, versus US causation studies, where it denotes qualitative evaluation), and still others, such as the term for 'evidence' when referring to social science research evidence, has a different level of meaning in particular countries (such as Sweden – where it conveys the sense of legal proof). It is important to check out meanings of any potentially confusing evaluation words when working at international or national levels.

11.3 Respond to the national impact challenge

The world of library impact evaluation is changing, as politicians wrestle with the fall-out from the global economic crisis and every type of service is called into question. Library service managers in North America and Western Europe are responding to the evaluation and advocacy demands of their new political environments in various ways. They may:

- commission general public or public library **user perception studies** which usually demonstrate positive attitudes to these libraries – even amongst people who don't use them!
- call on or collaborate with academic researchers to conduct **large-scale evaluations** of the economic and social effects of public libraries (Bryson, Usherwood and Streatfield, 2002; Becker et al., 2010), or of public access ICT users (Sciadas et al., 2012), or public access to computers and the internet through public libraries (e.g. Bertot et al., 2010, 2011; Hoffman, Bertot and Davis, 2012); or studies of school libraries (Todd, Gordon and Lu, 2011), the results of which can be used for advocacy (see Scholastic Research Foundation, 2008)
- hire consultants to evaluate the **economic impact** of their services by, for example, the British Library (Spectrum Strategy Consultants, 2004), or TNS Infratest (2010)
- engage in professional development to equip themselves and their staff to undertake **qualitative impact evaluation** of services, through action research, such as the Impact Implementation Programme involving 22 UK university library teams (Payne and Conyers, 2005; Markless and Streatfield, 2005, 2008) or through professional association workshops (Markless and Streatfield, 2006)
- join **international library development projects** with strong components of impact evaluation and advocacy at national level, such as GL, or, on a more limited scale, the 'Enabling access to knowledge through libraries in developing and transition countries' (EiFL) programme, which, amongst other things, collects advocacy data for public libraries through an ambitious public perceptions survey (TNS RMS East Africa, 2011; Elbert, Fuegi and Lipeikaite, 2012).

Other models of large-scale and strategic impact evaluation are likely to emerge. Meanwhile, what can we learn from what has gone before?

11.4   What can national or international library evaluation try to achieve?

We have already noted some reasons why library service managers get involved in impact evaluation, and national or international impact evaluators may have similar agendas, but there is wider scope here for encouraging change. In a recently published examination of the consequences of 23 research projects funded by Canada's International Development Research Centre, Fred Carden (2009) identifies three ways in which research can contribute to better governance, as:

1   Encouraging open inquiry and debate
2   Empowering people with the knowledge to hold governments accountable
3   Enlarging the array of policy options.

Although the IDRC projects are large in scale and international in scope, these three principles appear to present an appropriate challenge for library service evaluators.

Taking an optimistic view, as service evaluation and advocacy become increasingly part of the discourse of public sector development, more benign and democratic forms of evaluation are likely to be considered in many countries, echoing the academic debate of recent years. Within the library field, both GL and IFLA lead the way in encouraging localized approaches to evaluation and encompassing disadvantaged groups within the evidence gathering, if not yet full democratization of control of the evaluation programmes.

11.5   Are you ready for impact evaluation?

When we recently looked at how to use impact evaluation to support national development of public libraries in various countries (Streatfield and Markless, 2011) we started by gauging how ready countries are for such a move. The countries that we know something about fall into three categories:

1   In countries where there is no strong tradition of library development, evaluation of library services is usually confined to token gathering of performance statistics, unless there are externally funded projects. The priority for evaluation of funded projects is probably to provide the funder

with assurance that the project had been completed. Normally the main focus here is on change to the services on offer rather than changes to the users of services or to the communities affected. The exception is where funders insist that grantees collect evidence of the broader impact of services. This can create problems in such countries because there is limited expertise in impact evaluation.

2 In the former Communist states of Eastern Europe and in other countries where the government tends towards centralist authority, monitoring and evaluation requirements and data collection methods are usually prescribed centrally. The focus is likely to be on limited service performance data to confirm that the national plan is being successful; if there are prescribed targets there may be process or output indicators to show that these are being met. Public advocacy has little significance in this context although aligning library services with potentially influential political patrons could be important.

3 In other countries with more or less well developed education and public libraries, there is usually a growing awareness of, and interest in, more challenging forms of evaluation. This has sometimes been prompted by the advent of New Managerialism in the public services during the 1980s and 90s, or, more recently, by the growing political and economic effects of the global financial crisis. Unfortunately, at the point where the more malign effects of New Managerialist evaluation are being recognized (for example, leading to the abandonment of the draconian Best Value programme of public sector performance judgement in the UK), government austerity measures introduced in Europe in response to the financial crisis are likely to be facilitated by further selective evaluation based on public sector rationing criteria. Public advocacy based on impact evidence is being increasingly recognized as important to the survival of libraries in such volatile environments. (See examples below).

Each category poses particular challenges and it is important to take account of where you are and the implications of this when planning impact evaluation (or even deciding whether it is feasible yet and in what form).

11.6 Start evaluation with programme design – and learn as you go

The Global Libraries approach to impact planning and assessment (their preferred description for impact evaluation) is to introduce it at the beginning of their country programmes and incorporate it into all project phases. Although no other library development programme has the same level of management and resources, they can aspire (like GL) to design an evaluation that is 'rigorous and practical, a shared enterprise and timely' and reviewed at all stages of any development project.

Since the early work of the two precursor projects in Chile and Mexico which paved the way for the GL initiative, evaluation of the various country programmes has evolved gradually. Some of the strands in this evolution include:

1 Moving from a main focus on performance monitoring and measurement towards more ambitious efforts to evaluate the impact of public access ICT on people's lives.
2 A parallel movement from measurement and reporting towards what is essentially action research, in which what is learnt at each stage is fed into efforts to improve aspects of the service offered.
3 A gradual refocusing of IPA work in some countries, which are progressively targeting the aspects of their services which they see as important for further evaluation (such as economic value in Latvia or cultural activities in Poland).
4 A gradual shift towards more innovative evidence-collection methods, such as the use of pop-up surveys, computer-assisted telephone interviews and contingent valuation to explore the perceived economic value of public libraries.
5 Finally, all of the IPA specialists support efforts to use IPA results in sustained advocacy on behalf of public libraries, as discussed in more detail by Sawaya et al. (2011) and at a more general level by Streatfield and Markless (2011).

(Summary based on Streatfield et al., 2012, 9)

On a more modest scale, IFLA has learnt from their earlier experience with the FAIFE initiative, in which impact evaluation came fairly late and focused on their training programme. For Building Strong Library Associations they work on an impact evaluation framework from the beginning and are able to train their local programme facilitators in the basics of evaluation before evidence collection begins, so that the transition to collecting impact evidence and applying the results is more coherent.

11.7 Identifying a framework for national and international impact evaluation

Are there good models available for national-level evaluators who are thinking about evaluating the impact of libraries? Other potential large-scale funders will find obvious scope for learning from Global Libraries, but what can library developers at national level learn? We think that the GL framework provides a basis for systematic evaluation and one that can be adapted for use in countries which are not likely to receive the level of resourcing for their libraries that GL offers to public libraries in their grantee countries. We also think that the framework can be adapted for national-level evaluation of education and health libraries. (If you are interested in a fuller account of this framework, see Streatfield and Markless, 2009).

Before going on to outline our view of the GL approach to evaluation, it is important to state that what follows *is* our view, and should not be taken as representing the official view of Global Libraries or of the Bill and Melinda Gates Foundation.

11.7.1 Evaluating a development programme

What is the relationship between library service development, service monitoring and impact planning and assessment? For GL, evaluation is integral to development, as shown in Figure 11.1.

In this programme, the evaluators focus library service performance measurement mainly on public access to computers, since the programme is about introducing computers into libraries for public use and training library

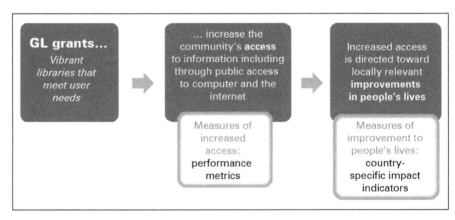

Figure 11.1 *Dimensions of GL IPA information collection (Fried, Kochanowicz and Chiranov, 2010)*

staff to support this process. The most challenging dimension of this work, the impact evaluation, is (so far) mainly undertaken at national level.

11.7.2 Exploring impact

The good news is that the GL definition of impact is almost identical to the one we offer at the beginning of this book. Fittingly, for a programme operating internationally over several years, the GL definition adds a dimension about the breadth and depth of change. An impact:

- may be wide-ranging, affecting many stakeholders, from library staff to library users and from local government officials to local community groups; or
- may be more specific, directly affecting only one group of stakeholders
- can occur on levels from the superficial to the life-changing.

The IPA Road Map stresses that:

GL does not expect grantees to undertake attribution studies. In the context of Global Libraries, IPA concentrates on planning to make a difference through the country grant program; on assessing implementation (what has been put in place); and on gathering evidence of benefits that have accrued or changes that have been made since the country grant program began. We can reasonably assume that the country grant program has contributed to the changes identified and has 'added value' but there may be other influences involved so we do not seek to prove a causal relationship.

For a large-scale programme such as the GL, it is important to strike a balance between the different levels and types of impact, as well as between limited and partial short-term impacts and difficult-to-evaluate longer-term effects.

Figure 11.2 on the next page shows the main levels at which a major programme can have an impact.

Clearly some of these areas of impact require long-term attention but you can collect evidence of impact about others within an annual planning cycle.

Grantees are encouraged to identify the most relevant impact areas for their own countries; themes where the country grant programme can potentially have a large impact on individuals, organizations and communities. The main areas suggested where public access to information in libraries can make a difference are:

Education   Agriculture
Health   Communication
Culture and Leisure   E-government
Economic development

Figure 11.2 *Levels of potential impact (Global Libraries Initiative 2008) (Streatfield and Markless, 2009)*

A matrix is provided in the *IPA Road Map*[39] that covers each of these impact areas in greater detail and shows outcomes for libraries and librarians, short-term impacts on communities and users, and longer-term impacts on the community and society. This matrix is designed to offer ideas to grantees when holding local discussions and making decisions to create their own impact framework. Grantees are encouraged to ask themselves which of these elements are most relevant to their community, government and other stakeholders and what their objectives should be in each of these areas of activity. They are also advised to avoid spending unnecessary resources on assessing elements that will not add much to the picture. One element of this matrix is shown in Example 11.1.

Example 11.1   IPA Road Map for impact area: Education

Outcomes for libraries and library workers (equivalent to our 'success criteria')
Local content developed by library workers to offer a wider range of learning opportunities
Library workers offer online reading programs
Libraries offer a wide variety of material to motivate children

Short-term impacts on community/users
Wider range of people take up learning opportunities (marginalized groups, unemployed etc.)
Acquire job-related skills and qualifications through access to online courses/tutorials (e.g. writing CV/résumé, marketing, ICT)
More school children and college students use ICT in the library

Longer term impacts on community/society
Enhanced quality of human capital
Increased capacity for participating in new economic domains
Improved quality of school/college work though access to up-to-date information
Improved literacy through increased motivation and reading programs

---

You should be able to develop a similar matrix for your own evaluation using the guidance in Part 2 of this book.

When grantees have decided on the locally relevant impacts that they want to achieve through their GL programme they are encouraged to formulate impact indicators to provide information on programme effectiveness in meeting impact goals. Help is then offered for the other stages in the impact evaluation process. This support provided to country impact specialists follows the general principles set out in this book.

In the interests of sanity, we will continue to use 'impact evaluation' in the same way that it is used in the remainder of this book. If you *are* interested in different views on what impact evaluation involves, please read the definition of **Impact planning and assessment** in the glossary, 'Impact and all that', at the beginning of this book.

11.8   Developing an approach to impact evaluation at national level

Global Libraries offers a well thought-through international intervention strategy with a strong evaluation emphasis focused on 'changing people's lives'. GL participants also show a willingness to learn and to share what is learned, as evinced by the recent special issue of the journal *Performance Measurement and Metrics*, which is devoted to impact planning and assessment of GL, and where all but one of the contributors are current or former country IPA specialists (in eight of the countries involved with GL) and all are committed to sharing what they are learning with library developers and national public library evaluation specialists in non-GL countries (Streatfield et al., 2012).

The GL IPA framework has developed over the past ten years as a process of continuous learning by GL IPA staff, impact consultants and grantee (country-level) IPA specialists. We have been lucky to be involved in this process, partly because it has enabled us to identify principles and key practical points that we think are important for national-level evaluation of libraries.

11.8.1 Some principles of impact evaluation

Turning to the principles first, we believe that:

- library managers and staff should be empowered to understand and conduct impact evaluation work
- key decisions about the scope and focus of this work should be influenced by those directly involved, including service users where feasible
- impact indicators should be appropriate for the service and not imposed by an outside agency for political purposes
- flexibility is needed in conducting impact evaluation, but based on rigorous application of appropriate evidence-collection methods
- given its relative novelty for most library service managers, impact evaluation should be viewed as a process of managing organizational change.

You may not agree with all or any of these principles, but we suggest that an effective programme of national impact evaluation should be based on a shared set of views about what impact evaluation means in practice, and that this set of views should be supported by all of the key participants in the process.

11.8.2 Doing national impact evaluation: key practical considerations

The GL approach to impact planning and assessment is enshrined in the 'IPA Road Map', which was created to support grantees (and especially the grantee IPA specialists). The IPA journey for grantees is presented in four stages, as shown in Figure 11.3.

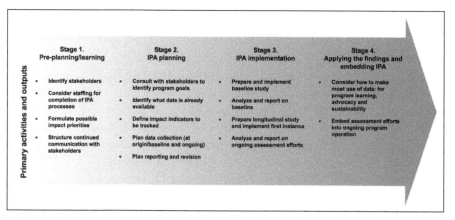

Figure 11.3 *The four stages of IPA (Fried et al., 2010)*

We do not slavishly follow the IPA Road Map (which we helped to create) here, because this was essentially produced to guide participants in the Global Libraries Initiative and to meet the requirements of that programme. However, there are clear points of correspondence with the IPA Roadmap and we acknowledge our debt to Global Libraries for helping us to shape and develop our ideas. Although the following questions and issues have emerged from our experience of national impact evaluations we believe that they are also relevant to more local or regional work.

11.8.3 Why are you doing impact evaluation – and how?

Before embarking on a national (or international) programme of impact evaluation it is important to be clear about what kind of evidence you want to gather and for what purpose. Who are you seeking to influence with your impact evidence and how will you use that evidence? What kind of performance measurement and impact evaluation base are you building on? What resources, including accessible expertise can you draw on to help?

Example 11.2   Small-scale international impact evaluation

We encourage evaluators to focus on the impact of innovations on service users, but this may not be the only focus. When IFLA adopts our general impact evaluation approach for its FAIFE work (Bradley, 2009), the planning team decides to focus their impact indicators on the effects of the programme training on the library staff who take part rather than on the users of their services. This choice of focus is dictated by the limited resources (time and people) available for evaluation work.

11.8.4 Who will lead the evaluation programme?

You will be lucky if you can recruit an impact evaluation specialist to lead this work who has the full set of skills and experience for the job, especially if you are in a developing or emergent country. Candidates are likely to have library performance measurement experience, social science research competence or international development evaluation expertise, but probably not all three. Global Libraries grantee experience of this kind of recruitment shows that new IPA specialists from any of these backgrounds rapidly learn what they need in order to undertake library evaluation. (It is probably easiest to make up any shortfall in library experience – if you have librarians involved in managing your evaluation.)

The same considerations apply if you are able to recruit a team of people to lead your impact work – your target should be to secure complementary skills across the team. If not, you may be able to get help from sub-contracted consultants or from 'friendly' academic staff.

How do you envisage collecting the evaluation evidence? The choices are likely to be between employing a survey organization, involving academic research staff or assembling a library organization-based team to orchestrate collection of evidence by library staff (or, of course, a combination of these). All have their merits and weaknesses:

1 Commissioned surveys are expensive, but if they are done well there are clear advocacy benefits in having a disinterested organization doing the work. If you make the right choice of vendor the work should be done well, if you have prepared a clear set of terms of reference for the work. Expressed cynically, if you don't ask for it you won't get it – unless you pay more.

2 Academic researchers are likely to be sympathetic to your real needs and you may be able to get some 'free' research done by students looking for dissertation topics, but you will have to commit time to supervising this type of work to ensure that it meets your need. Again being cynical, academic researchers are likely to be more interested in the underlying organizational research issues than library managers and may pursue their own research agenda rather than address your particular evaluation concerns.

3 In-house evaluation will be less immediately costly because you may be able to divert library manager time from other tasks. However, it does take time to build up the necessary level of expertise to design, manage and deliver an evaluation programme. The main drawback with this approach is that however good the evidence you assemble it will appear to be 'special pleading' – librarians evaluating libraries.

11.8.5 Who will influence the evaluation programme?

Since libraries are not developed in a political vacuum it is important to identify and if possible involve key players from central and local government, the academic world, business and other people who are interested in your libraries. You might aim to build up a sense of ownership of the process by getting key players involved in planning and designing the programme and, crucially, in helping to interpret the evaluation findings and their implications. You can strengthen this sense of ownership by ensuring that you communicate regularly with the key players, so that they know what you are doing and what your work is showing.

11.8.6 What will you focus on?

Where will you focus your impact evaluation efforts? If you are looking to bring about change in a political environment (such as health, education or public libraries) it probably makes sense to carefully relate what you are doing to national or local/organizational political priorities. (When Global Libraries decide to conduct a Pan-European survey of public perceptions of public libraries and of their role in public access computing, they start by conducting a review of European Union policies and where public libraries have, or might have, a role in helping to achieve these policies.)

This book draws attention to many of the areas where libraries can make a difference. You may like to initiate discussions with key stakeholders, including library managers and, crucially, library service users and potential users, to build up a picture of where you need to be able to show whether your libraries are likely to make a difference to people's lives. One of the impressive features of the Global Libraries Initiative is that countries interested in joining the programme are supported in preparing a full proposal. A key requirement is that they should engage with stakeholders to explore local priorities for developing the programme. This typically involves (amongst other elements) running focus groups for potential users to find out what benefits they anticipate from having public access to ICT. How many library development programmes commence with this level of user consultation?

11.9 Ethical evaluation

Throughout this book we encourage library service managers to work towards achieving high standards of evaluation. We draw attention to ethical behaviour when collecting evidence from respondents and in interpreting the evidence collected. Ethical evaluation becomes even more important when operating at national or international level, because the distorting effects of political pressures are likely to be greater and because distorted evidence is likely to have a greater negative effect when applied at national level. The reinterpretation of the nature of impact evaluation referred to in Chapter 3 extends to reconsideration of ethical evaluation or more general consideration of values in evaluation (House and Howe, 1999). This evaluation debate has led various evaluation professional bodies to seek a shared professional stance on ethical issues (e.g. the American Evaluation Association, 1995). The concept of ethical evaluation is being further pursued by individuals, such as Datta (1999) who examines whether published guiding principles are helpful in aligning a range of different interpretations of ethical positions. She concludes that:

- diverse evaluators *agree* that the evaluator should not be an advocate (or, presumably, an adversary) of a specific program in the sense of taking sides, of a preconceived position of support (or destruction)
- there is *agreement* that the evaluator should be an advocate for making sure that as many relevant cards as possible get laid on the table, face up, with the values (worth, merit) showing
- there is *agreement* that the evaluator must be aware of how less powerful voices or unpopular views, positions, information can get silenced and make special efforts to ensure that these voices (data, view, information) get heard.

We hope that evaluators looking at libraries from a national perspective will agree with these three points.

How do evaluation ethics affect national or international library service managers or evaluators? Here are some issues and points where we think that practical decisions are needed:

11.9.1 Some ethical considerations for service managers

The main issues for library service managers are about what is practical given the constraints of time and resources. Some of the practical decisions required are as follows:

1 **Whether to employ or train evaluators rather than rely on external experts** – if you secure in-house evaluation capacity, this gives you the flexibility to undertake short-term and small-scale evaluations of specific initiatives and should help to secure staff support for evaluation work. Many managers argue that it is better to do evaluation yourself rather than have arbitrary

impact indicators and targets imposed from outside. On the other hand, if you conduct evaluations internally this may give rise to suspicion that the results have been manipulated and only the most dedicated internal evaluator will be able to conduct the more sophisticated forms of evidence-gathering.

2 **How to align impact areas appropriately.** In some countries, decisions about impact areas and indicators may be reached without reference to library service managers. However, if you can make or recommend a choice, alignment with national or regional government priorities should make it easier to construct an advocacy case that resonates at policy levels. On the other hand, since each library service has a different history and current circumstances (including the state of the library) evaluation focused on local priorities may be more important. Whatever the choice, it is vital to ensure that you choose the impact areas and impact indicators to show what difference the library service can make; you won't be able to show this difference if you adopt a national or regional priority without indicating how the potential library contribution can be evaluated.

3 **Find enough time to assemble evidence.** In many countries there may be pressure on library services to conduct evaluations to fit within annual funding or planning cycles or, if international or national funding is involved, to complete evaluation programmes within two or at most three years. This is problematic at the one-year level, since you will find it difficult to assemble any evidence of significant change within such a short time period, but it may still be too early to evaluate change at the three-year level, since it is well established that major change (such as introducing public access ICT through public libraries) usually takes from three to five years (Fullan, 2007). If you hurry an evaluation this may lead to misdirection in focus onto what can be measured in time rather than what should be evaluated. The result if you do this may be insufficient evidence of good enough quality to make an effective advocacy case for service sustainability. (In this context, GL offers a good practice example by committing to a five-year programme.) It is interesting to note that there have been relatively few longitudinal studies of library service impact.

4 **Address social inclusion.** The literature on democratic evaluation emphasizes the importance of including marginalized people within evaluation programmes. This raises the issue of what social exclusion means in the context of library services. If people are excluded from equitable access to libraries through access problems, bureaucratic rules or other means, will this make it difficult to include them in service evaluation? How can such difficulties be overcome?

5 **Who takes the lead in advocacy?** Should library service managers take a
   leading advocacy role in interpreting evaluation findings and presenting
   messages to policy shapers and decision makers or should you rely upon
   respected 'champions' who are not seen to have a vested interest in
   libraries? Is it possible to take a leading advocacy role *and* to play a
   significant part in service evaluation or will this inevitably lead to focusing
   on only collecting positive evidence?

11.9.2 Some ethical considerations for evaluators

Although evaluators should be independent of the library services that they are
evaluating, in many smaller countries this may not be feasible in practice, since
evaluators, policy shapers and library service managers are all likely to operate
within the same circles. Retaining an independent stance becomes more
problematic if you are an evaluator employed by a library service or part of the
library community. Whatever your position, evaluators have a number of issues
to manage:

1 **Pressure from key participants.** Demands of funders, policy shapers and
   library service managers can all put pressure on evaluators to focus on
   evidence of success rather than evidence of fundamental change and to
   minimize the amount of evidence collection required, since this may put
   additional burdens on the library services. If you give way to this pressure
   this may lead you to make the wrong methodological choices for evidence
   collection (this usually results in over-reliance on routine performance data
   collection which tells the evaluator little about changes being produced by
   new or modified library services). In turn this may lead you to go through
   the motions of evaluation without focusing on significant change, or to
   focus on library activities instead of on their effects on users.
2 **Insufficient time for effective evaluations.** If you are over-optimistic about
   what level of change can be seen in one, two or three years, this may lead
   you to hurry evaluations, which may in turn lead to distortion in
   interpretation of results, especially by practitioner-evaluators who need to
   keep your own services going and who may be 'researching for survival.'
3 **Opting for the simple logic model of evaluation.** Although many
   organizational interventions are likely to be complicated or complex, it is
   perhaps not surprising that organizational managers or programme
   evaluators usually choose the politically expedient route of regarding impact
   evaluation as a simple logic mechanistic process (Ramirez, 2007). It is
   particularly difficult for the internal evaluator to propose and implement

more complex evaluation models, especially if these do not provide the option of comparing progress over time against baseline evidence.

4 **The evaluator as advocate.** If you are a library evaluator, can you sustain an ethical advocacy position when you are broadly (or in the case of evaluators employed by library services, specifically) identified with the existing services? Returning to Datta's principles of ethical advocacy for evaluators listed above:

- *As a library evaluator, are you inevitably an advocate of a specific programme in the sense of taking sides, of a preconceived position of support?*
- *Can you ensure that as many relevant cards as possible get laid on the table, face up, with the values (worth, merit) showing?*
- *To what extent can you ensure that less powerful voices or unpopular views get heard?*

11.10 Emergent evaluation revisited

Two difficulties are likely to arise when evaluating change at national level:

1 Some countries have little experience of evaluating the impact of library services on users. Faced with making the shift from performance measurement to impact evaluation, managers tend to be cautious about identifying impacts. They usually focus on changes to the library service and to library staff rather than on changes to people's lives. When this happens managers often hear anecdotal evidence of changes in what users do, how they use information and how they view libraries. Sometimes they then try to change the focus towards evidence of change to users. These 'stories of change' are really important when making the advocacy case for libraries but will be dismissed if they are not seen as supported by reliable evidence

2 Most plans for impact evaluation are not flexible enough to enable a shift in focus towards important areas of change. To combat this, it may be helpful to think about managing projects as a series of linked steps (for example, in the public library arena: buying and installing computers – training staff to use them – offering public access – training users; and, in parallel: measuring the level of use – assessing impact on users). This pattern may not work well when major change (such as introducing IT-based services) is introduced into a new setting (such as communities where there is little ICT access) and where the interests, concerns, expertise and communication networks of these communities are likely to be complicated

or complex. In this situation, the people designing new services usually don't know what changes these services may create.

People involved in assessing the impact of international development projects are well aware of these issues and have adopted two related and more flexible assessment approaches in response – 'emergent evaluation' and 'developmental evaluation'(we referred to both of these earlier). These approaches assume that when people introduce new services they will not know

- exactly how these services will work in the new setting
- all of the likely effects of these services on users
- which changes from the user perspective will be most important

– until the services are running.

We recommend that you continue with your evaluation programme but also collect as much relevant information as possible until you start to get a picture of what change is happening and who is affected. You should then be able to design an impact framework that takes account of these changes. We describe this problem when talking about emergent evaluation in Chapters 2 and 6 and discuss various ways of collecting such evidence, through stories, interviews and other means in Chapter 6. Developmental evaluation specialists recommend that if you are finding new evidence of change you should 'update the baseline as new understandings of the beginning situation emerge through engagement as change unfolds.' (Patton, 2011, 257). This should enable you to adjust the evaluation focus without undermining the impact evaluation work that is already going on. (There is likely to be an additional cost here for the design and piloting of questions added to surveys or other evidence collection approaches.)

11.11 Plan the evaluation

Once you have agreed on the focus you should be well placed, with a little help from this book, to identify your impact objectives and translate these into impact indicators. You should also be able to align these indicators with whatever performance measurement you already have in place. The main task then is to plan the evidence collection process in detail (who will do what, and when) and to think about what kinds of reports you will need and for what purposes.

11.12 Starting to enact your plan

The Irish banker Vincent Dooley once observed that 'The trouble with plans is that they have to degenerate into action.' This is the point we have reached and this is where the scale of your impact evaluation will determine how you implement your plans. The previous section of this book has described a process of impact evaluation that lends itself to year-on-year comparison. If you are taking this approach and if you are looking to develop and evaluate new services as part of that approach it is important to establish the baseline – by gathering evidence to see what the situation is before you begin to innovate so that you can reasonably argue that any changes were affected by (if not directly attributable to) your innovations.

11.13 Sustain the process

If you are embarking on an ambitious programme of evaluation, you will now be committed to a more or less continuous cycle of baseline evidence collection, analysis of results, reporting, preparing for the next phase of evaluation, evidence collection and so on.

Increasingly, you are likely to concentrate on using the evaluation findings (as evidence of change accumulates). You will probably want to combine data from your performance measurement work with in-depth illumination of the impact of the service captured in stories from users and library staff. You should be able to use these reports for service review and development purposes as well as for advocacy, where it is important to tailor the reports for the specific target audiences – what are the key messages from your evidence for this group?

If the programme of evaluation is successful you will have questions about how to sustain this work and build it into your normal ways of working. One effect of focusing on impact evaluation may be to strengthen library data collection at national level (judging by the experience in GL countries such as Latvia and Lithuania). You may also have scope for training library staff to conduct impact evaluation at local level to further embed an evaluation culture.

11.14 Thoughts on advocacy

This book is not about advocacy but anyone involved in national or international impact evaluation will have to consider the questions that arise when using the results of this work to influence decision makers. Here are some issues for anyone facing this challenge:

1 Gathering good-quality impact evidence and using it in advocacy on behalf of libraries is a worthwhile activity, but we should always remember that decisions about libraries are taken in the political world, where the most logical argument does not always win and may not even be heard. A soundly based case for change is most likely to work if the decision makers are already predisposed to make that change. Impact evidence can help but it is only part of the picture.

2 There is a tendency for the people who conduct the evaluation to interpret the results but this is not the only way. If you are seeking to strengthen libraries through a national programme, one sign of its strength (and a potentially useful impact indicator) is whether library service managers are involved in interpreting the results before they set firmly into the evaluation report. When conducting research or evaluation, we always try to involve the people who are being researched in formative workshops to look at the emerging findings and offer their interpretations of the findings and what they mean.

3 Impact evaluation takes time, energy and effort and when reporting on such work there is a strong temptation to show everyone how much work was involved by describing the research process and showing lots of tables of results. This is not helpful in advocacy. The evaluation report should concentrate on the key findings and their implications. Other evaluators may be interested in seeing all the results and how you obtained them – but almost nobody else. Avoid the temptation to show all your evidence.

4 The people who conduct the evaluation are probably not the best people to 'sell' the findings, because 'They would say that, wouldn't they?' Who can put the library case most credibly in your organization or community? Can you persuade people who are respected by the key decision makers in your community to act as champions for your libraries? If so, what key findings and supporting evidence can you provide them with so that your case is heard?

11.15 Some examples of impact evidence and advocacy

Advocacy based on impact evidence is mainly about deciding who you need to convince and looking carefully at your evidence (or gathering more evidence) to persuade them. But what does this mean in practice? Here are two examples drawn from the Global Libraries Initiative:

Example 11.3   European Union level

When the five EU countries that are part of the Global Libraries Initiative come together to think about how to raise awareness of the role that public libraries can play in supporting EU policies, they begin by identifying who they needed to influence. The list includes:

1 The European Commission and Directorates-General
2 National and local governments

- Ministries (including public libraries and those responsible for health, education, inclusion, communication, and economic development)
- National agencies
- Local authorities
- Municipalities
- Grantees and staff of the Global Libraries Initiative of the Bill and Melinda Gates Foundation
- Public libraries (including community libraries) and library officials
- Library sector stakeholders – European Bureau of Library, Information and Documentation Associations (EBLIDA); National Authorities on Public Libraries in Europe (NAPLE), IFLA, and national Library Associations
- The ICT for development community
- National/local media.

Their first thought is that they have a lot of evidence about the part that public access computing plays in connecting library users to Europe. However, they look more closely and find that there are gaps in this evidence and differences in how each country collects it, so more consistent evidence is needed.

The response is to commission a major cross-European survey of perceptions of public libraries in 18 EU member countries, which aims to provide public libraries in the EU, and the national/cross-national organizations that support these libraries, with valid impact data they can use for advocacy purposes.

Example 11.4   Country level

In this example from the 'Father's Third Son Development Project' in Latvia, the focus is on sharing learning about effective libraries within the country. To do this:

1 They run impact planning workshops with different stakeholders, where their expectations are discussed and agreement is made about desired outcomes.

(Two workshops are held – at the beginning of the project and during the revision of the impact evaluation framework).

2 They seek close co-operation with the authority responsible for national statistics of public libraries. Building co-operation in Latvia starts from the very beginning of the project. They agree to include impact indicators into the national statistics after the project impact studies end. The 'Cultural Map' information system that is used for collecting national statistics will be used in future for collection of impact data.

3 A conference for library managers, municipality leaders and other stakeholders is held after each impact study and in-depth study. In Latvia these are highly valued by librarians because participants are given an opportunity to learn how the studies are conducted, what the data mean, and to practise how to use data and evidence in practical sessions.

4 Regional workshops are run for librarians – there are 28 regional libraries in Latvia which regularly organize workshops for their local librarians. This is an opportunity for the project's Impact Specialist and/or Advocacy Specialist to share learning and explain/discuss study findings.

5 They hold brainstorming sessions with different stakeholders during the planning phase of the advocacy training programme – these are very valuable.

6 Various more attractive ways are found to share findings than just a formal report. In Latvia they use desk calendars to share main findings to stakeholders (sending them to each municipality and to the main stakeholders). Besides calendars, they produced notebooks and bookmarks that explain the study findings.

(Streatfield, et al., 2012, 60–61)

In the first example, weighing up the strength of the available impact evidence leads to a decision to gather more evidence in a different way. In the second case, efforts are made to involve the people who are engaged in library service delivery at various stages of the impact evaluation process.

11.16 Impact evaluation, advocacy and service sustainability

We wind up this chapter with three observations on the relationships between impact evaluation, advocacy and service sustainability. It is often asserted that evidence of impact is a key to service sustainability and we accept that this should be the case. However:

1 We have noted some tendency amongst national organizations to conflate impact assessment and advocacy, even to the extent of commissioning the collection of impact evidence to support the advocacy case.
2 There is also a tendency to 'cherry-pick' only the most positive evidence in making the advocacy case. In our view, impact evaluation should be seen as an independent process that may or may not give rise to evidence of success and should lead to a 'warts and all' approach to the presentation of findings for advocacy purposes. Most politicians at local or national level can readily identify the 'good news only' approach to presenting evidence and any such approach will rapidly undermine the case being presented.
3 Finally, although we confidently assert that rigorous impact evaluation combined with lucid advocacy should lead to service sustainability, there is comparatively little evidence to suggest that this is how key decisions are usually made. Evidence-based strategic decision making may be highly desirable, but are our societies ready for this? Or are we still at the stage of development characterized by the Irish dramatist George Bernard Shaw, when he said that 'Reformers have the idea that change can be achieved by brute sanity'?

Acknowledgement

The authors would like to express thanks to Monika Elbert and David Fuegi, who have helped to develop our thinking about IPA (as set out in this chapter), in their roles as independent consultants to GL, and to all the GL Grantee IPA Specialists who have so freely shared their knowledge and experience, as well as to Teresa Peters, Sandra Fried, Janet Sawaya and Jeremy Paley, who have all taken important roles within GL in helping to shape the GL approach to IPA.

12
Where do we go from here?

This chapter moves beyond the practical aspects of impact evaluation covered so far. It puts a toe in the water by introducing some issues and offers further sources to take up if you are interested in finding out more.

What else do you need to think about if you want to take impact evaluation seriously? Evaluation can be too narrow, too shallow, too short term or undertaken too soon. We discuss these concerns below and then look at the scope for benchmarking around impact and at where all this work fits with the increasing emphasis on evidence-based library work.

12.1 Getting impact evaluation right

The process introduced in the main part of this book is intended to be practical and to meet the immediate impact evaluation needs of library service managers looking at accountability or seeking to develop their services (or to survive). To keep things as straightforward as possible, we have concentrated on evaluating the impact of parts of your service, especially those parts where you are trying to make a real difference to specific target groups of users or potential users. We have tried to take account of the unprecedented major change that is going on in the library world, especially in relation to electronic service provision and digital literacies, as well as the funding crisis occurring in many countries.

Even so, there is a danger that impact evaluation carried out by service managers can miss important parts of the picture. In particular, there is a risk that impact evaluation can be too narrow in its focus (so that the big picture is missed), too shallow in its execution, too short term (getting instant feedback can be easy but may also be very misleading), and it may miss important change altogether if it is done too soon. How can we avoid these traps?

12.2   Getting beyond the narrow focus

12.2.1 Social capital

How can we look at the big questions about how libraries contribute to the cohesion and development of their communities or organizations? One way of exploring this theme is through the concept of social capital – defined as the stock of active connections among people in a community, or the trust, mutual understanding, and shared values and behaviours that bind the members of human networks and communities and make co-operative action possible (Cohen and Prusak, 2001). According to the World Bank (1999) social capital is not just the sum of the institutions which underpin a society – it is the glue that holds them together.

The basic premise is that interaction enables people to build communities, to commit themselves to each other, and to knit the social fabric. Developing a sense of belonging and getting involved in social networks can, it is claimed, bring great benefits to people, partly through the relationships of trust and tolerance that evolve (Smith, 2001). Without this interaction, on the other hand, trust decays; and eventually begins to manifest itself in serious social problems (Beem, 1999).

Evaluation of social capital focuses on the density of social networks that people are involved in; the extent to which they are engaged with others in informal, social activities; and their membership of groups and associations. A key dimension of social capital is whether interaction is **bonding** (exclusive) or **bridging** (inclusive). The former is more inward-looking and may reinforce exclusive identities and homogeneous groups. The latter is more outward-looking and may encompass people across different social divides (Putnam 2000).

Although the concept of social capital can readily be applied to communities, it is now being explored with firms and organizations as people become

> . . . increasingly suspicious of the 'people, processes, technology' mantra, 'ceaselessly intoned as a summary of the sources of organizational effectiveness'
>
> Cohen and Prusak (2001, 8)

Interestingly, the organizational benefits claimed include better knowledge sharing, due to established trust relationships, common frames of reference and shared goals.

In recent years social inclusion and community building have emerged as central themes in the policies of many governments. Libraries of all kinds have the potential to contribute to the development of social capital; indeed the notion that public libraries have a social impact is an old one and there are numerous examples of libraries setting out to become community hubs and reaching out to marginalized/disadvantaged groups. In the UK a new 'Community,

Diversity and Equality' Group within CILIP has social impact at its heart; and many of the GL countries have adopted a sustained focus on the library contribution to social cohesion and to community identity and heritage. Despite all this, the literature on the role of libraries in building social capital remains sparse (Vårheim, 2007) even though the scope for the approach is explored by Alan Bundy (2003a; 2003b) and by Hillenbrand (2005) in Australia; and Anne Goulding (2004) in the UK; and more recently in a four-year project (PLACE: Public Libraries – Arenas for Citizenship) funded by the Research Council of Norway (Vårheim, 2009). If you are sufficiently interested to explore the possibilities of social capital as a focus for library impact evaluation, Kathleen Swinbourne (2000) offers advice on conducting your own social capital audit (based on experience in Australian public libraries).

12.3 Digging deeper

Our model of impact evaluation should work if you can establish what sort of impact your service is having now and have some feel for what sort of impact it is likely to have one, three or five years hence. Problems arise if the programme that you want to evaluate is inherently innovatory, unpredictable or plain messy. As libraries of all kinds extend the possibilities of electronic information provision, use different types of social media or go beyond familiar ways of conceptualizing and delivering services, it is sometimes difficult to gauge what sort of impact services should be having, because there are no meaningful precedents.

To give an example, when a consortium of university libraries asks whether their joint cataloguing of e-resources (aimed at enhanced access by all kinds of higher education users) is having sufficient effect to justify further joint funding – the short answer is that they don't know enough to begin to predict likely impact over the next few years. Will regionally based resource discovery collaboration be redundant next year or within five years as search engine providers become more ambitious? Current evaluation criteria for this type of service are probably too heavily rooted in past traditions of study and research to be of much use. In this as in other areas where libraries are looking at and doing new things it may take time for evaluation to catch up, or we may have to think about how to evaluate in different ways.

To push this issue further, most approaches to evaluation (possibly including our own) expose service managers to the danger of sliding into utilitarian rationalism – omitting any place for imagination. You can't always specify appropriate objectives at the outset (although this is the first step in our approach). Even so, you may want to try something because it feels like a good idea or in response to a complex problem where you think your solution just might fit.

When looking for new ways to work alongside young people in Swedish libraries, the idea was hatched for young people to submit their own cultural products to be borrowed at libraries; the Demotek was born. It emerged differently in various locations from a shelf in some places to real collaboration with film and culture houses leading to film showings elsewhere. 'There are many different answers to how a Demotek has transformed a library both physically and virtually . . . set up the parameters as to what kind of participatory culture you want . . . daring to make the effort and daring to make the wrong decisions' (Larson, 2010, 76). This project doesn't provide much scope for evaluation based on limited predicted objectives! This is not an argument for jettisoning evaluation. In fact, it is probably more important to evaluate the impact of this type of initiative because it offers the prospect of dramatic improvement if it works. There is a strong case for evaluating the impact of initiatives that take time, energy and effort away from keeping the system working (moving beyond infrastructure maintenance) because this effort is inevitably using up precious energy squeezed out from the thousand and three things that you have to do to keep the system functioning adequately. You need to know whether your innovations are paying off, when you have worked out how to do this.

These difficulties may be relatively new for the library service impact evaluation arena, but other disciplines have been trying to find ways of evaluating messy and evolving innovations for years. To take a leaf from an educational evaluation book, if:

- your programme has complex goals that are difficult to define precisely
- your programme is dominated by 'special' influences, such as the particular character of the institution
- there is insufficient time, a paucity of standard data or uncertainty about what evaluation questions to ask (so that formalized evaluation designs are inappropriate)

then emergent evaluation is probably the answer. (It is a sobering thought that these points were being recognized and pursued in educational evaluation more than 30 years ago, by Parlett and Dearden, 1977). We have already outlined this approach (in Chapter 2) but commend it again here because it:

- gets past the need to specify objectives in advance
- allows you to engage with evaluation even when likely outcomes are hazy
- enables you to concentrate more and more on what emerges as important as you go along, through the idea of progressive focusing.

12.4   Looking long enough

Since most library services are more or less locked into an annual planning cycle and have only limited time to do evaluation, it is not surprising that much evaluation tends to be too short term and superficial to really pick up on impact.

12.4.1 Getting beyond the 'reactionnaire'

The classic post-event questionnaire used to get feedback at the end of most training events is of some use to event managers (to monitor whether participants have a good time, strongly dislike the idiosyncrasies of a trainer, or enjoy the food provided), which is why they are sometimes called reactionnaires. They are of little use in telling you whether the event is effective as an educational opportunity because they are administered too soon after the event for any learning or growth in confidence to be detected or for any enhanced skills or knowledge to be applied. It is feasible to get more useful impact evidence by following up with a selection of participants two to six months after the event to ask what they remember from the experience, whether they feel more confident as a result, what they have applied in their work since (changed behaviour) or what they have otherwise drawn upon, but this is more expensive than collecting 'reactionnaires'.

12.4.2 Premature evaluation

The follow-up interview may do a better job than the reactionnaire in getting at the impact of training events, but in asking about the impact of specific educational experiences we are in danger of over-simplifying a complex process. Race pointed to the dangers of pre-specifying educational targets and learning outcomes:

> In our target driven systems of post-compulsory education, there seems little room for 'Not-yet-successful learning' . . . the most complex ideas probably need to be grasped and lost several times before they are gradually retained more permanently and safely.
>
> Race (2005, 21)

Significant changes in people's behaviour may take a long time to get established. A lawyer may accept the argument for undertaking systematic database searches when working with clients, or a clinician might recognize the need to become more evidence-based in treatment decisions. It may still take months or even years, with follow-up support along the way, before this shift is translated into significant change in how they do their day-to-day work, if this happens at all.

Which of our programme evaluations is sufficiently flexible to pick up on this sort of learning? If you really want to find out the long-term effects of your interventions, it is necessary to think about evidence gathering months or years beyond the initial engagement and about using methods (such as the critical incident interview) that help respondents to identify the effects of your work long after the event.

12.4.3 Choose a longer time-frame

We have already said that the one-year planning cycle becomes an encumbrance if your innovation is complex and the outcomes are problematic. A variation on this theme that crops up in most libraries is the need for dust to settle after restructuring or reorganization. Your impact indicators may not work as well after the changes as before and may now be irrelevant. But since you can't be sure how the newly configured service is bedding down, a short interregnum is probably a good idea, before you decide on your success criteria and targets, once the managers have some experience of the new structures and ways of working.

Changes to library services may be large and complex, with any impacts likely to emerge over a long time period. To give two examples of structural changes in public library services in the UK, many public library service points are realigned as front-line service points incorporating a range of other user services offered by local authorities (such as housing advice or even marriage registration). Similarly, some local authority children's library services are incorporated within a wider range of education, social and health care services to children. In these examples, to judge the public library service impact in isolation makes no sense, but what differences do the converged services make to the library part of the new service and how should the library services change in response? Answers to these questions are only now beginning to emerge and clarity will take time.

In higher education, similar issues are encountered around convergence of libraries and other learning support services. Again, it makes sense to wait and look at impact when managers have some idea of realistic expectations for the new integrated service.

12.5   Getting help

The aim of this book is to enable you to undertake impact evaluation of your library service. However, we recognize that this may involve other people (such as members of your work team) and that not everyone takes naturally to evaluation work. When are they likely to need help and what sorts of help? Dorothy

Williams and her colleagues looked at impact evaluation support needs in a small survey carried out as a follow-up to their review of the available evidence about social, learning and economic impacts of museums, archives and libraries considered earlier (section 3.2). They found that:

> The respondents appeared to fall into two groups: those embarking on impact evaluation with limited experience who wanted help in the form of practical tools and examples of techniques and instruments, and those with greater understanding of the issues who viewed the resources in terms of maintaining professional awareness, keeping up to date and being provided with pointers to relevant resources outwith their normal professional sources of information.
>
> Williams et al. (2005, 546)

We hope that the suggestions in this book will move people beyond this set of problems. But what sorts of support are likely to be needed to undertake the evaluation process described in this book? The cluster of university library teams who adopted this general approach as the core of the action research programme referred to earlier (section 3.5.2) identified several practical problems in doing evaluation (Markless and Streatfield, 2006). They came up with three clusters of problems, which can be approached in different ways. Although these teams all work in academic libraries, both the problems and the pattern of useful support suggested are similar across all types of libraries undertaking impact evaluation.

12.5.1 Problems in managing the impact evaluation process

Most of these problems amount to variations on the usual issues in managing competing priorities and trying to move the service forward:

- what to prioritize and where to start, given the other competing demands on library management time
- conflict in timescales between the reporting needs of the service and the natural evidence-collection cycle for an initiative
- the cost of commercial software (affecting the thrust to digitize as well as access to e-information)
- how to organize appropriate professional development so that library colleagues can help to collect reliable evidence
- understanding current innovations in teaching and learning and how they affect library service provision.

If you are looking for outside help in these areas you should be able to find people who know their way around current ideas on managing change and who are skilled in facilitating this aspect of professional development.

Other management problems seem to be specific to impact evaluation:

- how to isolate the library contribution to joint initiatives (getting collaborators to comment on the effect of the library contribution)
- how to defend choices of research methods (particularly when reporting to academic colleagues, many of whom specialize in aspects of research)
- research design issues:

  - devising questionnaires (assessment tools) to test the skills you want to test
  - screening out library/academic jargon through adequate piloting
  - how to collect 'unadulterated' evidence, given the vested interests of those involved
  - choosing a timescale and timing that will take account of key features in the academic year.

However, all of these difficulties are regularly encountered by anyone managing social science research projects and this is the direction to look in if you want external help. These are also problems where a small amount of expert advice is likely to be a big help.

12.5.2 Practical research issues

Again, we are in the territory of the social science researcher. We have cheated here by offering ways forward [in brackets] after listing the problem, in case you run up against the same problem and would like a quick answer:

- how to overcome the tendency for respondents (e.g. academics/researchers) to tell you what they *should* be doing [ask them to choose from paragraphs giving vignettes/scenarios based on real practice, then to modify them by changing words, to make a closer fit to their own behaviour]
- what to do if users fail to recognize their information literacy limitations [timing is important: e.g. new students have no clear idea of what is expected of them at the beginning of a course of study]
- how to focus on use of websites when users may not know which sites they have used [try interviewing users while they are searching]

- how to deal with unresponsive/defensive/lying interview respondents [look for training in research interview technique]
- how to get feedback from academic staff when they mark student assignments that involve library use [brief them on what evidence you want before they do the marking, then contact them straight afterwards to get feedback].

What external help to look for here depends upon the amount of help that you need. Universities that offer courses in library and information studies should have staff who are experienced in qualitative research and who can facilitate group work for all types of libraries. They may also be able to offer help in evaluating the impact of aspects of your work (such as information literacy support) directly or by deploying students to do practical research in their dissertations. Using students is most effective if you are able and ready to give time to ensure that their evaluation approach and focus produces evidence that can help your library to develop. University faculties of education or departments of teaching and learning have staff who are experienced in evaluating educational interventions. Better yet, if they have the will, academic staff can collaborate creatively with library service managers and their staff to produce better evaluation.

12.5.3 Help in conducting action research

If you decide to adopt an action research approach, the key to any outside help is good facilitation. External facilitators need to choose carefully the nature of the support role at each stage in the process and be ready to act accordingly. They need a range of research, change management and facilitation skills to support this type of development activity (see Markless and Streatfield, 2006).

12.6   Towards impact benchmarking

When you have gathered your impact evidence you should be able to compare (or benchmark) the impact of your services with those of other people. Or should you? Before we look at the possibilities for this kind of comparison, what do we mean by benchmarking and how well is it done in the more traditional library service monitoring areas?

12.6.1 Output and process benchmarking

We commonly encounter two types of service benchmarking:

> **LAWS OF IMPACT EVALUATION 12**
> Benchmarking should be seen as the beginning of a journey of discovery – not as an end in itself. The aim should be to learn more about your service by comparing its impact with that of others – not to secure a place in a table of merit.

1 **Output (or data) benchmarking** – in which you relate the inputs (resources) to the outputs of a defined aspect of your service with one or more library services elsewhere. (For example, you can look at the direct purchase costs of loan materials in relation to the total loans in a given year.) It is fairly easy to achieve these sorts of comparisons, providing that you and the other managers involved define all your terms consistently and measure them equally accurately in each library (e.g. who exactly are included as 'users'?). You will also have to think about the underlying assumptions in such comparisons (in this case, that cheaper loans are better).

2 **Process benchmarking** – in which you look at what you do with the inputs to try to achieve specific outputs (ways of using resources to get particular effects). If you do process benchmarking with other library services, this offers some basis for comparing what processes are undertaken and how (e.g. between the point when a book is selected for purchase and its first loan). However, you again need to think about assumptions. (Is the simplest or cheapest set of processes automatically the best?) To be effective, you should conduct benchmarking with similar services (in size, state of development and aims) and get into discussion with the managers of the other services about any identified differences, to find out why they occur.

The common denominator between these two approaches is that you undertake them in an attempt to improve the quality of the services under review, or to provide a basis for organizational/federal/government service monitoring.

To introduce another layer of complexity, advocates of both output and process benchmarking commonly urge managers to make comparisons with the best comparable organizations in any sector – not just libraries. Output benchmarking, in particular, can degenerate into a control instrument for government agencies, ensuring that organizations commit disproportionate resources to outperforming their peers in narrowly prescribed areas and, in doing so, demonstrate that the service (or the government) is meeting more or less arbitrary improvement targets.

On a more positive note, outcomes-focused process benchmarking appears to be growing in popularity. For example, although Larry Brady of FMC, one of the biggest US corporations (quoted by Kaplan and Norton, 1993), is scathing about most output benchmarking, he is a strong advocate of process benchmarking:

> We ask our managers to go outside the organisation and determine the approaches that will allow achievement of their long-term targets . . . we want to stimulate thought about how to do things differently to achieve the target rather than how to do existing things better.

Taking this argument a step further, if we want to do things differently, it is important to know about the impact of what we are doing now, which brings us to the idea of benchmarking around impact.

12.6.2 Doing impact benchmarking

In order to benchmark around impact you need to be able to compare evidence of the impact of specific services directly with those in another library, as a starting point for thinking about how to deliver better services. As with process benchmarking, this works best if the organizations are similar in size and state of development, but such similarities are not enough. Our work has shown that even when libraries are doing roughly the same things (for example, designing and delivering critical appraisal skills workshops for hospital clinicians) their objectives and targets may well be different. Unless you limit your choice to 'like-minded' library services, you will have to take account of such differences when interpreting relative strength of impact.

There may, of course, be all sorts of reasons why one service has more impact than another, so it is also important to reduce the possibilities. The ideal here is to be able to compare the impacts of a particular service provided in two or more settings in which the same things are done in broadly the same way over a similar time period. It is equally important to use the same evidence-gathering instruments applied in the same way and at the same time. Ideally, you need toolkits of assessment instruments on which to draw (e.g. questionnaires or interview schedules), as well as precise and fully documented descriptions of the processes undertaken to achieve the impact in each setting, so that any subtle differences can be identified.

One of the keys to successful benchmarking is to do it at the right time. You will be ready for benchmarking after you have systematically worked out your service objectives and priorities. This should help in focusing on things that other people are doing that you might not otherwise think about. If benchmarking is started too early it may push you into someone else's agenda and solutions – you may get hooked into their outputs and processes which may not achieve the impact you want.

Is impact benchmarking with organizations other than libraries feasible? Probably not, at this stage. In principle, it should be possible to make meaningful comparisons with specific services offered by other carefully selected organizations. But whether the amount of necessary exploration of the differences between the work environments and organizational drivers is likely to be worthwhile in terms of lessons learnt through the comparisons is highly questionable.

12.7   Towards evidence-based working?

When we discussed evidence-based working earlier (section 1.1.6) we viewed it as part of the research environment but there are signs that evidence-informed and professionally based practice is creeping onto the agenda in libraries as well as in other work areas. What issues do we have to face in moving towards an impact evaluation-friendly environment? What can other work sectors tell us about creating the conditions for evidence-informed working?

12.7.1 Research dissemination and encouraging uptake

In most countries the infrastructure required to disseminate research findings across libraries and information services is generally weak, although as more research findings migrate to the internet there is probably more chance that people will find something relevant. Even so, library service managers may not know that there are any relevant research findings and implications relating to their current preoccupations. If they decide to look for evidence, there may be no immediately obvious source that will bring together the key research findings. If they find relevant evidence, how well are they equipped to interpret findings appropriately? The same is true in other sectors. For instance, although there is a lot of work being done on making research information available in the health field, key health service workers (including hospital consultants) still need help in learning how to look for and interpret research evidence. Most other sectors, such as education and social care, still have a long way to go on making research findings available effectively.

12.7.2 Debating the nature and basis of professional knowledge and practice

This is the issue that matters. Efforts to apply evidence-based approaches to social care and education, as well as to the public health end of the health service continuum, have raised questions about the nature of professional practice and knowledge:

- Advocates of evidence-based working tend to assume that professional practice follows a technical-rational model (emphasizing rules, laws, routines and prescriptions; efficient systems; technical expertise; fixed standards, knowledge seen as graspable and permanent, etc.)
- The role of professional judgement may be undervalued.
- Views of good practice arising from experience and peer discussion also tend to be discounted. This raises a real issue about what constitutes the evidence base.

Uncertainty, messiness, unpredictability and unique situations are part of the working life of most professionals. In such circumstances 'wise judgement under conditions of considerable uncertainty' is the best response available. Evidence-based working makes no allowance for this dimension. For these reasons, we prefer to advocate evidence-informed and professionally based practice. (Our colleague Andrew Booth prefers 'evidence-based and professionally informed', which opens up a further area of debate!)

12.8 Other visions

What changes will the next few years bring? Here are some possible scenarios:

1 Advances in the application of information and social networking technologies, coupled with political and corporate decisions about the relative merits of libraries and other services, will lead to the demise of libraries.
2 Libraries will survive by adapting to increasingly rapid changes and continually demonstrating their effectiveness. (The alternative scenario put forward by Dave Nicholas (2012) that libraries will 'sleepwalk to disaster', is at least equally possible.)
3 Libraries will play a pivotal part in the 'Age of Information' and digital communication by developing and adapting services to match our increasing understanding of information literacy, how people learn and the differentiated information seeking and use behaviour of all major service user groups. This will depend upon researchers who work in such areas as information retrieval and 'information seeking in context' making common cause with library service managers to apply research knowledge in practice. (For a review of some of the potentially fertile areas of application see Kuhlthau, 2005.) In this vision of the future, some specialist libraries will evolve by moving from use of the present simplistic information retrieval

systems to engagement with semantic management of information resources.

And how is the world of impact evaluation likely to change? We conclude by offering one version of the present and immediate future – even though it was written more than two decades ago!

> The evaluation agenda has expanded . . . from an initial focus on student learning outcomes to the study of cases . . . as a better way of understanding the problems and effects of change. Evaluators have become the storytellers and theorists of innovation. . . . Evaluation is an interrogative activity intended to yield useful knowledge about social action.
>
> Kushner and MacDonald (1987)

Does this offer a future for library service managers as the storytellers and practitioners of innovation? We hope so.

References and further reading

Aabø, S. (2005) Are Public Libraries Worth Their Price?: A contingent valuation study of Norwegian public libraries, *New Library World*, **106** (11/12), 487–95, http://dx.doi.org/10.1108/03074800510634973.

Aabø, S. (2009) Libraries and Return on Investment (ROI): a meta-analysis, *New Library World*, **110** (7/8), 311–24, http://dx.doi.org/10.1108/03074800910975142.

Aabø, S. and Audunson, R. (2002) Rational Choice and Valuation of Public Libraries: can economic models for evaluating non-market goods be applied to public libraries? *Journal of Librarianship and Information Science*, **34**, 5–15, http://dx.doi.org/10.1177/096100060203400102.

Aabø, S., Audunson, R. and Vårheim, A. (2010) How do Public Libraries Function as Meeting Spaces? *Library and Information Science Research*, **32** (1), 16–26.

Abma, T. A. (2006) The Practice and Politics of Responsive Evaluation, *American Journal of Evaluation*, **27** (1), 31–43.

American Evaluation Association, Task Force on Guiding Principles for Evaluators (1995). In Shadish, W. R., Newman, D. L., Scheirer, M. A. and Wye, C. (eds) *Guiding Principles for Evaluators*, New Directions for Program Evaluation no. 66, Jossey-Bass, San Francisco.

Ankem, K. (2008) Evaluation of method in systematic reviews and meta-analyses published in LIS, *Library and Information Research*, **32** (101), 91–104.

Arnold, R. (1998) *Target Setting: school and LEA in partnership*, Slough, Education Management Information Exchange, National Foundation for Educational Research.

Audunson, R., Vårheim, A., Aabø, S. and Holm, E. (2007) Public Libraries, Social Capital and Low Intensive Meeting Places. Proceedings of the Sixth International Conference on Conceptions of Library and Information Science – 'Featuring the Future', *Information Research*, **12** (4), 1–13, http://informationr.net/ir/12-4/colis20.html.

Banks, M. A. (2008) Friendly Skepticism about Evidence Based Library and Information Practice, *Evidence Based Library and Information Practice*, **3** (3), 86–90.

Becker, S., Crandall, M. D., Fisher, K. E., Kinney, B., Landry, C. and Rocha, A. (2010) *Opportunity for All: how the American public benefits from Internet access at U.S. Libraries*, Institute of Museum and Library Services, Washington DC, http://tascha.washington.edu/usimpact.

Beem, C. (1999) *The Necessity of Politics: reclaiming American public life*, Chicago, University of Chicago Press.

Bell, J. (2010) *Doing Your Research Project: a guide for first-time researchers in education and social science*, 5th edn, Buckingham, Open University Press.

Bertot, J. C., Jaeger, P. T., and McClure, C. R. (eds) (2011) *Public Libraries and the Internet: roles, perspectives, and implications*, Westport, CT, Libraries Unlimited.

Bertot, J. C., Langa, L. A., Grimes, J. M., Sigler, K. and Simmons, S. N. (2010) *2009–2010 Public Library Funding and Technology Access Survey: survey findings and results*. Report submitted to American Library Association Office for Research and Statistics, Center for Library and Information Innovation, www.plinternetsurvey.org/sites/default/files/publications/2010_plftas.pdf (www.clii.umd.edu).

Bertot, J. C., Sigler, K., McDermott, A., DeCoster, E., Katz, S., Langa, L. A. and Grimes, J. M. (2011) *2010–2011 Public Library Funding and Technology Access Survey: survey findings and results*. Information Policy and Access Center: University of Maryland, www.plinternetsurvey.org.

Bielavitz, T. (2010) The Balanced Scorecard: A systemic model for evaluation and assessment of learning outcomes? *Evidence Based Library and Information Practice*, **5** (2), 35–46, http://ejournals.library.ualberta.ca/index.php/EBLIP/article/view/6928.

Booth, A. (2006) Counting What Counts: performance measurement and evidence-based practice, *Performance Measurement and Metrics*, **7** (2), 63–74.

Booth, A. (2009) Using Evidence in Practice: eleven steps to EBLIP service, *Health Information and Libraries Journal*, **26** (1), 81–4.

Booth, A. and Brice, A. (2004) *Evidence-based Practice for Information Professionals: a handbook*, London, Facet Publishing.

Boston, J., Martin, J., Pallot, J. and Walsh, P. (1996) *Public Management in the New Zealand Model*, Oxford University Press, Auckland, New Zealand.

Bradley, F. (2009) IFLA, Sustainability and Impact Assessment, *Performance Measurement and Metrics*, **10** (3), 167–71.

Brenner, M., Brown, J. and Canter, D. V. (eds) (1985) *The Research Interview: uses and approaches*, London, Academic Press.

Brettle, A. (2012) Learning from Others About Research Evidence, *Evidence Based Library and Information Practice*, **7** (2), 1–3.

Brice, A. and Booth, A. (2004) Consider the Evidence, *CILIP Update*, **3** (6), (June), 32.

Brigham, C. (1999) *EFQM Excellence Model*, London, Improvement and Development Agency.

Brophy, P. (2002) The Evaluation of Public Library Online Services: measuring impact, The People's Network 2002 Workshop series Issues Paper no.1, www.mla.gov.uk/documents/pn_impact.

Brophy, P. (2008) Telling the Story: qualitative approaches to measuring the performance of emerging library services, *Performance Measurement and Metrics*, **9** (1), 7–17.

Brophy, P. (2009) *Narrative-based Practice*, Ashgate Publishing, Surrey.

Brophy, P. and Craven, J. (2004) *Longitude II: a library networking impact toolkit for a user-driven environment*, London, Museums, Libraries and Archives Council, http://books.google.co.uk/books/about/Longitude_II.html?id= QbnjNwAACAAJ&redir_esc.

Bruce, C. S. (1997) *The Seven Faces of Information Literacy*, Adelaide, Auslib Press.

Bryson, J., Usherwood, R. C. and Streatfield, D. R. (2002) *Social Impact Audit for the South West Museums, Libraries and Archives Council*, Centre for Public Library and Information in Society, University of Sheffield, Sheffield.

Bundy, A. (2003a) Best Investment: the modern public library as social capital. Paper presented at the AGM of Friends of Libraries of Australia, Altona, Victoria, 27 August.

Bundy, A. (2003b) Vision, Mission, Trumpets: public libraries as social capital. Paper presented to NSW Country Public Libraries Association Conference,

Public Libraries Light Up Lives, Tweed Heads, NSW, 3 July,
http://trove.nla.gov.au/work/153094145.

Burrows, J. and Berardinelli, P. (2003) Systematic Performance Improvement:
refining the space between learning and results, *Journal of Workplace
Learning*, **15** (1), 6–13.

Caplan, N., Morrison, A. and Stambaugh, R. (1975) *The Use of Social Science
Knowledge in Policy Decisions at the National Level*, Ann Arbor, Institute of
Social Research, University of Michigan.

Carden, F. (2009) *Knowledge to Policy: making the most of development
research*, Sage/IDRC, Thousand Oaks, CA,
www.idrc.ca/openebooks/417-8/.

Carr, E. H. (1961) *What is History?*, Harmondsworth, Middx, Penguin.

Chamberlain, D. (2003) A Pilot Study of the Use of Inter-library Loans by
Clinical Staff, *Health Information and Libraries Journal*, **20** (4),
(December), 235–9.

Chase, S.E. (2005) Narrative Inquiry: multiple lenses, approaches, voices. In
Denzin, N. K. and Lincoln, Y. S. (eds) *The Sage Handbook of Qualitative
Research*, 3rd edn, Thousand Oaks, CA, Sage, 651–79.

Chiranov, M. (2011) Applying Pop-up Survey Software to Incorporate Users'
Feedback into Public Library Computing Service Management, *Performance
Measurement and Metrics*, **12** (1), 50–65.

Chiranov, M. (2012) Combining Qualitative and Quantitative Evidence: forming
strategic collaborations – and telling stories. In Streatfield, D. R., Paberza, K.,
Lipeikaite, U., Chiranov, M., Devetakova, L. and Sadunisvili, R. (2012)
Developing Impact Planning and Assessment at National Level: addressing
some issues, *Performance Measurement and Metrics*, **13** (1), 63–5.

Chung, H. K. (2008) The Contingent Valuation Method in Public Libraries,
Journal of Librarianship and Information Science, **40** (2), 71–80,
http://dx.doi.org/10.1177/0961000608089343.

Cohen, D. and Prusak, L. (2001) *In Good Company: how social capital makes
organizations work*, Boston, MA, Harvard Business School Press.

Covey, D. T. (2002) Academic library assessment: new duties and dilemmas,
New Library World, **103** (1175/1176), 156–64.

Coward, C. T. and Fisher, K. E. (2010) Measuring Indirect Access: indicators
of the impact of Lay Information Mediary Behavior (LIMBS), World
Library and Information Congress: 76th IFLA General Conference and
Assembly 10–15 August, Gothenburg, Sweden,
http://conference.ifla.org/past/ifla76/72-coward-en.pdf.

Crawford, J. (2006) *The Culture of Evaluation in Library and Information
Services*, Witney, Oxon, Chandos.

Creaser, C. and Spezi, V. (2012) Working Together: evolving value for academic libraries: a report commissioned by Sage, Loughborough, LISU, Loughborough University, http://libraryvalue.files.wordpress.com/2012/06/ndm-5709-lisu-final-report_web.pdf.

Datta, L. (1999) The Ethics of Evaluation: neutrality and advocacy, *New Directions for Evaluation*, **82** (Summer), 77–88.

Davis, D., Clark, L. and Bertot, J. C. (2010) *Libraries Connect Communities: Public Library Funding and Technology Access Study: 2009–2010.* Chicago, IL: American Library Association, http://americanlibrariesmagazine.org/archives/digital-supplement/summer-2010-digital-supplement.

Deem, R., Hillyard, S. and Reed, M. (2007) *Knowledge, Higher Education, and the New Managerialism: the changing management of UK universities,* Oxford Scholastic Online Monographs.

Elbert, M., Fuegi, D. and Lipeikaite, U. (2012) Public Libraries in Africa – Agents for Development and Innovation? Current perceptions of local stakeholders, *IFLA Journal*, **38** (2), 148–65.

Eraut, M. (2004) Practice-based Evidence. In Thomas, G. and Pring, R. (eds) (2004) *Evidence-based Practice in Education*, Maidenhead, Open University Press, McGraw-Hill Education, 91–101.

Fels Institute of Government (2010) *The Economic Value of The Free Library In Philadelphia*, University of Pennsylvania, Fels Institute of Government, www.freelibrary.org/about/felsstudy.htm.

Fisher, K. E., Erdelez, S. and McKechnie, E. F. (2005) *Theories of Information Behavior*, Medford, NJ, Information Today, Inc.

Fisher, K. E., Landry, C. F. and Naumer, C. M. (2007) Social Spaces, Casual Interactions, Meaningful Exchanges: an information ground typology based on the college student experience. *Information Research*, **12** (2), http://InformationR.net/ir/12-2/paper291.html.

Fitz-Gibbon, C. T. (1996) *Monitoring Education: indicators, quality and effectiveness*, London, Cassell.

Fitz-Gibbon, C. T. and Kochan, S. (2000) School Effectiveness and Education Indicators. In Teddlie, C. and Reynolds, D. (eds) *The International Handbook of School Effectiveness Research*, London, Falmer Press.

Francis, B. H., Lance, K. C. and Lietzau, Z. (2010) *School Librarians Continue to Help Students Achieve Standards: The Third Colorado Study*, Denver, CO, Library Research Service, www.lrs.org/documents/closer_look/CO3_2010_Closer_Look_Report.pdf.

Fried, S., Kochanowicz, M. and Chiranov, M. (2010) Planning for Impact, Assessing for Sustainability, *Performance Measurement and Metrics*, **11** (1), 56–74.

Fullan, M. (2007) *The New Meaning of Educational Change*, 4th edn, New York, NY, Teachers College Press.

Glaser, B. G. (1992) *Basics of Grounded Theory Analysis*, Mill Valley, CA, Sociology Press.

Glaser, B. G. and Strauss, A. L. (1967) *The Discovery of Grounded Theory: strategies for qualitative research*, Chicago, Aldine.

Goodhart, C. (1983) *Monetary Theory and Practice: the UK experience*, London, Macmillan, 96.

Goulding, A. (2004) Libraries and Social Capital. *Journal of Librarianship and Information Science*, **36** (1), 3–6.

Grant, M. J. and Booth, A. (2009) A typology of reviews: an analysis of 14 review types and associated methodologies, *Health Information and Libraries Journal*, **26** (2), 91–108.

Gray, J. and Wilcox, B. (1995) *'Good School, Bad School': evaluating performance and encouraging improvement*, Buckingham, Open University Press.

Greene, J. C. (2006) Evaluation, Democracy and Social Change. In Shaw, I.F., Greene, J.C. and Mark, M.M. *Handbook of Evaluation: policies, programs and practices*, London, Sage.

Griffiths, J-M., King, D. W. and Aerni, S. (2006) *Taxpayer Return of Investment in Pennsylvania Public Libraries*, www.statelibrary.state.pa.us/libraries/lib/libraries/PAROIreportFINAL7.pdf.

Griffiths, J-M., King, D. W., Tomer, C., Lynch, T. and Harrington, J. (2004) *Taxpayer Return on Investment in Florida Public Libraries: Summary Report*, State Library and Archives of Florida, http://dlis.dos.state.fl.us/bld/roi/FinalReport.cfm.

Guba, E. G. and Lincoln, Y. (1987) *Fourth Generation Evaluation*, London, Sage.

Harada, V. M. (2005) Librarians and Teachers as Research Partners: reshaping practice based on assessment and reflection, *School Libraries Worldwide*, **11** (2), (July), 49–72.

Heinström, J. (2003) Fast Surfers, Broad Scanners and Deep Divers as Users of Information Technology: relating information preferences to personality traits, *Proceedings of the American Society for Information Science and Technology*, **40** (1), 247–54.

Hillenbrand, C. (2005) Public Libraries as Developers of Social Capital, *Australasian Public Libraries and Information Services*, **18** (1), 4–12.

Hinchliffe, J. and Oakleaf, M. (2010) Sustainable Progress Through Impact: the Value of Academic Libraries project, World Library and Information Congress: 76th IFLA General Conference and Assembly 10–15 August, Gothenburg, Sweden.

Hoffman, J., Bertot, J. C. and Davis, D. M. (2012) *Libraries Connect Communities: Public Library Funding and Technology Access Study 2011–2012*. Digital supplement of *American Libraries* magazine, (June), http://viewer.zmags.com/publication/4673a369.

Holt, G. E., Elliott, D. and Dussold, C. (1996) A Framework for Evaluating Public Investment in Urban Libraries, *Bottom Line*, 9 (4), (Summer), 4–13. Feature article in a special issue.

House, E. R. (1993) *Professional Evaluation: social impacts and political consequences*, Sage, Newbury Park, CA.

House, E. R. (2005) Qualitative Evaluation and Changing Social Policy. In Denzin, N. K. and Lincoln, Y. S. *The Sage Handbook of Qualitative Research*, Sage, London, 1069–81.

House, E. R. (2006) Democracy and Evaluation, *Evaluation*, 12 (1), 119–27.

House, E. R. and Howe, K. R. (1999) *Values in Evaluation and Social Research*, Thousand Oaks, CA, Sage.

Huysmans, F. and Oomes, M. (2012) Measuring the Public Library's Societal Value: a methodological research program, paper at IFLA World Library and Information Congress, 78th IFLA General Conference and Assembly, 11–17 August 2012, Helsinki, Finland.

Information Policy and Access Center (2012) *Public Libraries and Access*, Maryland, IPAC, University of Maryland.

Information Policy and Access Center (2012) *Public Libraries and E-government*, Maryland, IPAC, University of Maryland.

Jantii, M. and Tang, K. (2011) *Return on Investment and Value of Libraries – Bibliography*, Council of Australian University Libraries (CAUL), www.caul.edu.au/.

Johnson, C.A. (2010) Do Public Libraries Contribute to Social Capital? A preliminary investigation into the relationship, *Library and Information Science Research*, 32 (2), 147–55.

Kaplan, R. S. and Norton, D. P. (1992) The Balanced Scorecard: measures that drive performance, *Harvard Business Review* (Jan–Feb).

Kaplan, R. S. and Norton, D. P. (1993) Putting the Balanced Scorecard to Work, *Harvard Business Review*, Sept–Oct. [Both articles reprinted in *Harvard Business Review on measuring corporate performance*, Boston, USA Harvard Business School Press, 1998.]

Kaufmann, P. T. (2008) The Library as Strategic Investment: results of the Illinois Return on Investment study, *Liber Quarterly*, **18** (3/4), http://liber.library.uu.nl/index.php/lq/article/view/7941.

Kinnell, M., Usherwood, R. and Jones, K. (1999a) *Improving Library and Information Services Through Self-assessment: a guide for senior managers and staff developers*, BLR+I Report 172, London, Library Association Publishing.

Kinnell, M., Usherwood, R. and Jones, K. (1999b) *The Library and Information Services Self-assessment Training Pack*, BLR+I Report 172, London, Library Association Publishing.

Knight, P. (2003) *Reducing Uncertainty*, Discussion Paper no. 4, York, Higher Education Academy.

Kochanowicz, M. (2012) Impact Planning and Assessment – Making it Happen: Poland, *Performance Measurement and Metrics*, **13** (1), 32–7.

Koufogiannakis, D. and Wiebe, N. (2006) Effective Methods for Teaching Information Literacy Skills to Undergraduate Students: a systematic review and meta-analysis, *Evidence Based Library and Information Practice*, **1** (3), http://ejournals.library.ualberta.ca/index.php/eblip/issue/view/9.

Kuhlthau, C. C. (2005) Towards Collaboration Between Information Seeking Research and Information Retrieval, *Information Research*, **10** (2), (January), Paper 225, http://Informationr.net/ir/10-2/paper225.htm.

Kushner, S. and MacDonald, B. (1987) The Limitations of Programme Evaluation. In Murphy, R. and Torrance, H. (eds) *Evaluating Education: issues and methods*, London, Harper and Row.

Lance, K. C. and Hofschire, L. (2012) *Change in School Librarian Staffing Linked with Change in CSAP Reading Performance, 2005 to 2011*, Denver, CO, Library Research Service. http://www.lrs.org/documents/closer_look/CO4_2012_Closer_Look_Report.pdf.

Lance, K. C., Rodney, M. J. and Schwarz, W. (2010) *Idaho School Library Impact Study 2009: how Idaho school librarians, teachers and administrators collaborate for student success*, RSL Research Group and Idaho Commission for Libraries, http://libraries.idaho.gov/files/Full%20rpt.pdf.

Larson, J. H. (ed.) (2010) *Nordic Public Libraries 2.0*, Copenhagen, Danish Agency for Libraries and Media.

Law, D. (2006) Evaluating the Impact of Your Library, *Library Review*, **55** (9), 636–7.

Limberg, L. (2005) Experiencing Information Seeking and Learning: research on patterns of variation. In Maceviĉiūtė, E. and Wilson, T. D. (eds) *Introducing Information Management: an information research reader,* London, Facet Publishing, 68–80.

Limberg, L., Sundin, O. and Talja, S. (2012) Three Theoretical Perspectives on Information Literacy, *Human IT* [accepted for publication.]

Linley, R. and Usherwood, R. C. (1998) *New Measures for the New Library,* British Library Research and Innovation Centre Report 89, Sheffield, Centre for the Public Library in the Information Society, University of Sheffield.

Loertscher, D. V. with Todd, R. J. (2003) *We Boost Achievement! Evidence-based Practice for School Library Media Specialists,* Salt Lake City, UT, Hi Willow Research and Publishing. Project Achievement was based on the work published here.

Lonsdale, M. (2003) *Impact of School Libraries on Student Achievement: a review of the research report for the Australian School Library Association,* Victoria, Australian Council for Educational Research.

Luther, J. (2008) *University Investment in the Library: What's the return? A case study at the University of Illinois at Urbana-Champaign,* San Diego, CA, Elsevier.

MacBeth, J. et al. (2001) *The Impact of Study Support,* Research Report 273, London, Department for Education and Skills.

Macfarlane, B. (2009) *Researching with Integrity: the ethics of academic enquiry,* London, Routledge.

Manjarrez, C. A., Cigna, J. and Bajaj, B. (2007) *Making Cities Stronger: public library contributions to local economic development,* Urban Libraries Council, Evanston, IL, www.urban.org/publications/1001075.html.

Markless, S. (ed.) (2009) *The Innovative School Librarian: thinking outside the box,* London, Facet Publishing.

Markless, S. and Streatfield, D. R. (2000) *The Really Effective College Library,* Library and Information Commission Research Report 51, Twickenham, Information Management Associates for the Library and Information Commission [Phase 2 project report].

Markless, S. and Streatfield, D. R. (2004) *Improve your Library: a self-evaluation process for secondary school libraries and learning resource centres,* 2 vols, London, Department for Education and Skills, www.informat.org/schoollibraries/secondarynewuser.html.

Markless, S. and Streatfield, D. R. (2005) Facilitating the Impact Implementation Programme, *Library and Information Research,* **29** (91),

(Spring), 10–19. The whole of this special issue of LIRN is devoted to the
Impact Implementation Programme.

Markless, S. and Streatfield, D. R. (2006) Gathering and Applying Evidence
of the Impact of UK University Libraries on Student Learning and
Research: a facilitated action research approach, *International Journal of
Information Management*, **26** (1), 3–15.

Markless, S. and Streatfield, D. R. (2008) Supported Self-evaluation in
Assessing the Impact of HE Libraries, *Performance Measurement and
Metrics* **9** (1), 38–47.

Mays, R., Tenopir, C. and Kaufman, P. (2010) Lib-Value: Measuring Value and
Return on Investment of Academic Libraries, *Research Library Issues: A bi-
monthly report from ARL, CNI, and SPARC*, **271** (August), 38–42.

McKernan, J. (1991) *Curriculum Action Research: a handbook of methods and
resources for the reflective practitioner*, London, Kogan Page.

McNiff, J. and Whitehead, J. (2010) *You and Your Action Research Project*,
Abingdon, Routledge.

Mertens, D.M. (2003) The Inclusive View of Evaluation: implications of
transformative theory for evaluation. In Donaldson, S.I. and Scrivens, M.
(eds) *Evaluating Social Programs and Problems: visions for the new
millennium*, Mahwah, NJ, Lawrence Erlbaum Associates.

Mintzberg, H. (1973) *The Nature of Managerial Work*, New York, NY, Harper
and Row [and subsequent editions].

Muir Gray, J. (1997) *Evidence-based Health Care: how to make health policy
and management decisions*, New York, NY, Churchill Livingstone.

Murray, D. (2003) Whom Do You Serve?, *CILIP Update*, **2** (2), (February),
23.

Nicholas, D. (2012) Disintermediated, Decoupled and Down, *CILIP Update*,
(April), 29–30.

Nicholas, D. and Rowlands, I. (2008) *Digital Consumers: reshaping the
information professions*, London, Facet Publishing.

Nicholas, D., Rowlands, I. and Jamali, H. R. (2010) E-textbook Use,
Information Seeking Behaviour and its Impact: case study business and
management, *Journal of Information Science*, **36** (2), 263–80.

Oakleaf, M. (2010) *The Value of Academic Libraries: a comprehensive research
review and report*, Association of College and Research Libraries, Chicago,
IL, American library Association,
www.ala.org/acrl/sites/ala.org.acrl/files/content/issues/value/val_report.pdf.

Paberza, K. (2010) Towards an Assessment of Public Library Value: statistics
on the policymakers' agenda, *Performance Measurement and Metrics*, **11**
(1), 83–92.

Paberza, K. (2012) *Economic Value of Public Libraries in Latvia* [slideshow], www.slideshare.net/bibliotekare/economic-value-of-public-libraries-in-latvia.

Paberza, K. and Rutkauskiene, U. (2010) Outcomes-based Measurement of Public Access Computing in Public Libraries: a comparative analysis of studies in Latvia and Lithuania, *Performance Measurement and Metrics*, **11** (1), 75–82.

Parasuraman, A., Zeithaml, V. A. and Berry, L. L. (1988) SERVQUAL: a multiple-item scale for measuring consumer perceptions of service quality, *Journal of Retailing*, **64** (1), 12–40.

Parlett, M. and Dearden, G. (eds) (1977) *Introduction to Illuminative Evaluation: studies in higher education*, Cardiff-by-the-Sea, CA, Pacific Soundings Press, and Guildford, Society for Research into Higher Education.

Parlett, M. and Hamilton, D. (1972) Evaluation as Illumination: a new approach to the study of innovatory programmes. Republished in Parlett, M. and Dearden, G. (eds) (1977) *Introduction to Illuminative Evaluation: studies in higher education*, Cardiff-by-the-Sea, CA, Pacific Soundings Press, and Guildford, Society for Research into Higher Education.

Patton, M. Q. (2011) *Developmental Evaluation: applying complexity concepts to enhance innovation and use*, New York, NY, The Guilford Press.

Patton, M. Q. (2012) *Essentials of Utilization-focused Evaluation*, Thousand Oaks, CA, Sage.

Payne, P. and Conyers, A. (2005) Measuring the Impact of Higher Education Libraries: the LIRG/SCONUL Impact Implementation Initiative, *Library and Information Research*, **29** (91), (Spring), 3–9.

Poll, R. (2011) *Bibliography: 'Impact and Outcome of Libraries'*, www.ifla.org/files/statistics-and-evaluation/publications/Bibl_Impact_Outcome-Jan2011.pdf.

Poll, R. and Boekhorst, P. (eds) (2007) *Measuring Quality: performance measurement in libraries*, 2nd rev. edn, IFLA Publications Series 127, Munich, K. G. Saur.

Poll, R. and Payne, P. (2006) Impact Measures for Libraries and Information Services, *Library Hi Tech*, **24** (4) 547–62.

Popper, K. R. (1969) *Conjectures and Refutations: the growth of scientific knowledge* [new edn London, Routledge 2002].

Porter, M. E. (1985) *Competitive Advantage: creating and sustaining superior performance*, New York, NY, Free Press.

Punie, Y., Zinnbauer, D. and Cabrera, M. (2008) *A review of the impact of ICT on learning*, Joint Research Centre – Institute for Prospective Technological

Studies, Luxembourg, Office for Official Publications of the European
Communities.
Putnam, R. D. (2000) *Bowling Alone: the collapse and revival of American
community*, New York, NY, Simon and Schuster.
QMW (1999) Achieving Effective Performance Management and
Benchmarking in the Public Sector, Queen Mary Public Policy Seminars,
University of London, 14 October.
Race, P. (2005) *Making Learning Happen*, London, Sage.
Ramirez, R. (2007) Appreciating the Contribution of Broadband ICT within
Rural and Remote Communities: stepping stones towards an alternative
paradigm, *The Information Society*, **23** (2), 85–94.
Research Information Network (2008) *Mind the Skills Gap:
information handling training for researchers: A report commissioned by the
Research Information Network*, London, RIN,
www.rin.ac.uk/system/files/attachments/Mind-skills-gap-report.pdf.
Research Information Network (2011a) *E-journals: their use, value and impact
– final report*, London, RIN,
www.lrs.org/documents/closer_look/CO4_2012_Closer_Look_Report.pdf.
Research Information Network (2011b) *Reinventing Research? Information
practices in the humanities. A Research Information Network Report*,
London, RIN,
www.rin.ac.uk/our-work/using-and-accessing-information-resources/
information-use-case-studies-humanities.
Research Information Network and the British Library (2009) *Patterns of
Information Use and Exchange: case studies of researchers in the life
sciences. A report by the Research Information Network and the British
Library*. London, RIN. www.rin.ac.uk/our-work/using-and-accessing-
information-resources/patterns-information-use-and-exchange-case-studie.
Research Information Network and Research Libraries UK (2011) *The Value of
Libraries for Research and Researchers. A RIN and RLUK report*, London,
RIN,
www.rin.ac.uk/our-work/using-and-accessing-information-resources/
value-libraries-research-and-researchers.
Research Information Network, Institute of Physics, Institute of Physics
Publishing and the Royal Astronomical Society (2011) *Collaborative Yet
Independent: information practices in the physical sciences*, London, RIN,
http://rinarchive.jisc-collections.ac.uk/our-work/using-and-accessing-
information-resources/physical-sciences-case-studies-use-and-discovery-

Robinson, S. and Pidd, M. (1998) Provider and Customer Expectations of Successful Simulation Projects, *Journal of the Operational Research Society*, **49** (3), 200–9.

Rogers, P. J. (2008) Using Programme Theory to Evaluate Complicated and Complex Aspects of Interventions, *Evaluation*, **14** (1), 29–48, http://evi.sagepub.com/cgi/content/abstract/14/1/29.

Sawaya, J., Maswabi, T., Taolo, R., Andrade, P., Grez, M. M., Pacheco, P., Paberza, K., Vigante, S., Kurutyte, A., Rutkauskiene, U., Jezowska, J. and Kochanowicz, M. (2011) Advocacy and Evidence for Sustainable Public Computer Access: experiences from the Global Libraries Initiative, *Library Review*, **60** (6), 448–72.

[Scholastic] Research Foundation (2008) *School Libraries Work!*, 3rd edn, Research Foundation Paper Danbury, CT, Scholastic Library Publishing, www2.scholastic.com/content/collateral_resources/pdf/s/slw3_2008.pdf.

Sciadas, G. with Lyons, H., Rothschild, C. and Sey, A. (2012) *Public Access to ICTs: Sculpting the profile of users*, Seattle, WA, Technology and Social Change Group, University of Washington Information School.

Sey, A. and Fellows, M. (2009) *Literature Review on the Impact of Public Access to Information and Communication Technologies*, CIS Working Paper no. 6, Seattle, WA, Center for Information and Society, University of Washington, http://library.globalimpactstudy.org/sites/default/files/docs/ CIS-WorkingPaperNo6.pdf.

Sharp, C. et al. (1999) *Playing for Success: an evaluation of the first year*, London, Department for Education and Employment.

Sharp, C. et al. (2000) *Playing for Success: an evaluation of the second year*, London, Department for Education and Skills.

Shaw, I. F., Greene, J. C. and Mark, M. M. (2006) *Handbook of Evaluation: policies, programs and practices*, London, Sage.

Silverman, D. (2007) *A Very Short, Fairly Interesting and Reasonably Cheap Book About Qualitative Research*, Thousand Oaks, CA, and London, Sage.

Simons, H. (2006) Ethics in Evaluation. In Shaw, I. F., Greene, J. C. and Mark, M. M., *Handbook of Evaluation: policies, programs and practices*, London, Sage.

Smith, M. K. (2001) Social Capital. In the Encyclopedia of Informal Education, www.infed.org/biblio/social_capital.htm.

Spectrum Strategy Consultants and Independent Consulting (2004) *Measuring Our Value: results of an independent economic impact study*,

London, British Library,
www.bl.uk/aboutus/stratpolprog/increasingvalue/measuring.pdf.

Stake, R. E. (2004) *Standards-based and Responsive Evaluation*, Thousand
Oaks, CA, Sage.

Stanley, T. and Killick, S. (2009) *Library Performance Measurement in the UK
and Ireland*, Washington, DC, Association of Research Libraries and
SCONUL.

Steffen, N., Lietzau, Z., Lance, K. C., Rybin, A. and Molliconi, C. (2009)
*Public Libraries – A Wise Investment: A Return on Investment Study of
Colorado Libraries*, Denver, CO, Library Research Service.
www.lrs.org/documents/closer_look/roi.pdf.

Strathern, M. (1997) Improving Ratings: audit in the British university system,
European Review, **5** (3), 305–21.

Streatfield, D. R. (2012) Impact Planning and Assessment of Public Libraries:
a country-level perspective, *Performance Measurement and Metrics*, **13** (1),
8–14.

Streatfield, D. R., Allen, D. K. and Wilson, T. D. (2010) Information literacy
training for postgraduate and postdoctoral researchers: a national survey and
its implications, *Libri*, **60** (3), 230–40.

Streatfield, D. R. and Markless, S. (1994) *Invisible Learning? The contribution
of school libraries to teaching and learning*, Library and Information
Research Report 98, London, British Library Research and Development
Department.

Streatfield, D. R. and Markless, S. (1997) *The Effective College Library*,
British Library Research and Innovation Report 21, Developing FE Series
1 (8), London, Further Education Development Agency [Phase 1 project
report].

Streatfield, D. R. and Markless, S. (2002a) *Critical Evaluation of the LIC
Value and Impact Programme: report to Resource: the Council for Museums,
Libraries and Archives*, London, Resource.

Streatfield, D. R. and Markless, S. (2002b) *Review of the Benefits of Library
Use in Schools, briefing paper* prepared for the Department for Education
and Skills, Twickenham, Information Management Associates.

Streatfield, D. R. and Markless, S. (2003) Gathering Evidence of What We
Do, *School Libraries in View*, **18** (Summer), 8–10.

Streatfield, D. R. and Markless, S. (2004) *Improve your Library: a self-
evaluation process for primary schools*, London, Department for Education
and Skills, http://dera.ioe.ac.uk/5293.

Streatfield, D. R. and Markless, S. (2009) What is Impact Assessment and Why is it Important? *Performance Measurement and Metrics*, **10** (2), 134–41.

Streatfield, D. R. and Markless, S. (2011) Impact Evaluation, Advocacy and Ethical Research: some issues for national strategy development? *Library Review*, **60** (4), 312–27.

Streatfield, D. R., Paberza, K., Lipeikaite, U., Chiranov, M., Devetakova, L. and Sadunisvili, R. (2012) Developing Impact Planning and Assessment at National Level: addressing some issues, *Performance Measurement and Metrics*, **13** (1), 58–65.

Streatfield, D. R., Quynh Truc Phan, Triyono, P., Rosalina, T., Devetakova, L., Chiranov, M., Kochanowicz, M., Taolo, R., Paberza, K., Lipekaite, U. and Sadunisvali, R. (2012) Assessment of Public Libraries: a country level perspective, *Performance Measurement and Metrics*, **13** (1), 15–57.

Streatfield, D. R., Shaper, S. and Rae-Scott, S. (2011) *School libraries in the UK: a worthwhile past, a difficult present – and a transformed future? Report of the UK national survey*, London, School Libraries Group of the Chartered Institute of Library and Information Professionals (CILIP) and Information Management Associates, www.cilip.org.uk/get-involved/special-interest-groups/school/pages/news.aspx.

Streatfield, D. R. et al. (2000) *Rediscovering Reading: public libraries and the National Year of Reading* (with Library and Information Commission), Research Report 30, Twickenham, Information Management Associates for the LIC.

Strode, I., Vanags, A., Strazdina, R., Dirveiks, J., Dombrovska, H., Pakalna, D. and Paberza, K. (2012) *Economic Value and Impact of Public Libraries in Latvia: study report*, Riga, Trešais Trêva Dêls.

Survey Working Group (2012) *Global Impact Study Surveys: methodologies and implementation*. Seattle, WA, Technology and Social Change Group, University of Washington Information School.

Swinbourne, K. (2000) *A Safe Place to Go: libraries and social capital*, Sydney, State Library of New South Wales Appendix 1, www.sl.nsw.gov.au/services/public_libraries/docs/safe_place.pdf.

Taticchi, P., Balachandran, K. and Tonelli, F. (2012) Performance Measurement and Management Systems: state of the art, guidelines for design and challenges, *Measuring Business Excellence*, **16** (2), 41–54.

Taticchi, P., Tonelli, F. and Cagnazzo, L. (2010) Performance Measurement and Management: a literature review and a research agenda, *Measuring Business Excellence*, **14** (1), 4–18.

Taylor, D. and Balloch, S. (eds) (2005) *The Politics of Evaluation: participation and policy implementation,* The Policy Press, Bristol.

Tenopir, C. and Volentine, R. with King, D.W. (2012) *UK Scholarly Reading and the Value of Library Resources,* JISC Collections, www.jisc-collections.ac.uk/news/Uk-scholarly-reading

Tenopir, C., King, D., Mays, R., Wu, L. and Baer, A. (2010) Measuring Value and Return on Investment of Academic Libraries, *Serials,* **23** (3), 182–90.

Thomas, G. (2004) Introduction: evidence and practice. In Thomas, G. and Pring, R. (eds) *Evidence-based Practice in Education,* Maidenhead, Open University Press, McGraw-Hill Education.

TNS Infratest (2010) *The TIB – a Future with Added Value: a study of the value and benefits of the German National Library of Science and Technology,* Hanover, TIB, www.tib-hannover.de/fileadmin/presse/tib-studie-2010-engl.pdf.

TNS RMS East Africa (2011) *Perceptions of public libraries in Africa report,* TNS RMS, www.eifl.net/perception-study.

Todd, R. J. (2001) Presentation to the International Association of School Librarianship Conference, Auckland, New Zealand, 9–12 July.

Todd, R. J., Gordon, C. A. and Lu, Y-L. (2011) *One Common Goal: student learning. Report of findings and recommendations of the New Jersey School Library Survey Phase 2,* New Jersey, Center for International Scholarship in School Libraries (CISSL), School of Communication and Information Rutgers, The State University of New Jersey. http://cissl.rutgers.edu/images/stories/docs/njasl_phase%20_2_final.pdf.

Todd, R. J. and Kuhlthau, C. C. (2005) Student Learning Through Ohio School Libraries, part 1. How effective school libraries help students, *School Libraries Worldwide,* **11** (1), 63–88. This special issue of the International Association of School Librarianship journal is devoted to the Ohio Project.

Underwood, J. (2009) *The Impact of Digital Technology: a review of the evidence of the impact of digital technologies on formal education,* Coventry, BECTA.

University of North Carolina, School of Information and Library Science (2006) *Taxpayer Return-on-Investment (ROI) in Pennsylvania Public Libraries, Report for the Commonwealth of Pennsylvania,* University of North Carolina, School of Information and Library Science, Chapel Hill, NC, www.palibraries.org/associations/9291/files/FullReport.pdf.

Urquhart, C. and Weightman, A. (2008) *Assessing the Impact of a Health Library Service: best practice guidance.* Based on research originally funded by LKDN (now sponsored by National Library for Health). Version for National Library for Health.

Usherwood, R. C., Evans, M. and Jones, K. (1999) *Assessment Tools for Quality Management in Public Libraries*, BLR+I Report 155, Sheffield, Centre for the Public Library in the Information Society, University of Sheffield.

Vakkari, P. (2012) Internet Use Increases the Odds of Using the Public Library, *Journal of Documentation*, **68** (5), www.emeraldinsight.com/journals.htm/journals.htm?articleid=17036852.

Vakkari, P. and Serola, S. (2012) Perceived Outcomes of Public Libraries, *Library and Information Science Research*, **34** (1), 37–44.

Vårheim, A. (2007) Social Capital and Public Libraries: the need for research, *Library and Information Science Research*, **29** (3), 416–28.

Vårheim, A. (2009) Public Libraries: places creating social capital? *Library Hi Tech*, **27** (3), 372–81.

Vestman, O. K. and Conner, R. F. (2006) The Relationship between Evaluation and Politics. In Shaw, I. F., Greene, J. C. and Mark, M. M., *Handbook of Evaluation: policies, programs and practices*, London, Sage.

Voogt, J. and Knezek. G. (eds) (2008) *International Handbook of Information Technology in Primary and Secondary Education*, Berlin, Heidelberg, New York, NY, Springer.

Wavell, C., Baxter, G., Johnson, I. and Williams, D. (2002) *Impact Evaluation of Museums, Archives and Libraries: available evidence project*, prepared by the School of Information and Media, Faculty of Management, Robert Gordon University, London, Resource, http://www4.rgu.ac.uk/files/imreport.pdf.

Weightman, A. L., Urquhart, C., Spink, S. and Thomas, R. (2009) The Value and Impact of Information Provided Through Library Services for Patient Care: developing guidance for best practice, *Health Information and Libraries Journal*, **26** (1), 63–71, www.ncbi.nlm.nih.gov/pubmed/19245645.

Weightman, A. L. and Williamson, J. (2005) The Value and Impact of Information Provided through Library Services for Patient Care: a systematic review, *Health Information and Libraries Journal*, **22** (1) (March), 4–25. [Work conducted on behalf of the Library and Knowledge Development Network (LKDN), Quality and Statistics Group].

Whelan, D. (2004) 13,000 Kids Can't be Wrong, *School Library Journal*, (January), www.schoollibraryjournal.com/article/CA377858.html.

White, H. (2010) A Contribution to Current Debates in Impact Evaluation, *Evaluation*, **16** (2) 153–64, http://evi.sagepub.com/content/16/2/153.

Williams, D. and Wavell, C. (2001) *The Impact of the School Library Resource Centre on Learning*, Library and Information Commission Research Report 112, Aberdeen, Faculty of Management, Robert Gordon University.

Williams, D., Wavell, C. and Coles, L. (2001) *Impact of School Library Services on Achievement and Learning: critical literature review*, London, DfES and Resource.

Williams, D., Coles, L. and Wavell, C. (2002) *Impact of School Library Services on Achievement and Learning in Primary Schools: critical literature review*, London, DfES and Resource.

Williams, D. A. et al. (2005) Implementing Impact Evaluation in Professional Practice: a study of support needs within the museum, archive and library sector, *International Journal of Information Management*, **25** (6), 533–48.

Woodcock, B. (1998) *Measuring Up: an introduction to theories and concepts of performance in public services*, London, CIPFA.

World Bank (1999) What is Social Capital?, http://web.worldbank.org/WBSITE/EXTERNAL/TOPICS/ EXTSOCIALDEVELOPMENT/EXTTSOCIALCAPITAL/0,,contentMDK: 20185164~menuPK:418217~pagePK:148956~piPK:216618~theSitePK: 401015,00.html.

Yin, R. K. (2008) *Case Study Research: design and methods*, 4th edn, London, Sage.

Zhang, L., Watson, E. M. and Banfield, L. (2007) The Efficacy of Computer-Assisted Instruction Versus Face-to-Face Instruction in Academic Libraries: A systematic review, *Journal of Academic Librarianship*, **33** (4), 478–84.

Notes

1   For our use of 'libraries' (and 'information services') in the text please see 'Impact and all that: use of some key terms in this book' on page xv.
2   http://eblip7.library.usask.ca/.
3   http://ejournals.library.ualberta.ca/index.php/EBLIP/.
4   www.gatesfoundation.org/libraries/Pages/united-states-libraries.aspx#.
5   www.idea.gov.uk/idk/aio/6056931.
6   The Evidence for Policy and Practice Information and Co-ordinating Centre (EPPI-Centre) is part of the Social Science Research Unit at the Institute of Education, University of London, http://eppi.ioe.ac.uk/cms/.
7   www.whatworks.ed.gov/.
8   This concern, and what to do about it, was a major theme of the International Research Colloquium on School Libraries organized by the Center for International Scholarship in School Libraries, Rutgers University, held in New York in April–May 2005. The research methods group at this event was led by Keith Curry Lance – the last comment is his.
9   www.inspiringlearningforall.gov.uk.
10 A distinction is drawn here between systematic reviews for weighing up published research evidence, which is a meticulous, exhaustive and expensive process, and semi-systematic reviews, which are less rigorous and usually only cover recent reports, but in which the selection criteria, scope and methodology are all specified. Systematic reviews, as developed by the Cochrane Collaboration in the health field and as applied to education, social care and other areas by the Campbell Collaboration and others, involve an apparatus of rigorous selection and operational processes, such as independent expert panels, double reviewing and systematic exclusion of reports that do not meet all the specifications.

11   www.lrs.org/public/roi/.
12   http://iilresearch.wordpress.com/2011/03/.
13   www.globalimpactstudy.org/about/.
14   www.libraryservices.nhs.uk/healer/researchguidelines/.
15   Brace, I. (2004) *Questionnaire design: How to plan, structure and write survey material for effective market research*, London, Kogan Page.
16   LibQUAL+(TM) is a suite of services that libraries use to solicit, track, understand, and act upon users' opinions of service quality. These services are offered to the library community by the Association of Research Libraries, www.libqual.org.
17   http://library.hud.ac.uk/blogs/projects/lidp/.
18   The Best Value and Better Performance in Libraries Project was conducted by a consortium led by Information Management Associates and also involving David Haynes Associates, the London Borough of Hammersmith and Fulham, and Wiltshire and Swindon Learning Resources. The project team consisted of David Streatfield, Sharon Markless and Ray Swan (IMA); Noeleen Schenk (DHA); David Herbert (Hammersmith); and Susan McCulloch (Wiltshire). The main output from this project can be found at the IMA website: www.informat.org (click on Best Value in the drop-down menu).
19   This programme was organized and led by the Library and Information Research Group and the Society of College, National and University Libraries.
20   These self-evaluation models and support materials were distributed widely to schools in England in the summer of 2004. The primary schools version can be found at: http://dera.ioe.ac.uk/5293/. The secondary schools version is at: www.informat.org/schoollibraries/secondarynewuser.html.
21   www.ifla.org/success-stories/.
22   www-01.ibm.com/software/analytics/spss.
23   www.qsrinternational.com/products.aspx.
24   http://ipac.umd.edu/sites/default/files/publications/ EgovBrief2012_0.pdf.
25   http://ipac.umd.edu/sites/default/files/publications/ CommunityAccessBrief2012_0.pdf.
26   www.continuumbooks.com/series/detail.aspx?SeriesId=1940.
27   http://informationr.net/ir/.
28   www.researchresources.net.
29   www.socialresearchmethods.net.
30   http://gsociology.icaap.org/methods/.

31 www.qual.auckland.ac.nz.
32 http://comminfo.rutgers.edu/professional-development/childlit/
researchmethods.html.
33 www.researchinglibrarian.com/journals.htm.
34 http://informationr.net/rm/.
35 www.lrs.org/cor.php.
36 http://nnlm.gov/mcr/evaluation/calculator.html.
37 http://nnlm.gov/mcr/evaluation/roi.html.
38 FAIFE, the Committee on Freedom of Access to Information and
Freedom of Expression, is an initiative within IFLA to promote freedom
of access to information and freedom of expression, related to libraries
and librarianship. We were asked to help create a framework to evaluate
the impact of the FAIFE training programme offered to library staff in
various countries. See: http://www.ifla.org/en/about-faife. Building
Strong Library Associations is a comprehensive programme offering a
strategic and coordinated approach to capacity building and sustainability
of library associations. The programme helps library associations and
their members increase their potential to improve services for library
users, provide equitable access to information and develop the library
and information profession. See: http://www.ifla.org/en/bsla.
39 The GL IPA Road Map is a guide to impact planning and assessment
aimed at IPA specialists in GL countries, made available on the GL
Intranet for participants in the Initiative.

Index

academic achievement and libraries
    45
academic libraries
    and evaluation 7, 67, 45
    economic value 44, 51
    evidence-gathering methods 124–5
    focus 71
    impact 50–2, 55, 56, 67
    indicators 93–4, 98–9
    interpreting evidence 164
    pressure to evaluate 7
academic researchers
    information literacy support for 51
    information-related behaviour 51
academic staff
    and academic libraries 51
    as evaluation collaborators 215
    impact of services; evidence 124
academic students, information-
    related behaviour 45, 51
access to libraries; evaluation of 6
accompanied visits 129
accountability and evaluation 7–8,
    14–15, 19–21
achievement
    definition xv, 25
action planning 177
action research 121, 157–60
    help 215

activities 105–8
    confusion with objectives 76
    for readers of this book 65–7, 73,
      76–7, 90, 101, 107, 119
    link to objectives 106, 107
    when to consider 105
advocacy 201–5; confusion with
    evaluation 15, 115–16, 168–70
affective change, evidence-gathering
    methods 122
aggregated outputs 24
aims and objectives, definition xvi
Alexandria Library; scholarly
    excursion 3
American Library Association and
    Information Institute xiv
analysing data 162–4
anthropological perspective 168
Arnold, Ronald 173
assessment, definition xvi
attribution studies 189
axial coding 164

balanced scorecard 15–16, 34–5
baseline evidence; shifting 158
    impact information 64, 172
bearing, evidence having positive
    161
behavioural change 80, 123

impact indicators (*continued*)
  as quantities 89–90
  as questions 88–9
  as statements 89
  clarity in 84
  corruptible 86
  corrupting 86
  definition 83
  focused on intended changes 87
  frameworks 95–101
  inflexible 86
  objectives and 90–4
  postponing selection of 85–6
  provisional character 87
  qualitative 88
  review of 87, 171–2
  small number of 85, 87
  validity of 85
  writing 88–94
impact measurement
  definition xviii
  targets 172–5
impact objectives 73–8
impact planning and assessment,
  definition xviii
impact process model
  described 62–3
  initial questions 65–6
  limitations of 209
  points to watch 63–5
impact targets 172–5
  definition xxii
indicators, definition 69
inferring change 121
informal
  comments 137
  learning *see* learning
  observation 129
information
  and communication technologies;

    evaluation of 4–7, 11–12, 13–14, 18
  and competitive advantage 9
  availability; and impact 4–7
  electronic 5, 12
  literacy 45, 48, 51, 67; skills 5, 48
  management and evaluation 9
  services
    explanation xx; impact evidence 113–23; impact indicators 91–3; process indicators 109
  skills *see* information literacy
information-seeking behaviour 42, 45, 51
innovations, evaluation 209–10
input
  measures 23
input, process, output model xix, 23–4
Inspiring Learning for All 37–8, 95–8
intentionality 87
international development evaluation 40
International Federation of Library Associations 57
  approach to impact evaluation 187
  impact evaluation focus 193
  Success Stories Database 157
international-level
  development goals 185
  ethical impact evaluation 196
  focus of impact evaluation 190, 193
  framework for impact evaluation 188–91, 192–3
  impact areas 190–1
  impact evaluation principles 190–1
  library development projects 184
  library impact evaluation 183–205
internet access, evaluation 5

Williamson, Jane 49
workplace libraries *see* special
    libraries
writing impact

indicators 88–94
targets 172–3

Yin, Robert 167

Evaluating and Measuring the Value, Use and Impact of Digital Collections
Lorna Hughes, editor

A huge investment has been made in digitizing scholarly and cultural heritage materials through initiatives based in museums, libraries and archives, as well as higher education institutions. The 'Digital Economy' is an important component of institutional planning, and much attention is given to the investment in digital projects and programmes. However, few initiatives have examined the actual use, value and impact of digital collections, and the role of digital collections in the changing information environment.

As the creative, cultural and educational sector faces a period of restricted funding, it is timely to re-examine the use of the digital collections that have been created in the past twenty years, and to consider their value to the institutions that host them and to the communities of users they serve.

This book brings together a group of international experts to consider the following key issues:

- What is the role of digital resources in the research life cycle?
- Do the arts and humanities face a 'data deluge'?
- How are digital collections to be sustained over the long term?
- How is use and impact to be assessed?
- What is the role of digital collections in the 'digital economy'?
- How is public engagement with digital cultural heritage materials to be assessed and supported?

This book will be of interest to academics, librarians, archivists and the staff of cultural heritage organizations, as well as funders and other key stakeholders with an interest in the development and long term sustainability of digital collections.

Lorna M Hughes is the University of Wales Chair in Digital Collections at the National Library of Wales

2011; 224pp; paperback; 978-1-85604-720-3; £49.95

Measuring Library Performance
Principles and techniques
Peter Brophy

'This book is an essential resource for libraries and librarians who are serious about measuring their impact on customers, patrons, and society at large...Measuring Library Performance will benefit library and information-science students, professors, and busy information professionals, too.'   *Public Libraries*

Measuring the performance of a library's services is one of the most crucial parts of providing a good service. This important book is the first to provide an accessible account of current thinking on the evaluation of library services, both traditional and - importantly - electronic library services. Illustrated throughout with a range of international examples across different types of libraries, this book will become the standard work on performance measurement.

The book is structured to focus first of all on the intended user of the services (outcome and impact perspectives), then to look at the management of the service (output and process issues), then at evaluating the building blocks of services (input issues) and finally to draw together these strands by examining some of the broader frameworks for evaluation which have emerged. The book ends with an extensive Appendix with a description of key methodologies and suitable references. Each chapter includes suggestions for further reading as well as key references.

The key areas addressed include:

- user satisfaction
- impact on users
- economic impact
- inputs
- evaluating processes
- counting the outputs
- acquiring content
- staff
- evaluating infrastructure
- benchmarking and balanced scorecard
- standards based approaches.

The emphasis on principles and techniques in the book means that it is perfect reading for busy practitioners but it is also eminently suitable for students and researchers trying to get to grips with this tricky area.

2006; 256pp; hardback; 978-1-85604-593-3; £49.95